Dear Laura,
This is a [illegible] of
Riverside Cemetery.

My love,

Aunt Betty
Young Mauken

IMAGES
of America

ASHEVILLE'S RIVERSIDE CEMETERY

P.S.

I believe in Resurrection and in Heaven with hope eternal. "The Messiah", an Oratorio by G. F. Handel. It isn't Christmas to me without listening to the Christmas portion, nor is it Easter without that listening to that portion by Handel, also. My sharing the event of the first ever national radio broad-cast in 1952 at Appalachian State Teachers College in Boone, N.C. is an unforgetable, hilarious rendition of practice endless and a very deep snow and dear classmates singing with gusto and beauty!

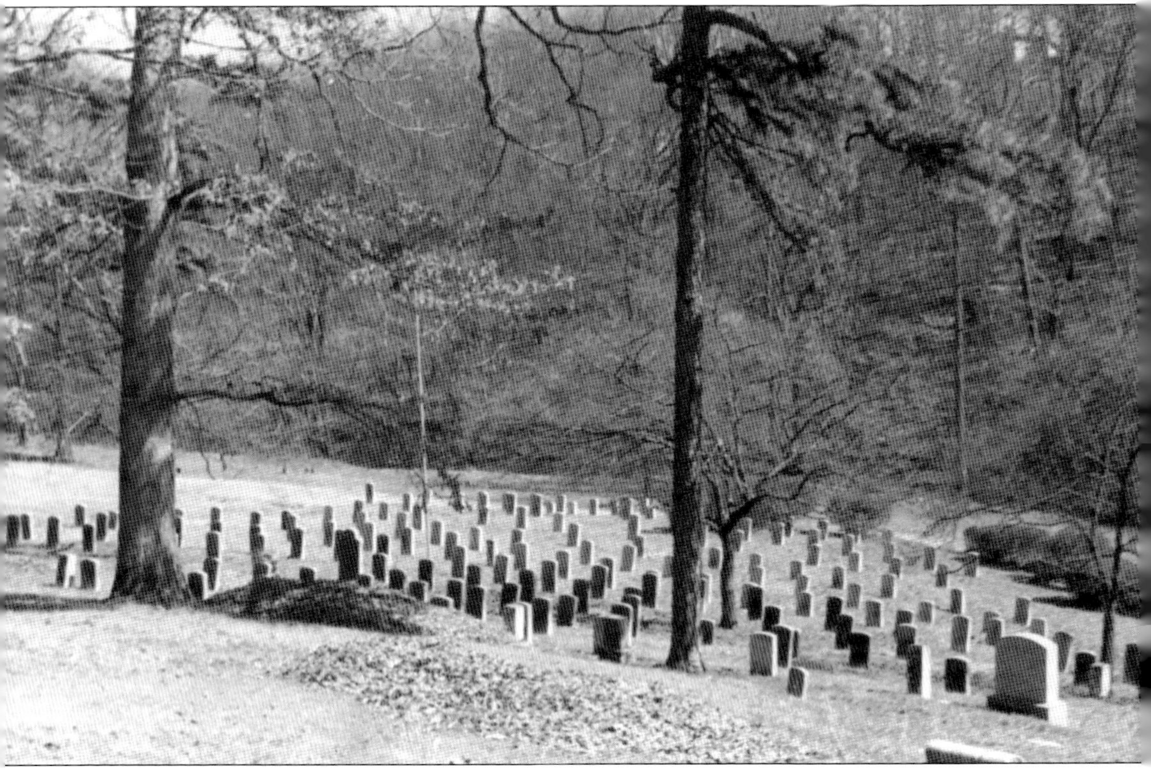

Pictured is Riverside's Veteran's Section. This section was Western North Carolina's original veteran's cemetery and served as the burial ground for those who passed away while patients at the Oteen military hospital in East Asheville. The section contains the resting places of soldiers from the Civil War to the Vietnam War. (Author's collection.)

ON THE COVER: This 1931 photograph shows German ambassador Dr. F.W. von Prittwitz alongside members of the Kiffin Rockwell Post of the American Legion in Section M of Riverside during the dedication of a monument to 18 German merchant marines who passed away while being held captive during World War I. The service was one of Riverside's largest and was broadcast live in both the United States and Germany. (E.M. Ball.)

IMAGES
of America

Asheville's Riverside Cemetery

Joshua Darty

ARCADIA
PUBLISHING

ISBN 978-1-4671-2819-3

Published by Arcadia Publishing
Charleston, South Carolina

Printed in the United States of America

Library of Congress Control Number: 2017953918

For all general information, please contact Arcadia Publishing:
Telephone 843-853-2070
Fax 843-853-0044
E-mail sales@arcadiapublishing.com
For customer service and orders:
Toll-Free 1-888-313-2665

Visit us on the Internet at www.arcadiapublishing.com

To my amazing wife, Katie, whose love and encouragement mean the world to me, and to our little girl, Charlie, who makes everyday a new adventure.

Contents

ACKNOWLEDGMENTS

It is my wish that anyone who picks up a copy of this book will find within its pages a view of Asheville and its history that they have never encountered before through the lives and deaths of some of our most notable citizens. I wish first to thank the incredible people of Asheville who helped build and shape the mountain oasis and who now lie entombed in the hallowed grounds of Riverside Cemetery. Their memory and those who helped to preserve it form the basis of this book. This book would not have been possible without the help and assistance of many fine people and organizations in Asheville. Special thanks go to Gary Clark of Tours by Clark, Buddy Reisenberg of Temple Beth HaTephila, the staff of the North Carolina Room at Pack Library, Colin Reeve at Ramsey Library Special Collections, Tom Muir at the Thomas Wolfe Memorial, and the City of Asheville Parks & Recreation staff. Additionally, I would like to thank Mike Kinsella and Caroline Anderson of Arcadia Publishing who first approached me about writing this book and guided me along the way. Finally, I would like to thank my wife, Katie, and my wonderful family who encouraged me to undertake this project and who have always been a source of love, understanding, and unwavering support.

Unless otherwise noted, all images are from the author's collection. The sources of the images found in this volume include the Riverside Cemetery Archives (RCA), the North Carolina Collection, Pack Memorial Public Library (NCC), the Thomas Wolfe Collection, Pack Memorial Public Library (TWC), the E.M. Ball Collection, D.H. Ramsey Library Special Collections, UNC Asheville (E.M. Ball), the Library of Congress (LOC), and the Adolph Thierbach Collection, Madison County Library (ATC).

Introduction

As the 19th century began drawing to a close, the small mountain city of Asheville entered into a period of booming population growth. Tradesmen, doctors, merchants, and anyone looking to cash in on Asheville's newfound status as a health and tourist mecca began flocking to the city to enjoy the cool climate and boundless opportunities. As the rapidly increasing population began to change the face of the city, Asheville's civic and business leaders began devising ways to bring progress to the city. At the forefront of their plans was the idea to create a modern cemetery that could serve as the burial ground for all of Asheville's great and good as well as bringing in more tourists by becoming the city's largest and most beautiful public park. To this end, the Asheville Cemetery Company was incorporated in August 1885 by a group of local politicians, businessmen, and community leaders. The first order of business for the new company was to find a suitable place for its cemetery. At the urging of Thomas Walton Patton and Richmond Pearson, a tract of land just outside of downtown overlooking the French Broad River was chosen. The majority of the property had belonged to the late Nicholas Woodfin, friend and business partner of Patton and an early proponent of the creation of the cemetery. The land was densely forested and included an area that had for many years been the location of one of the largest settlements of Cherokees in Buncombe County, as evidenced by the many artifacts found there.

In just four short months after the property was acquired, workers under the direction of noted English landscape architect Charles T. Colyer were able to clear trees, grade the steep hillsides, and create the wide carriageways that divided Riverside's five tiers. A large iron and granite gate was set at the end of the newly created Cemetery Street, and white gravel was laid on the main roads leading to the small wooden office constructed for the cemetery superintendent in the center of the property. W.S. Cornell, the first superintendent, began creating and mapping the sections of Riverside and laying out the first burial lots for the Asheville Cemetery Company in December 1885. The company advertised that the new cemetery was to be opened to the public on January 1, 1886, with the first burials to be those of the Patton family who were being disinterred from the Presbyterian Cemetery on Church Street. This plan was not to be, however. Instead, the cemetery opened quietly three weeks ahead of schedule when Charles Hill, the younger brother of Asheville businessman J.J. Hill, passed away unexpectedly while in Florida. Hill appealed to W.S. Cornell and was able to acquire a lot for his brother in the new cemetery and have him interred. Thus the yet-unnamed cemetery was officially opened on December 12, 1885.

The following year, the *Asheville Citizen* opined about Riverside: "It must be visited to be known; and then we are sure it will soon be learned that what Mt. Auburn is to Boston, Greenwood to New York, Hollywood to Richmond, Bonaventure to Savannah, Riverside will become to Asheville." These words proved to be prescient. Over the next several years, Riverside quickly established its reputation as one of the foremost cemeteries in the South, with its magnificent mountain views, carefully planned landscapes, imposing mausoleums, and unique monuments. Above all, a genuine commitment from the cemetery's caretakers and the citizens of Asheville to care for and adorn the cemetery pushed it to prominence as a place of beauty and reflection.

Artisans and craftsmen have always been drawn to the green slopes of Riverside to take inspiration from and contribute to the funerary art scattered among the trees. Many of the first moved to Asheville at the request of the Vanderbilt family in order to undertake the construction of the grand Biltmore Estate just up the French Broad River. After the completion of the estate, stonecutters and monument masons remained in Asheville and turned their talents to shaping the face of Asheville through the buildings, monuments, and sculptures that stand to this day. There is no place where the skill of these master craftsmen shines through more than the landscapes of Riverside, where original designs have been created by famous sculptors such as Samuel Isaac Bean, Fred Miles, Robert Sharp Smith, and W.O. Wolfe. Their art, enhanced by being surrounded by the natural beauty of the parklike setting of Riverside, has long drawn in tourists from around the globe.

Apart from the great beauty of Riverside, much of its famous reputation has derived from its notable occupants, both the famous and infamous. The best known among them are undoubtedly the literary giants Thomas Wolfe and William Sydney Porter, better known by his nom de plume O. Henry. Wolfe's ties to Riverside were especially close, as he had accompanied his father installing monuments within the cemetery as a child and attended the funerals of so many of his close family members before being interred himself in the family lot at just 37 years of age. Wolfe included Riverside in many of his writings, notably calling it "a pleasant place on a hill." Other notable Ashevillians interred within the grounds of Riverside include North Carolina governors Zebulon Vance and Locke Craig, politicians Thomas Clingman and Robert Rice Reynolds, artists Kenneth Noland and Vadim Bora, and Civil War heroes such as Medal of Honor recipient Andrew J. McGonnigle and James Posey, bodyguard to Pres. Abraham Lincoln.

Though a journey past the gates can invoke a sense of a time long past with its century-old monuments and stately oaks, Riverside has continued to fulfill the promise of its founders by remaining a modern cemetery. To this end, Riverside has stayed a leader among area cemeteries by being the first to catalog its gravesites through GIS technology, digitizing its interment archives and making them available to researchers and genealogists, and using ground-penetrating radar and drone photography to ascertain the location of unmarked graves. In recent years, Riverside has increased in popularity as a tourist destination, with over 35,000 visitors and 50 guided tours given annually. It continues to be an active cemetery, with around 75 internments every year.

Riverside, like all cemeteries, was created with the intention of honoring and remembering those entombed within its hallowed grounds. Through the efforts of cemetery staff, volunteers, and the citizens of Asheville, this aim has been continually met. British prime minister William Gladstone once said, "Show me the manner in which a nation or a community cares for its dead and I will measure with mathematical exactness the tender mercy of its people, their respect for the law of the land, and their loyalty to high ideals."

By this measure, Riverside demonstrates that the people of Asheville now and have always embodied the virtues of honor, respect, and the very highest of ideals.

One

The Asheville Cemetery Company

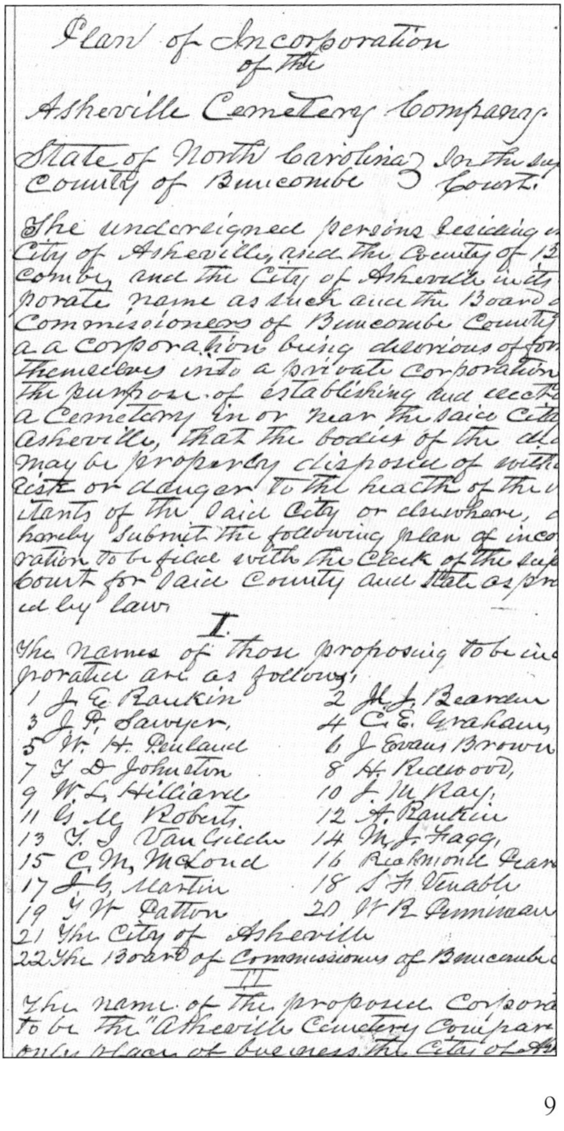

Plan of Incorporation
of the
Asheville Cemetery Company.

State of North Carolina } In the Su
County of Buncombe } Court.

The undersigned persons residing in
City of Asheville, and the County of B
combe, and the City of Asheville in its
porate name as such and the Board o
Commissioners of Buncombe County
a corporation being desirous of form
themselves into a private corporation
the purpose of establishing and erect
a Cemetery in or near the said City
Asheville, that the bodies of the de
may be properly disposed of with
risk or danger to the health of the i
itants of the said City or elsewhere, d
hereby submit the following plan of inco
oration to be filed with the Clerk of the Sup
Court for said County and State as pr
ed by law.

I.

The names of those proposing to be in
porated are as follows:

1 J. E. Rankin 2 M. J. Bearden
3 J. P. Sawyer 4 C. E. Graham
5 W. H. Penland 6 J. Evans Brown
7 T. D. Johnston 8 H. Redwood,
9 W. L. Hilliard 10 J. M. Ray,
11 G. M. Roberts 12 A. Rankin
13 T. J. Van Gilder 14 M. J. Fagg,
15 C. M. McLoud 16 Richmond Pear
17 J. G. Martin 18 S. H. Venable
19 T. W. Patton 20 W. R. Penniman
21 The City of Asheville
22 The Board of Commissioners of Buncombe

II

The name of the proposed Corpor
to be the "Asheville Cemetery Compan
Its place of business The City of Ash

The Asheville Cemetery Company was incorporated in August 1885 by prominent citizens of Asheville to provide a suitable burial ground for the growing city. The initial board, led by T.W. Patton and M.J. Bearden, sought to attract investors to the venture by offering 20 lots in the highest part of the cemetery to each stockholder. Forty investors were found, including the City of Asheville and Buncombe County governments. (RCA.)

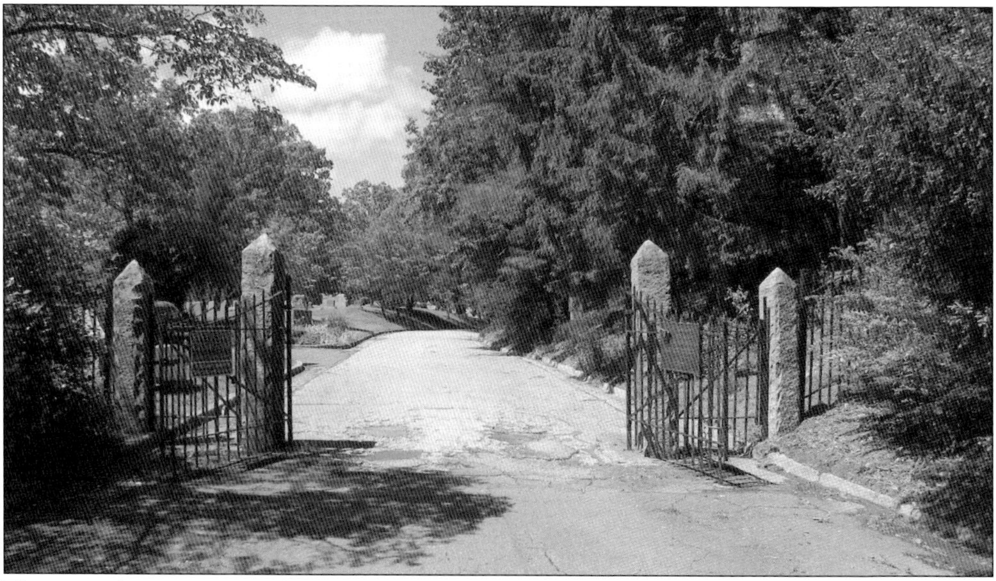

The wrought iron gates and granite pillars of Riverside Cemetery have welcomed mourners and visitors alike for over a century. This is the second gate built for Riverside, as the first gate, with its arch bearing the inscription "The Asheville Cemetery," was removed and donated as part of the scrap metal drives during the First World War.

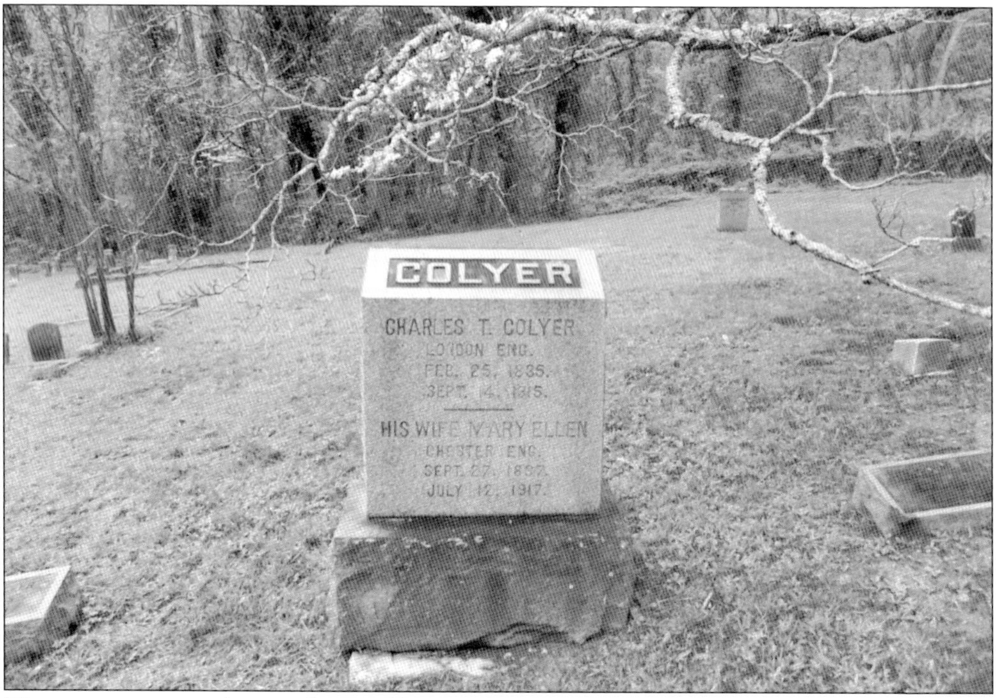

The cemetery grounds were designed by noted English landscape architect Charles T. Colyer, who also designed the grounds of the Grove Park Inn. His fashioned the grounds as a "garden cemetery" that was meant to serve as both a burial ground and the region's first public park. Riverside quickly became one of Asheville's most popular spots for walking and picnicking upon its opening in December 1885.

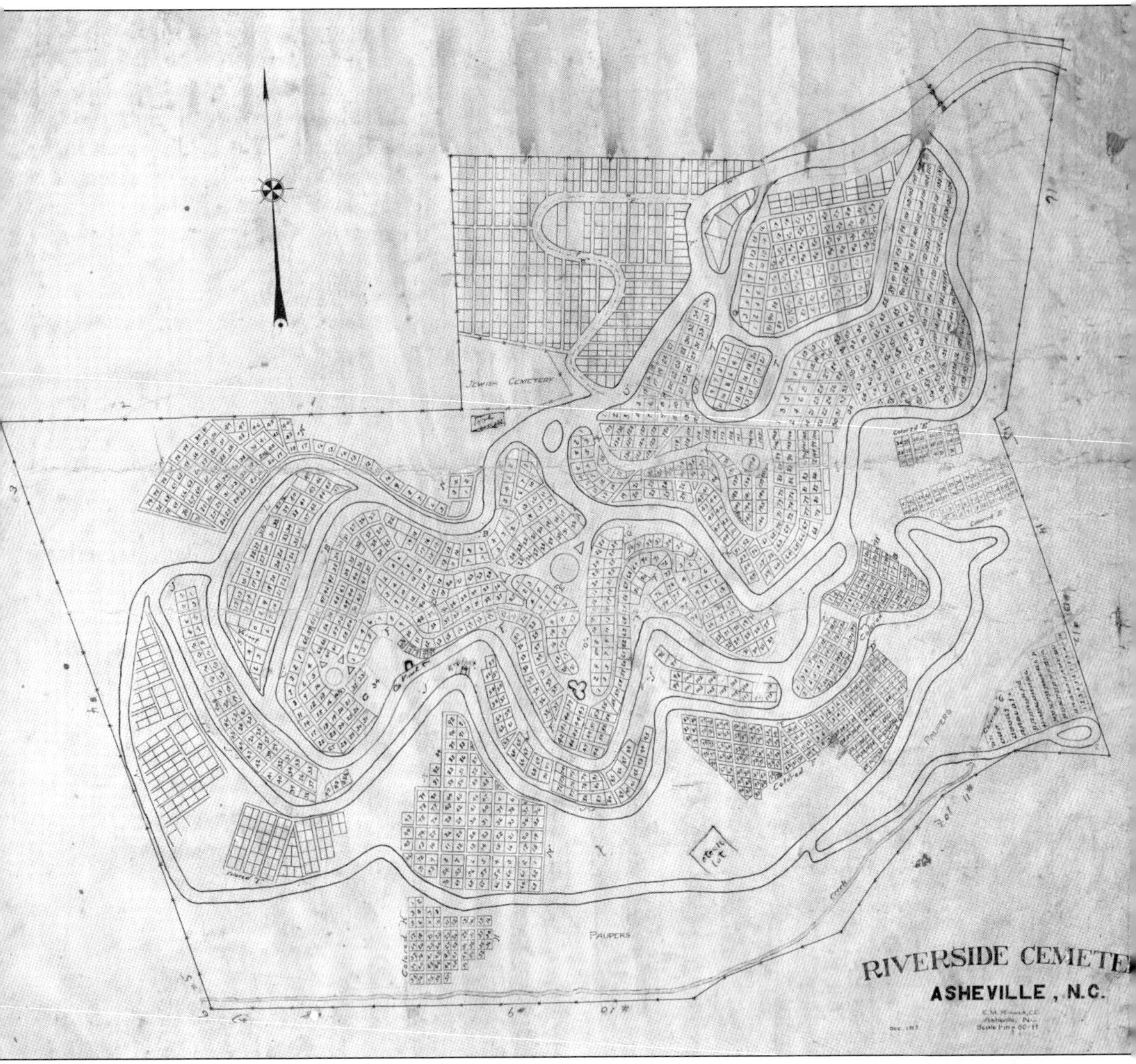

This 1919 map is the earliest complete map of Riverside. It was drawn to replace those lost when the office was destroyed by fire earlier in the year. C.T. Colyer designed Riverside to be laid out into five tiers, with white gravel carriageways encircling each. The first four tiers were to be reserved for the burial of white Christians. The fifth was to be used as a burial ground for African Americans and paupers. A separate entrance to the lower level was created at the southwest corner of the cemetery, closest to the French Broad River. The tiers were divided into sections with letter designations. Forty-five sections were created in all: 32 for whites, 8 for African Americans, 2 for paupers, and 3 for the Beth HaTephila Jewish congregation. The first to be sold were in Section A, at the center of the cemetery, and were reserved for the original stockholders of the Asheville Cemetery Company. (RCA.)

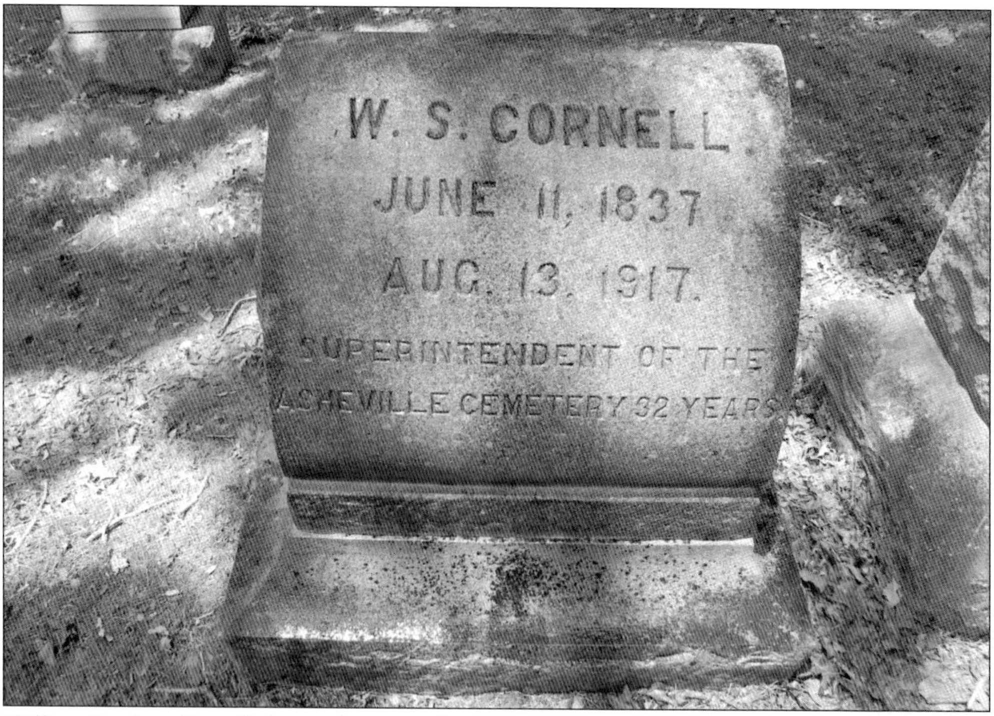

William Stephen Cornell, former farmer and manager of the Elk Mountain Cheese Factory, became the first superintendent of Riverside Cemetery and was its longest-tenured employee, working until his death in 1917 at 80 years old. Cornell, according to his obituary, said management of the cemetery was "the idol of his heart." He was known throughout Asheville for his long white beard and for standing at the cemetery gates singing hymns as processions came in.

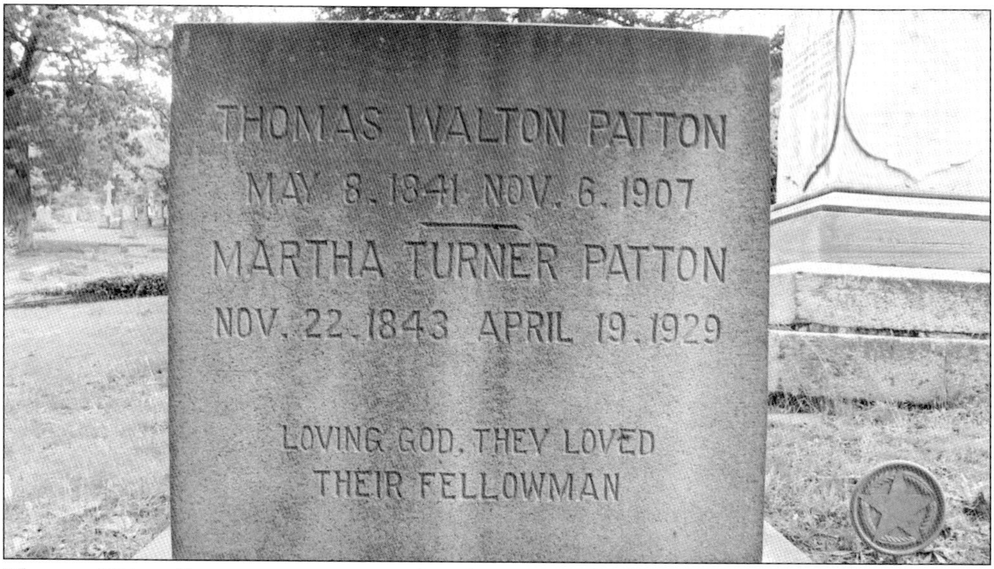

Thomas Walton Patton, among many other things, was the driving force behind the creation of Riverside. He organized the initial meetings of the Asheville Cemetery Company and served as its first secretary and treasurer, donated much of his money to hire the best he could find to design and build the cemetery grounds, and hired one of his closest friends—W.S. Cornell—as manager.

Throughout the life of the Asheville Cemetery Company (ACC), the Bank of Asheville served as its headquarters. The bank was centrally located to the offices of many of the stockholders in the ACC, and its directors, J.P. Sawyer, James Rankin, Richmond Pearson, and T.W. Patton, were heavily invested in the concept of providing a "modern" cemetery to Asheville. (HathiTrust, Harriet Sawyer Collection.)

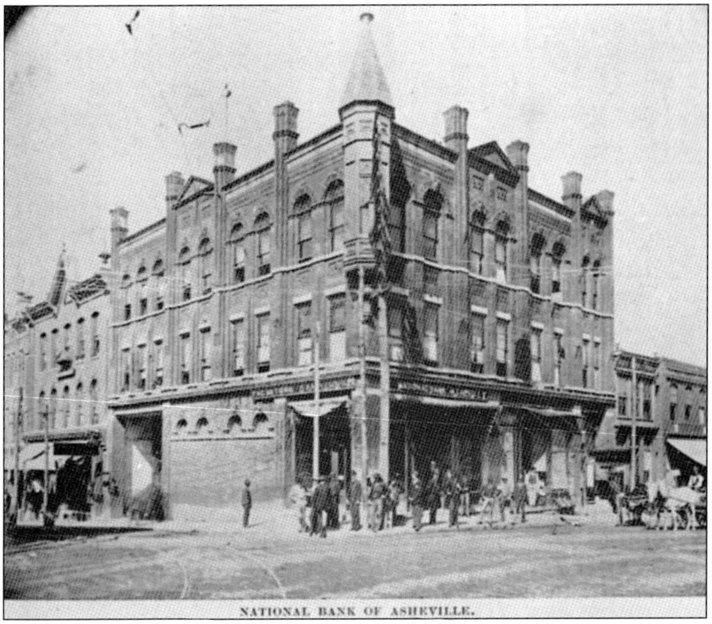

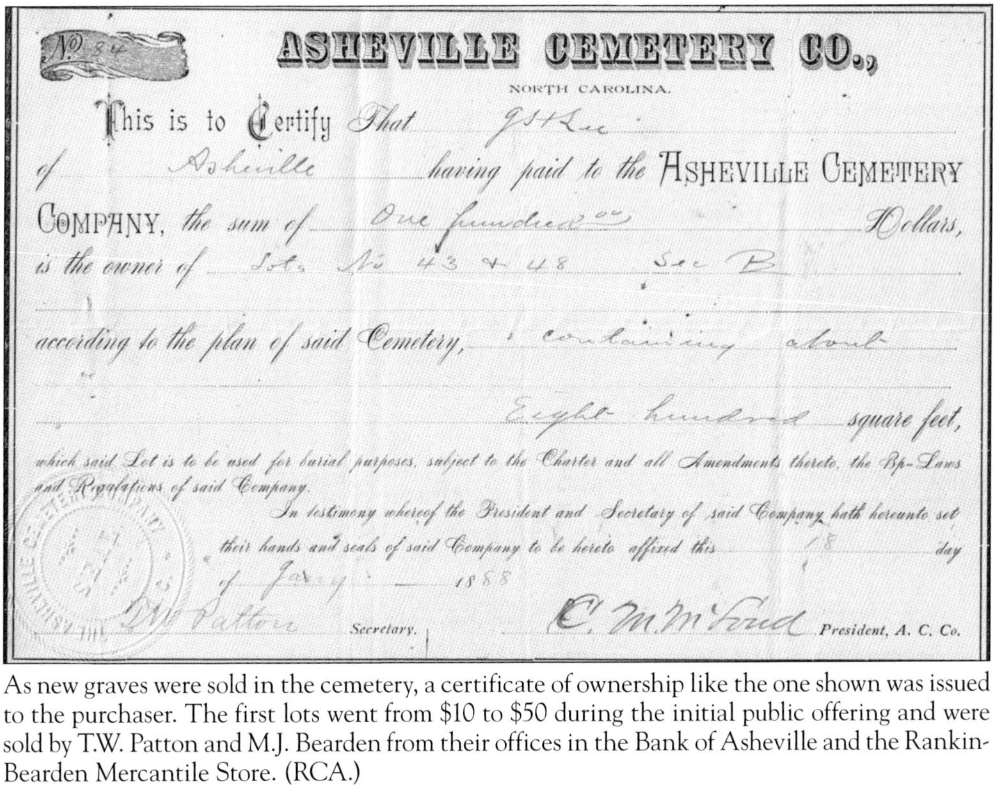

No. 84

ASHEVILLE CEMETERY CO.,

NORTH CAROLINA.

This is to Certify That J S Lee

of Asheville having paid to the ASHEVILLE CEMETERY COMPANY, the sum of One hundred 00 Dollars, is the owner of Lots No 43 & 48 Sec B

according to the plan of said Cemetery, containing about

Eight hundred square feet,

which said Lot is to be used for burial purposes, subject to the Charter and all Amendments thereto, the By-Laws and Regulations of said Company.

In testimony whereof the President and Secretary of said Company hath hereunto set their hands and seals of said Company to be hereto affixed this 18 day of Jany 1888

T W Patton Secretary. C. M. McLoud President, A. C. Co.

As new graves were sold in the cemetery, a certificate of ownership like the one shown was issued to the purchaser. The first lots went from $10 to $50 during the initial public offering and were sold by T.W. Patton and M.J. Bearden from their offices in the Bank of Asheville and the Rankin-Bearden Mercantile Store. (RCA.)

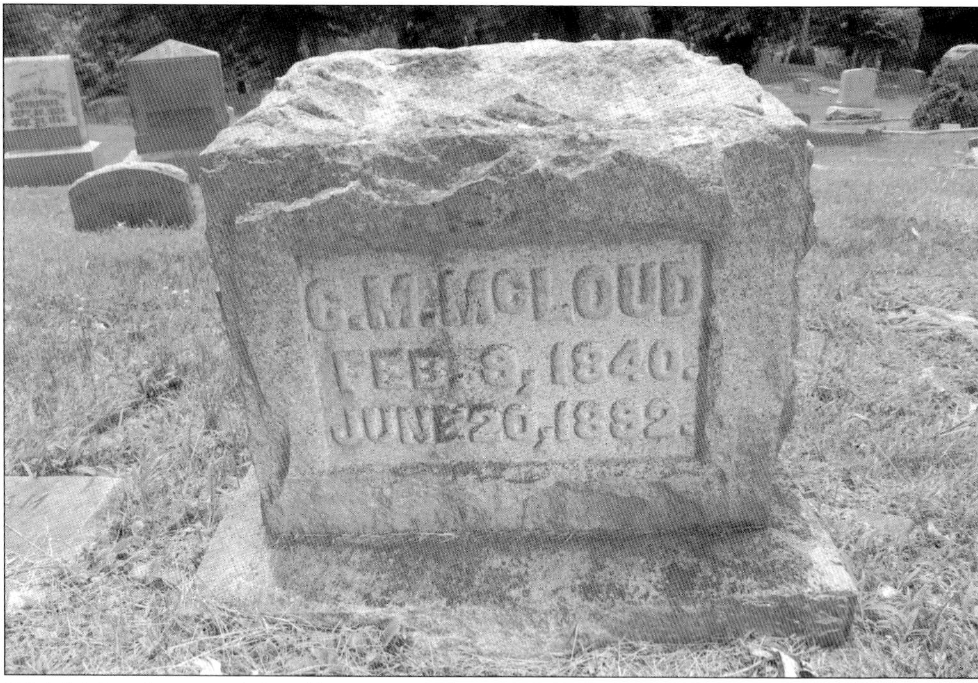

C.M. McLoud was an Asheville attorney who was instrumental in connecting Asheville to the rest of the state through the telegraph and railroads. He was named the first president of the Asheville Cemetery Company. McLoud held this responsibility for only seven short years before his untimely death in 1892.

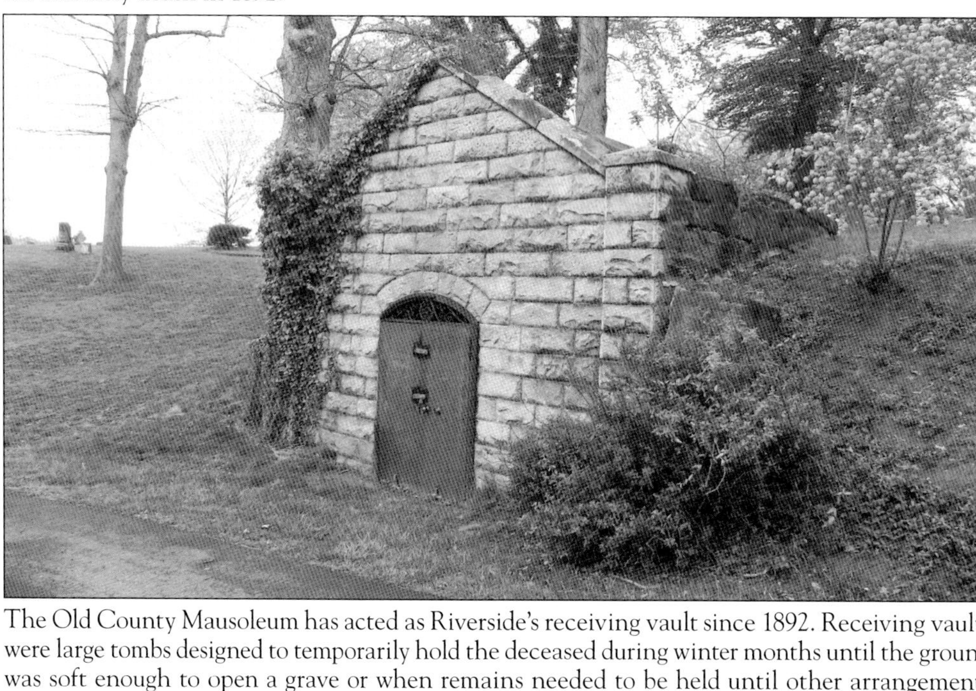

The Old County Mausoleum has acted as Riverside's receiving vault since 1892. Receiving vaults were large tombs designed to temporarily hold the deceased during winter months until the ground was soft enough to open a grave or when remains needed to be held until other arrangements could be made. As technology improved, the mausoleum was no longer needed for this purpose, and it has stood empty for almost 100 years.

The first burial in the newly opened Riverside Cemetery occurred on December 12, 1885, when 20-year-old Charles Hill of Florida was brought to Asheville by his brother James for burial. Hill's grave is unmarked. Just above it stands the first marker installed in the cemetery (pictured), a memorial marker for members of the influential Brown family of Pennsylvania.

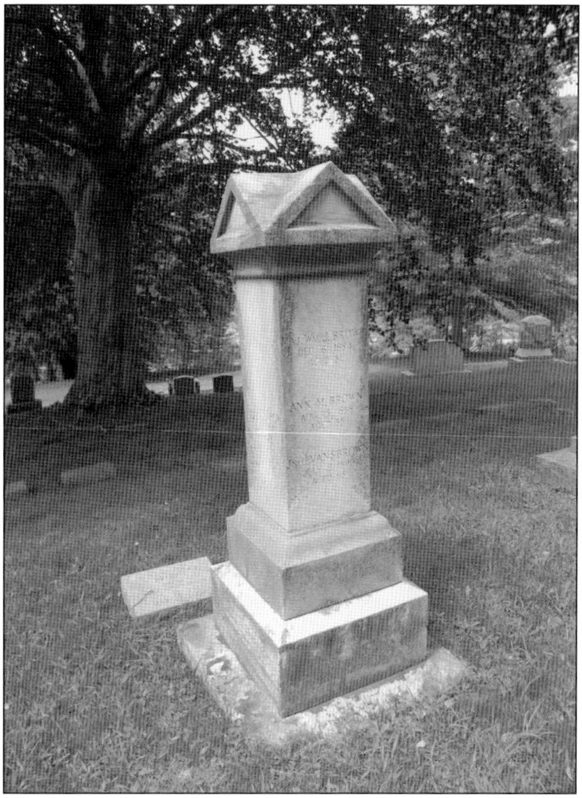

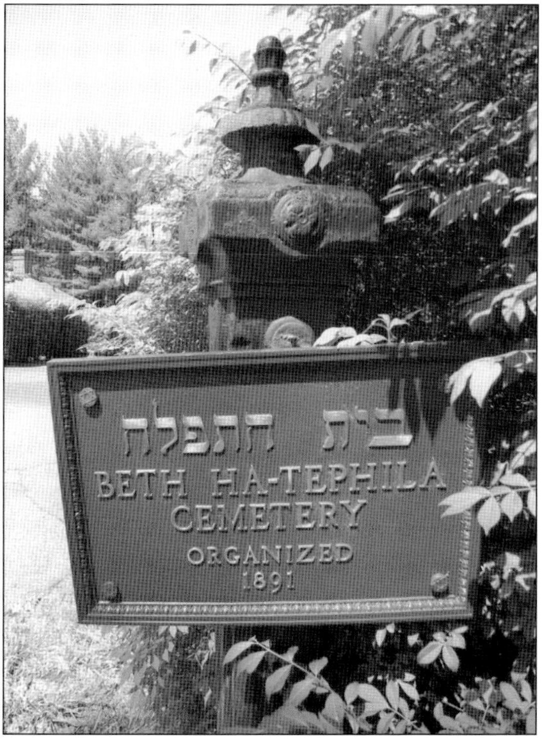

Founded in 1891, the Congregation Beth HaTephila cemetery is not technically a part of Riverside, though it is completely surrounded by Riverside's property. Members of the congregation who were among Asheville's leading businessmen, civic leaders, and philanthropists purchased three acres from the Asheville Cemetery Company beside the cemetery office and installed heavy wrought iron gates to separate it from the rest of the cemetery. (Congregation Beth HaTephila.)

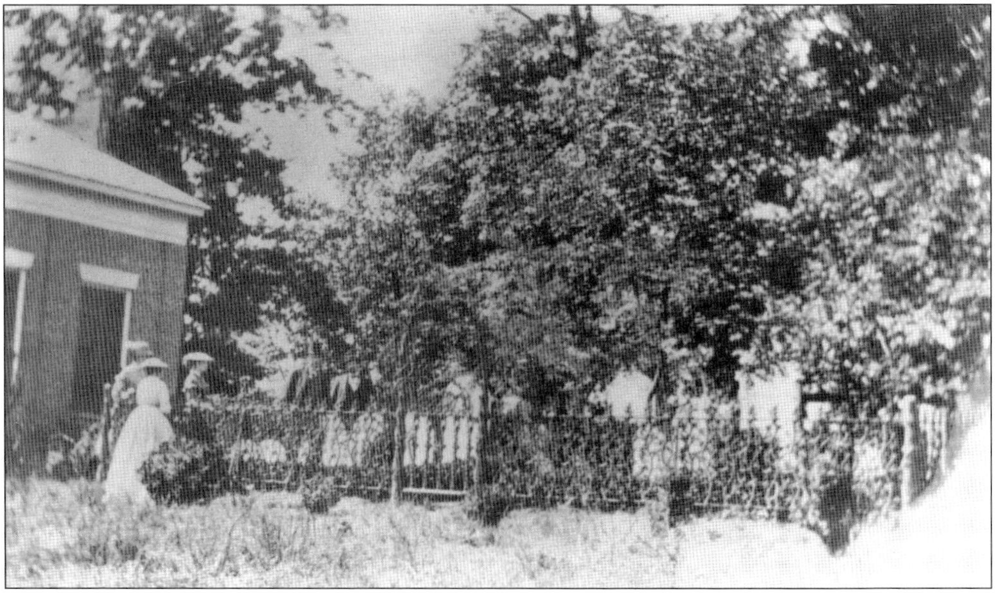

Though Riverside was established in 1885, many of the graves inside are much older. When Riverside opened its gates, other cemeteries within Asheville disinterred and moved families to Riverside, where the lots were promised to be well maintained. The first cemetery in Asheville had been located at the corner of Eagle and Market Streets before being moved within the Presbyterian cemetery on Church Street (above). The Presbyterian cemetery was almost entirely moved to Riverside between 1885 and 1901. Thus, many of the graves in Riverside date back to the early 1800s. The oldest of these relocated graves is that of Barbara Patton, matriarch of the influential Patton family, who died in 1807. (Above, NCC.)

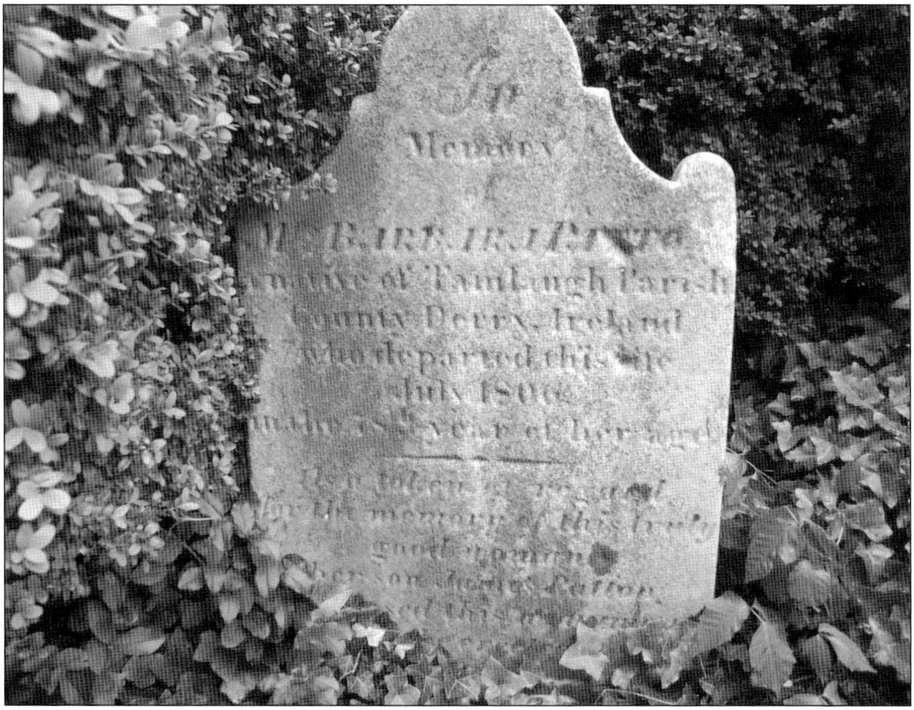

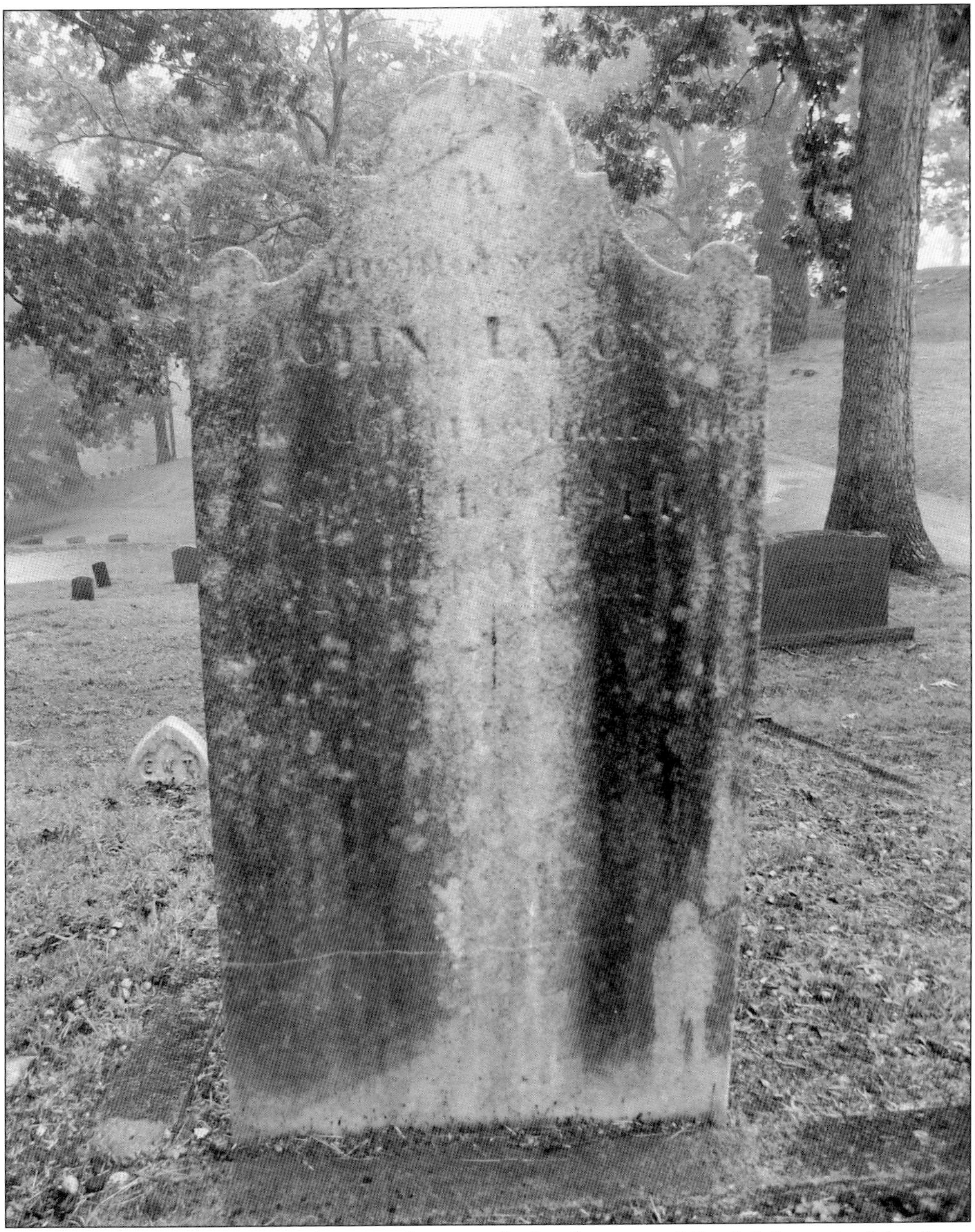

Though Barbara Patton passed away a few years before him, noted English botanist John Lyon has the distinction of having the oldest gravestone in Riverside and by some accounts the oldest engraved monument in Western North Carolina. Lyon passed away at the Eagle Hotel after succumbing to maladies that he presumably contracted as a result of his work. Lyon's marker was shipped to Asheville by his relations in Edinburgh, Scotland, after they received news of his passing. As an agent of King George II and later as manager of the Woodlands Estate in Philadelphia, Lyon was well known throughout America and Europe as a master in his field who was responsible for introducing rare American plants to Europe and was credited with introducing 31 new plants into horticulture. As a tribute to the man, one of his most popular finds, mountain fetterbush, has been planted around the base of his grave.

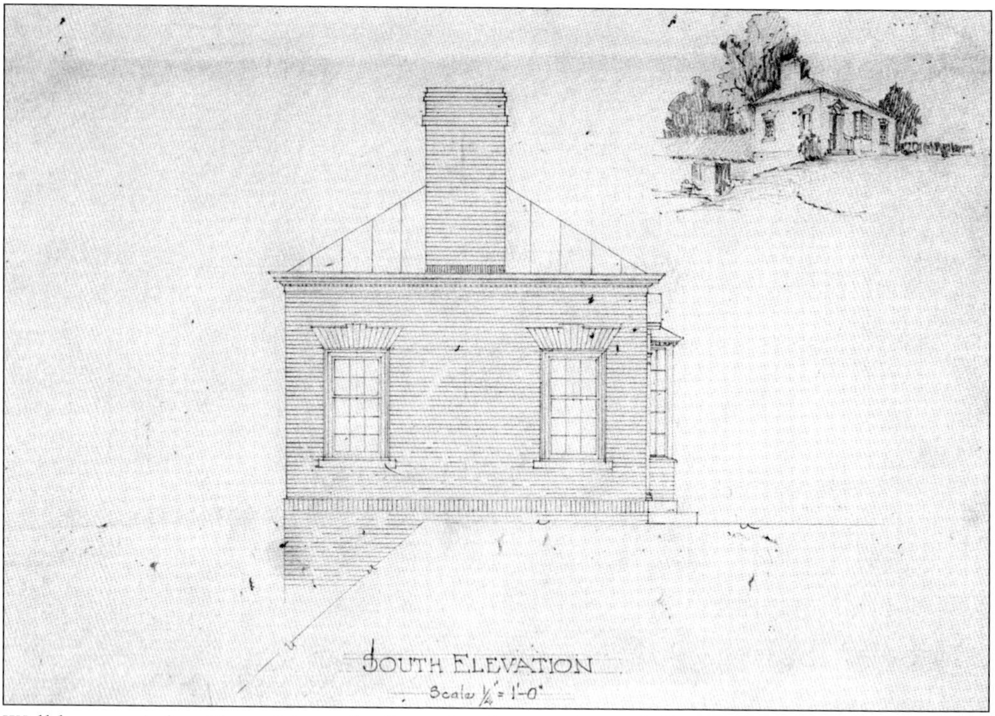

Well-known Asheville architect Anthony Lord created two different designs for the cemetery office for Edwin J. Atwood, superintendent for the Asheville Cemetery Company in 1934, to choose between. The building was quickly constructed using reclaimed brick and plaster. Several of the windows and one of the interior doors were also salvaged from the original structure. Over the years, the interior has been renovated several times to add modern conveniences, though the exterior of the building has remained basically untouched and looks much the same as it did over 83 years ago. (Both, NCC.)

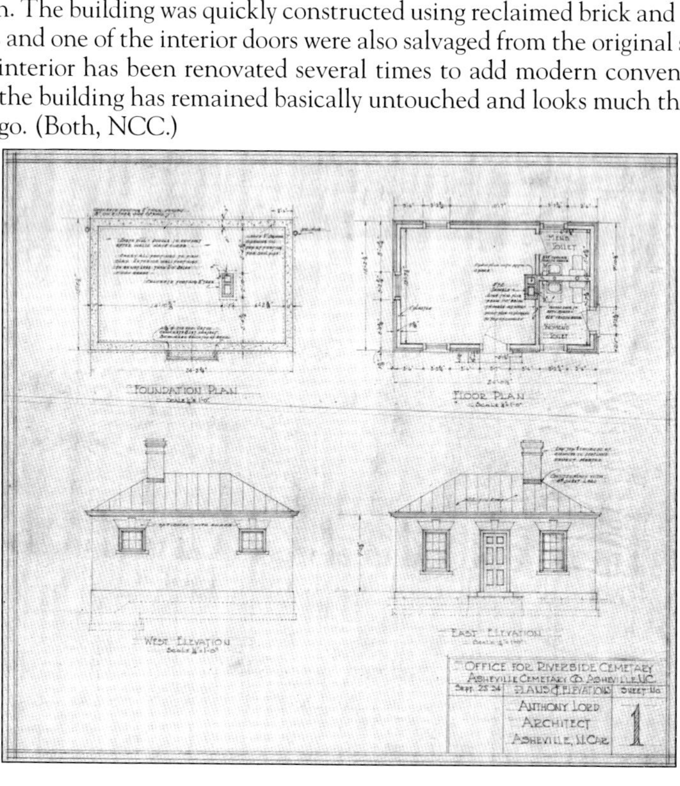

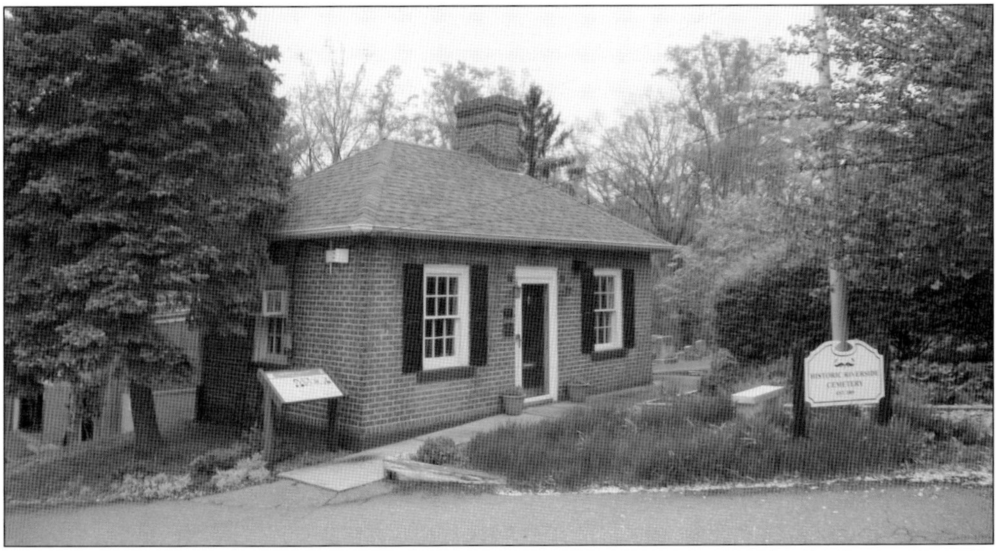

The 1934 office of Riverside Cemetery replaced the wooden structure that had served as the original office building and tool house. Anthony Lord, working with his father, designed the building to take in a lot of natural light, a necessity considering that electricity was not available in the cemetery until 1954.

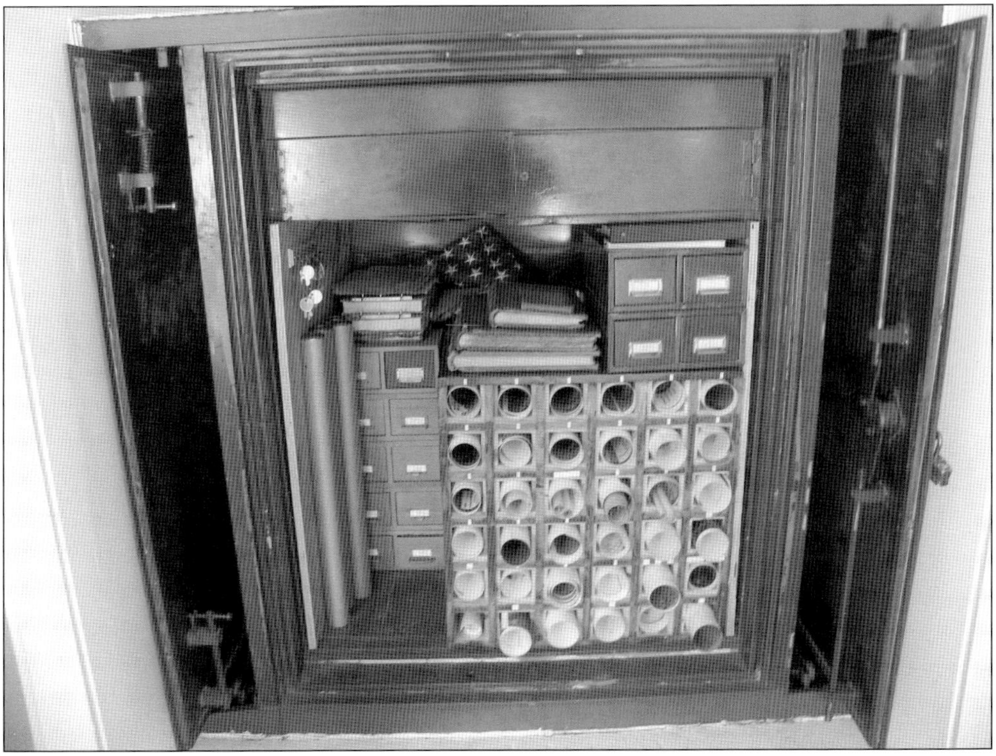

This 1905 Safe Cabinet Company safe has been used by Riverside to hold lot maps and interment records since it was brought over from the Bank of Asheville in 1920 by James Rankin, vice president of the bank. The safe is so large that when the wooden structure that served as an office was torn down to build the current one, the builders built around the safe rather than move it.

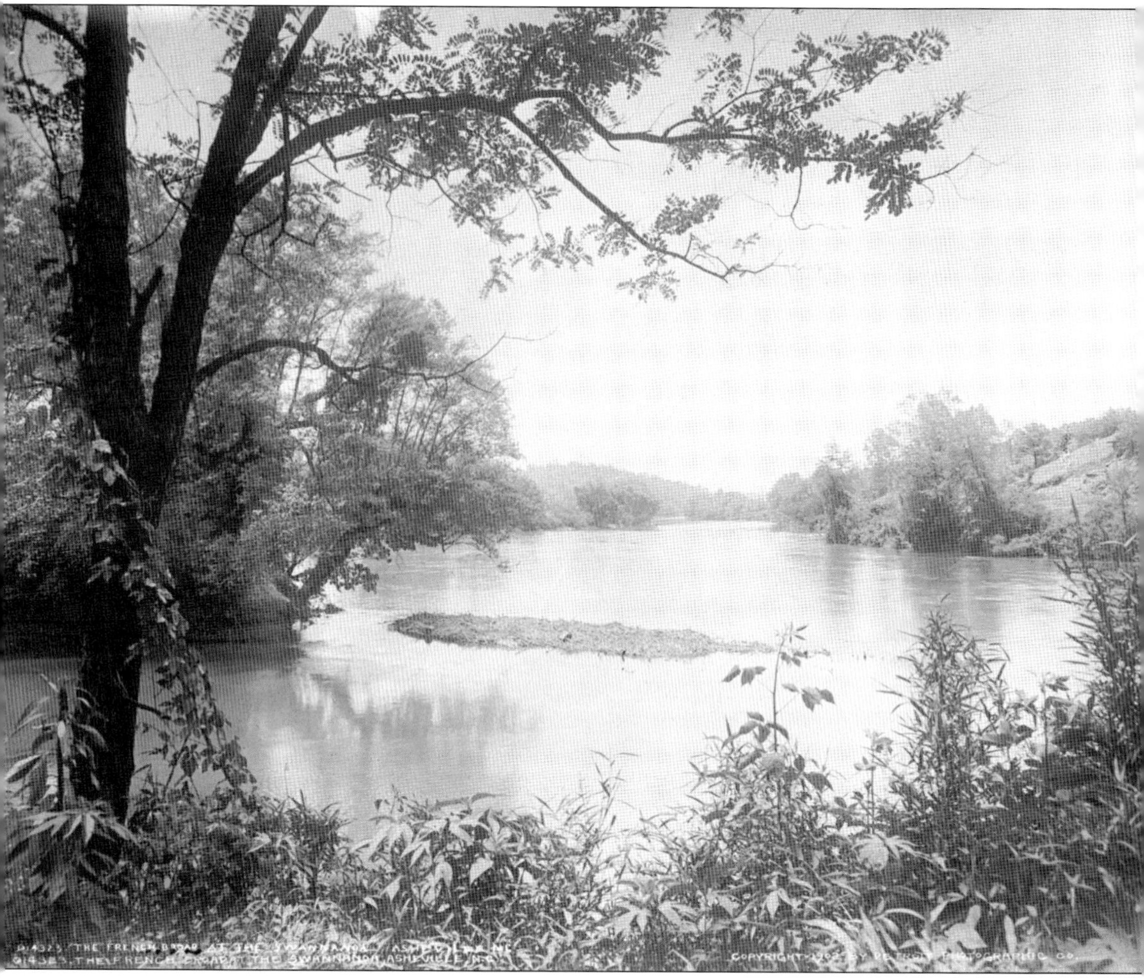

The French Broad River, running through the heart of Asheville, is on the eastern side of the cemetery, though it can only be seen in winter months. Originally, the cemetery grounds ran all the way down to the river before the property was taken for the railroad right-of-way. Real estate agent A.J. Lyman, who was tasked with selling graves in the cemetery by the Asheville Cemetery Company, was the one who first proposed calling the cemetery Riverside. As he told the *Asheville Citizen* at the time, Lyman suggested "Riverside" for "the music of the word, the presence of flowing waters, and the sound of the stream itself sending up murmur to mingle with the wailings of the mourner." The ACC heeded Lyman's suggestion, and the name Riverside Cemetery was adopted. (LOC.)

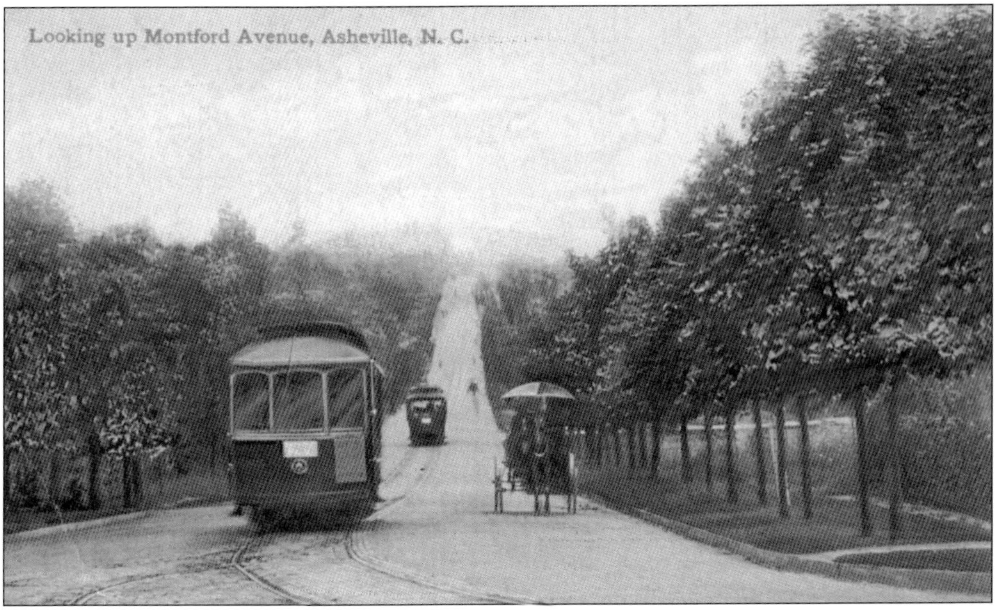

Riverside Cemetery is located in the heart of the Montford Historic District. Montford has long attracted Asheville's finest and most fashionable residents. Many of the stately houses were designed by architects now at rest within the confines of Riverside. Just a stone's throw away from downtown Asheville, the Montford community offers a quiet respite that brings visitors back to a bygone era. (NCC.)

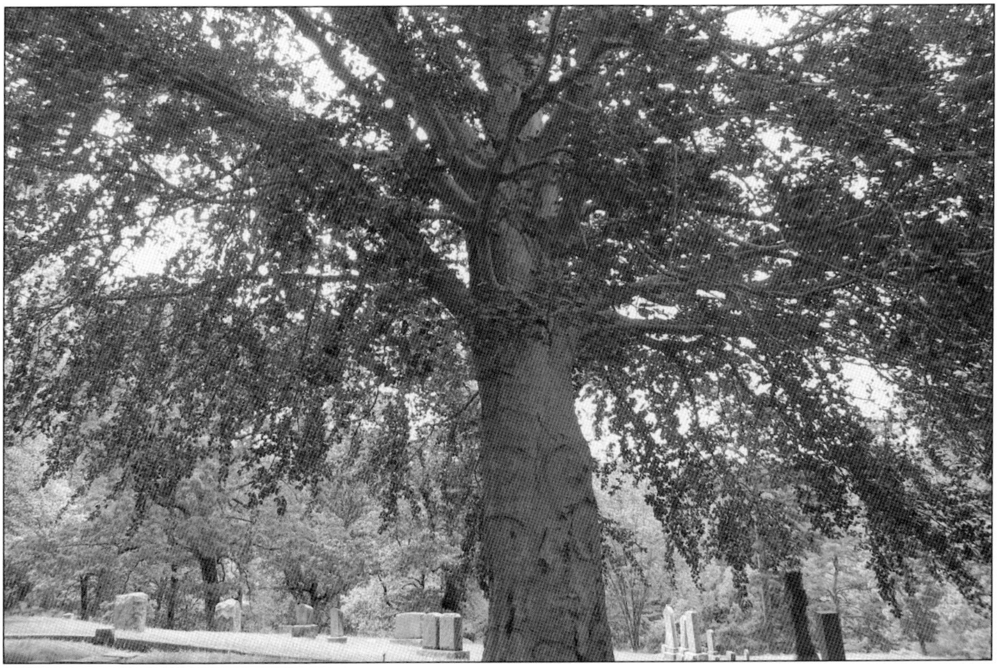

Ancient oaks, hollies, and beeches have given Riverside its status as a Buncombe County Treasure Tree Preserve. Pictured here is a purple European beech dated back to the 1830s, making it one of the oldest trees of its type in the world. The smooth, silvery bark of the tree attracted vandals for over a century. High up the trunk of the tree, the old carvings can just be seen.

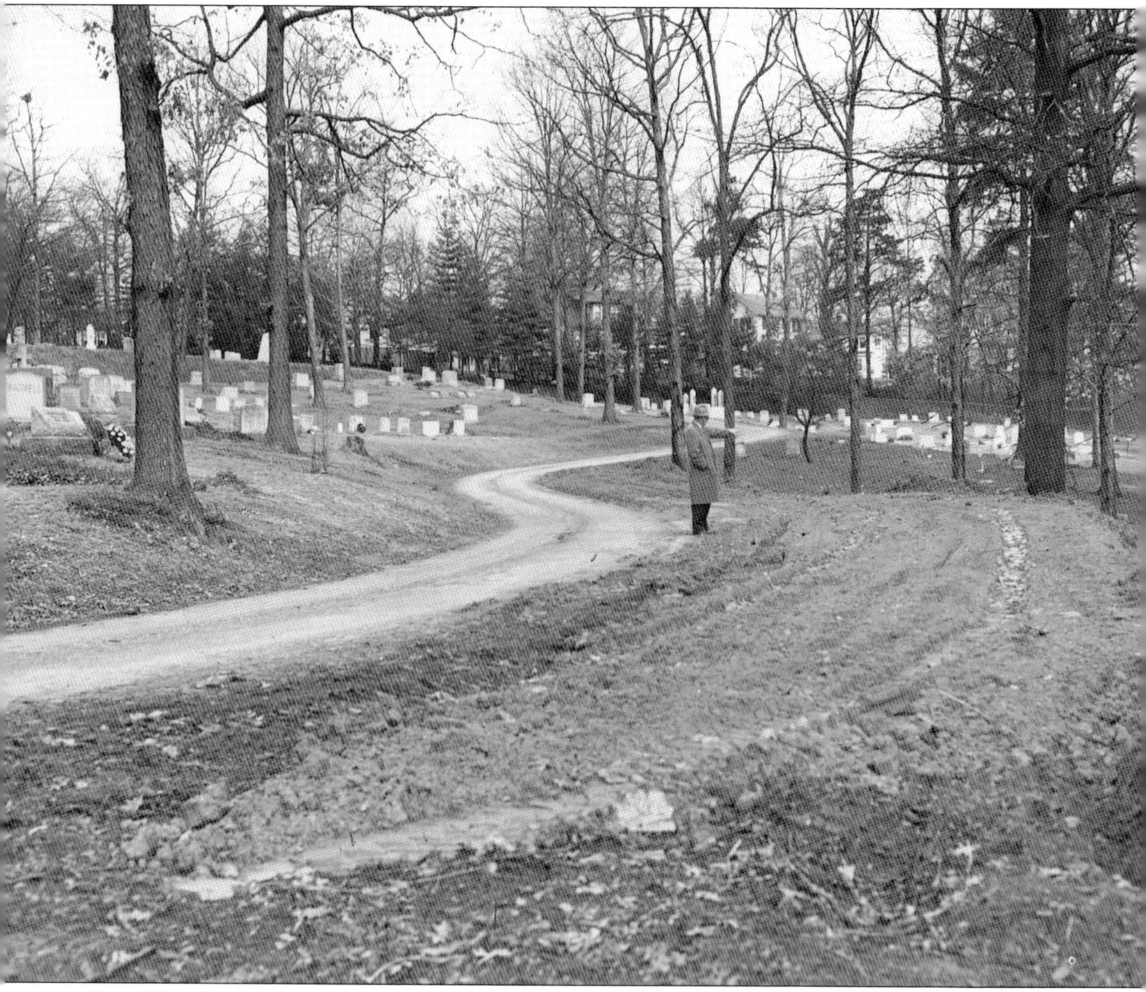

In 1952, the Asheville Cemetery Company found itself in dire financial straits. It appealed to the City of Asheville to assume operation of Riverside in order to preserve the cemetery. After much public debate and noted opposition from some of the owners of other cemeteries in the region, the city agreed to purchase the cemetery for a grand total of $10. City manager Weldon Weir appointed funeral product salesman Charles "Chick" Hunter (pictured) to be the cemetery's new manager and to restore it to prosperity. In a speech to the American Cemetery Association in 1956, Chick described the state in which he found the cemetery as "unkempt, with a bumper crop of honeysuckle, and an encroachment of weeds and poison ivy on every lot" The office to this point had never had electricity and was still relying on an old kerosene lamp. Chick quickly moved to set things right and, with the help of City of Asheville, soon had the cemetery back to its former glory. (RCA.)

Two

The Old Soldiers

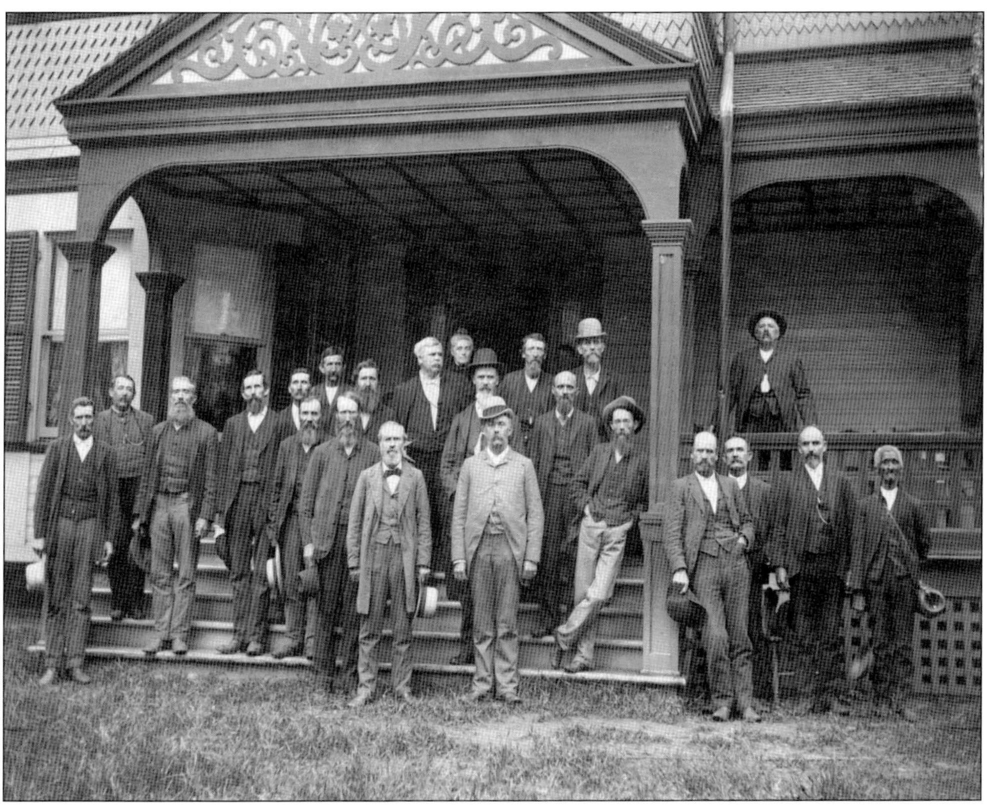

Though there was only one battle fought in Asheville during the course of the Civil War, it became a major military center for the Confederacy. Many of the men who took up arms for either side during the conflict came back to settle down in Asheville after its conclusion. Pictured here is a reunion of Confederate soldiers in 1890 at Gov. Zebulon Vance's house in Black Mountain, Gombroom. (NCC.)

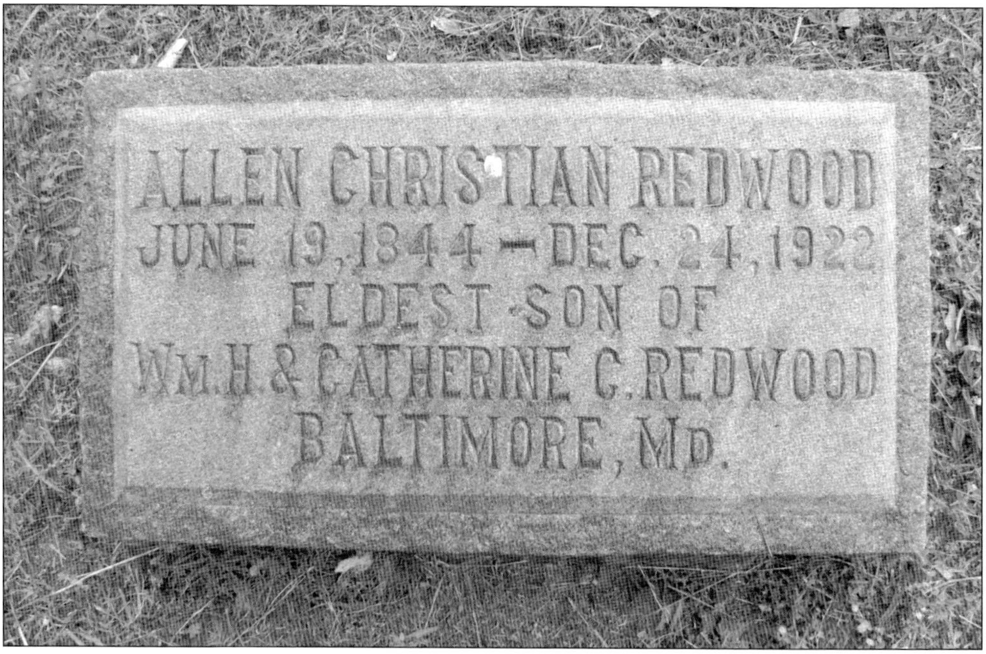

Allen Christian Redwood was a private in the Confederate army who served in both the 55th Virginia Infantry and 1st Maryland Cavalry. He was captured twice by Union forces and wounded three times. He was best known as a writer and illustrator both during and after the war. He depicted battles and everyday military life with astonishing detail for *Harper's Weekly* and was credited with the popularization of the character Johnny Reb. The engraving below is from *Battles and Leaders of the Civil War*, for which Redwood provided 50 illustrations. (Below, LOC.)

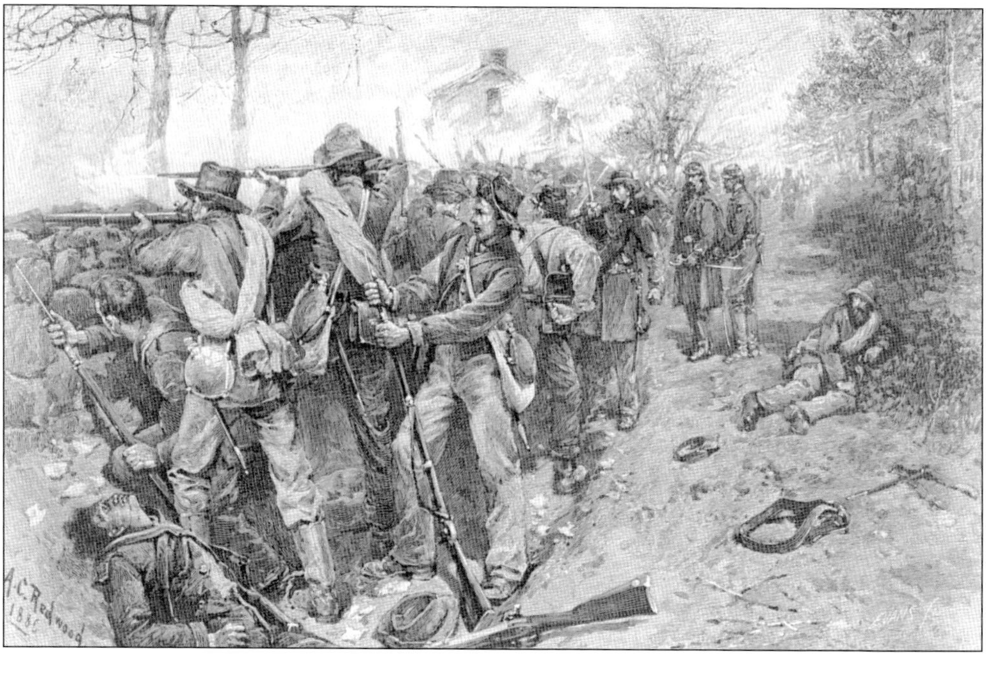

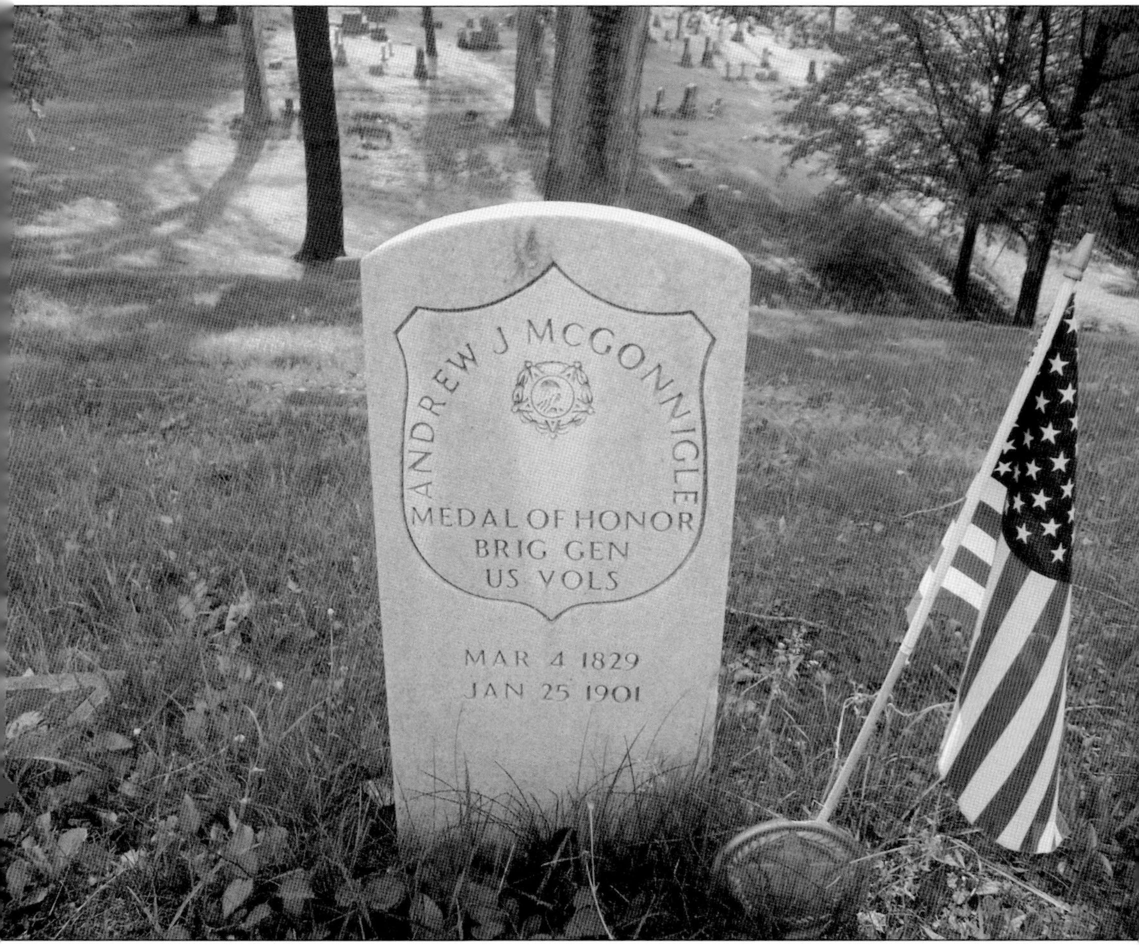

Andrew Jackson McGonnigle was a captain of volunteers for the Union army who was awarded the Medal of Honor for heroism during the Battle of Cedar Creek, fought near Middletown, Virginia, on October 19, 1864. Acting as chief quartermaster for Gen. Philip Sheridan, McGonnigle was severely wounded while leading a brigade of infantry during the battle. His charge helped turn the tide of the decisive engagement of the Shenandoah Valley Campaigns of 1864. The victory, just three weeks before the presidential election, encouraged Northerners and was instrumental to boosting President Lincoln to a second win at the polls. McGonnigle was commended for the greatest gallantry by General Sheridan following the battle and was transferred to the regular army, where he remained until his retirement as a major. He was awarded the Medal of Honor by Pres. William McKinley on July 21, 1897, just four years before his death. McGonnigle is one of only two Union soldiers to be buried in Riverside following the war.

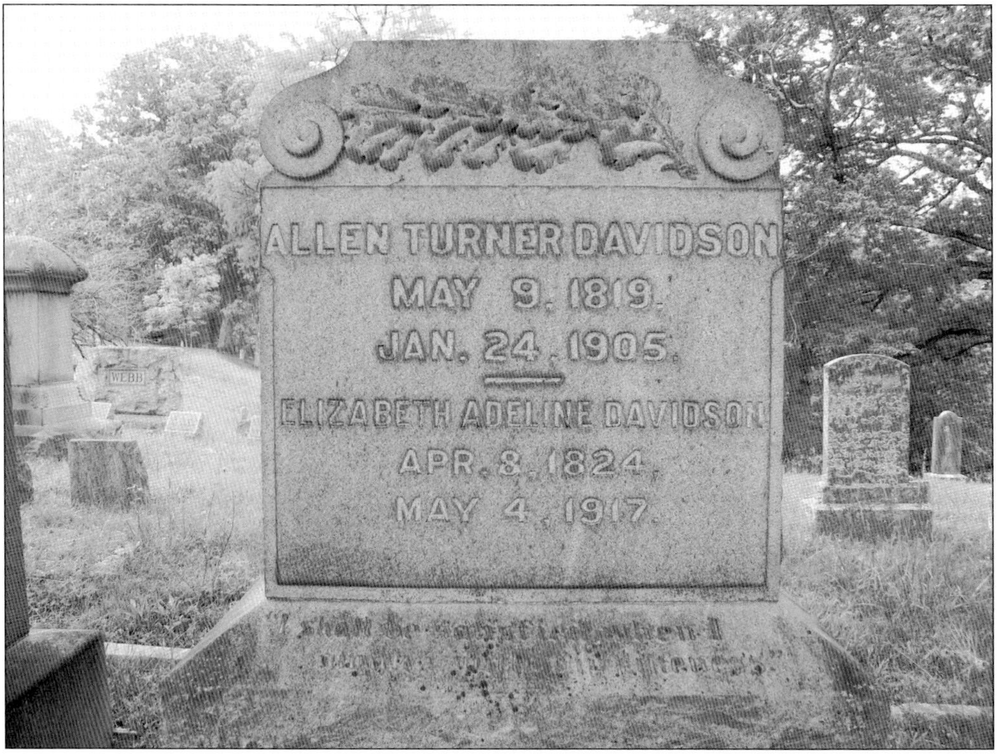

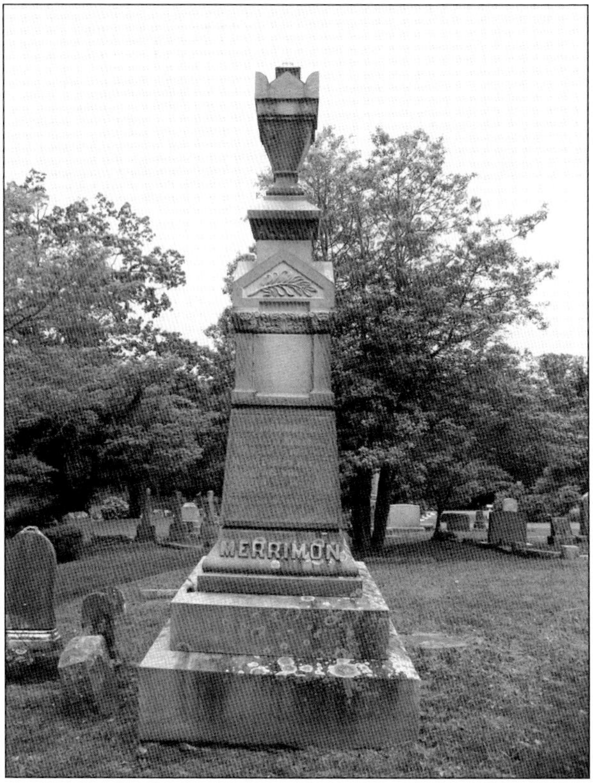

Allen Turner Davidson was elected to the North Carolina Secession Convention and the Provisional Congress of the Confederacy before being serving in the House of Representatives of the Confederate Congress in 1862. Davidson served only one term, being forced out because of his more moderate views and distaste for secession, but he later served on the council of state of his cousin, Gov. Zebulon Vance.

James Harvey Merrimon was the youngest of three brothers to enter into service for the Confederate army. He volunteered as adjutant for Company F of the 7th North Carolina Cavalry Battalion in 1862, though he only saw limited action, having primarily administrative duties. After the war, Merrimon was a prominent lawyer and superior court judge. Merrimon Avenue was named in his honor.

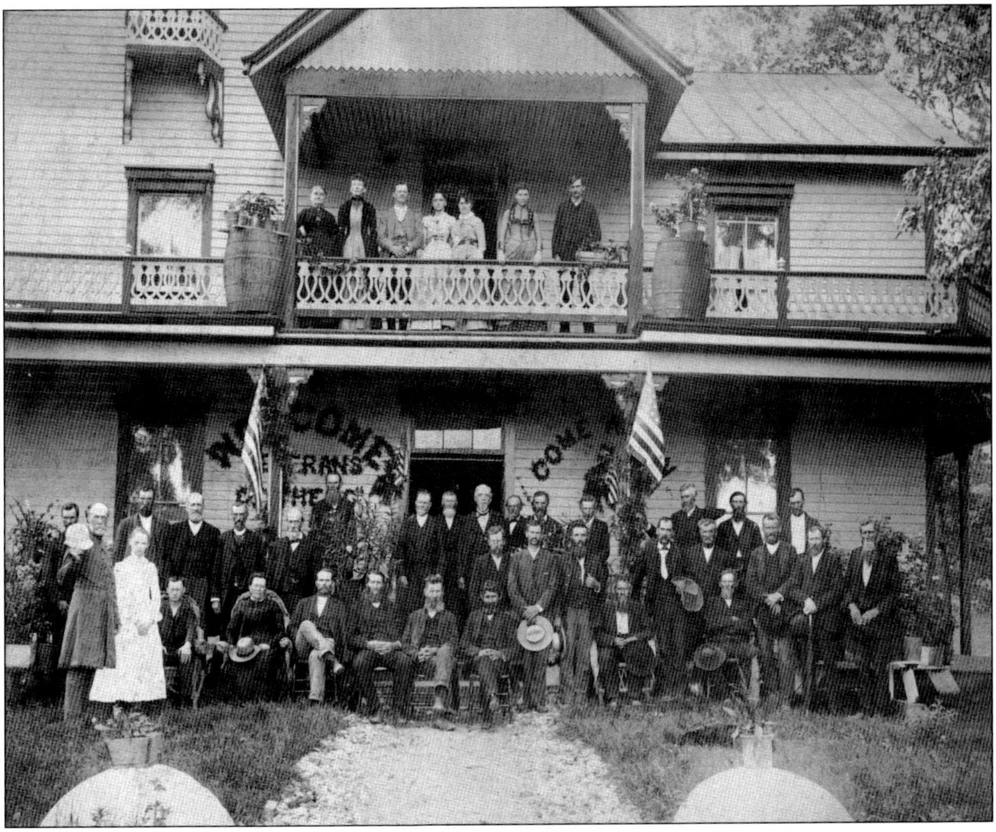

Col. Stephen Lee, cousin to Gen. Robert E. Lee, was a Charleston lawyer who came to Asheville with the intention of starting a school. Lee's Select School for Boys became well known throughout the South for its discipline and rigorous curriculum. Lee taught there until the onset of the war, upon which he joined the Confederacy at the age of 60 along with all nine of his sons. Of the nine, four gave their lives to the cause. Lee commanded the 16th North Carolina Regiment for most of the war before returning to Buncombe County to form the Silver Grays (many of whom are pictured above at an 1889 reunion). Though less than 300 in number, this company, composed of mainly older men and young boys, was able to repel a Union force of over 1,100 men in the Battle of Asheville, one of the last actions of the Civil War. (Above, NCC.)

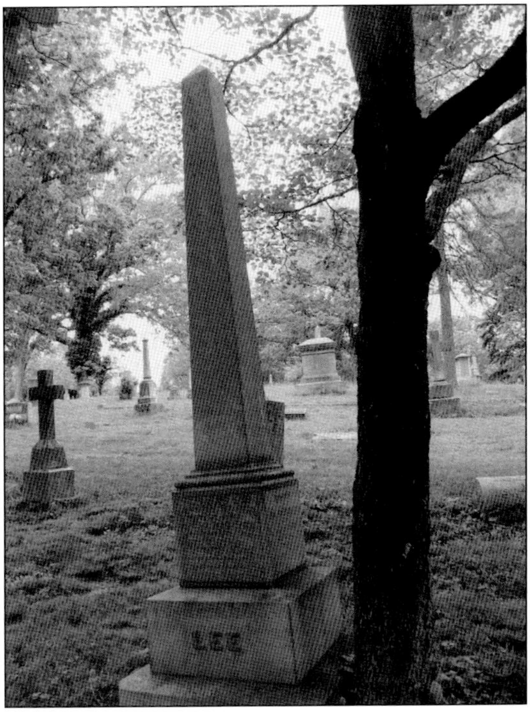

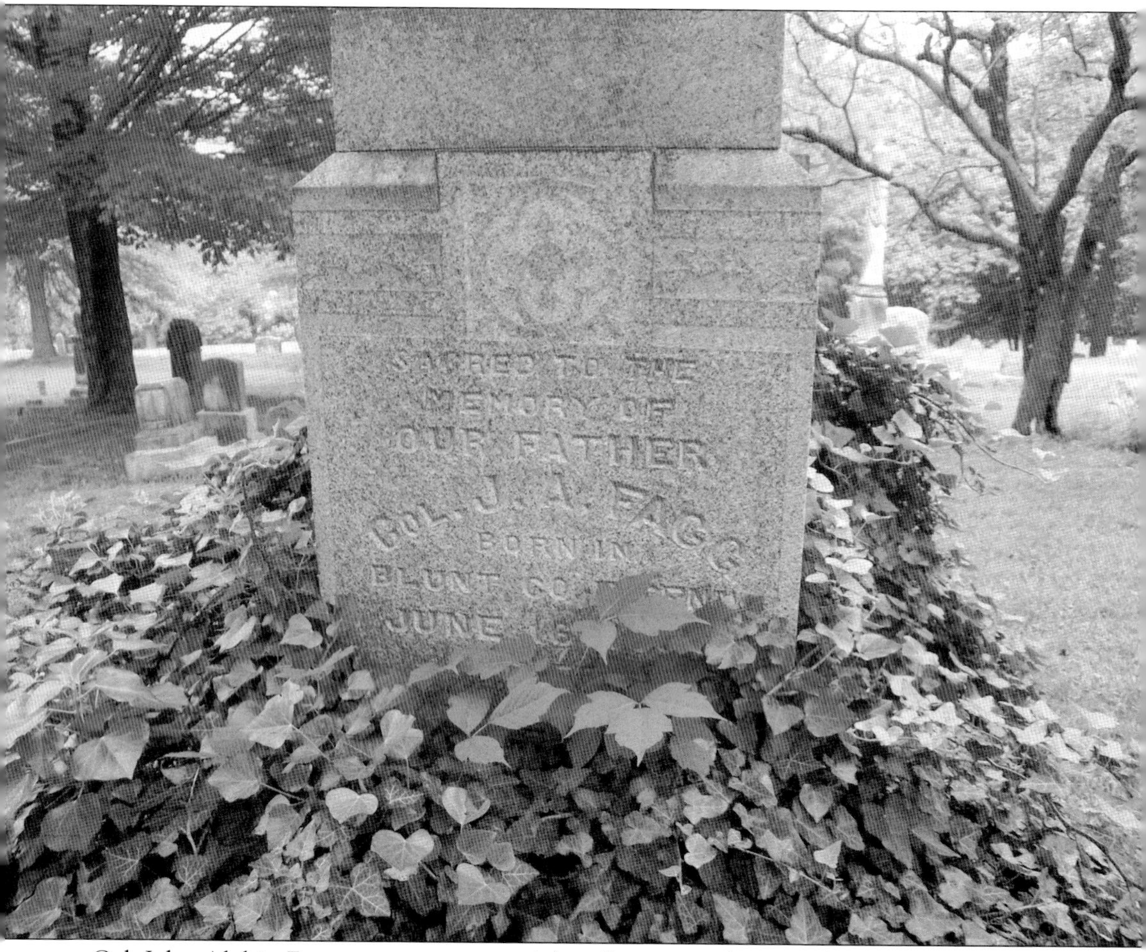

Col. John Alphin Fagg was a prominent Asheville citizen who served with distinction in the Mexican-American War. Upon his death in May 1888, the *Asheville Citizen* wrote of a touching instance of affection from his two beloved terriers. The dogs had been his constant companions is his later years and were inconsolable upon being separated from their master when he passed away. They went from room to room of his home looking for the colonel and then wandered off to the homes of other family members where they had been with him before. Eventually, the female dog, who had been closest to Colonel Fagg, found her way to his gravesite in the cemetery, though she had not been present at his burial. The dog rested upon his grave for the next several weeks and eventually passed away there. W.S. Cornell had her buried at the foot of Colonel Fagg's grave to reunite them once more.

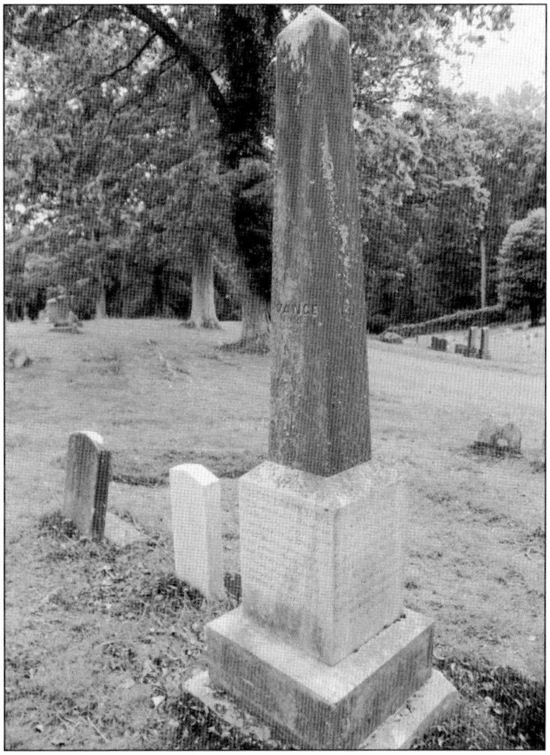

Robert Brank Vance was the older brother of Gov. Zebulon Vance and is often overlooked because of his famous sibling. However, Robert had an arguably more notable military career, and his political successes rivaled those of Zebulon. Robert was commissioned by Jefferson Davis as a brigadier general and commanded the 11th Tennessee Infantry following the death of James E. Raines at the Battle of Murfreesboro. During the battle, Robert was nearly killed himself by a shell that killed his horse beneath him. After contracting typhoid fever, he was transferred back to North Carolina, where he served until captured by Union troops at Crosby's Creek, Tennessee. He was held at Fort Delaware until the war's end. Following the war, Robert was elected to the US House of Representatives six consecutive times from 1873 until 1885. (Below, LOC.)

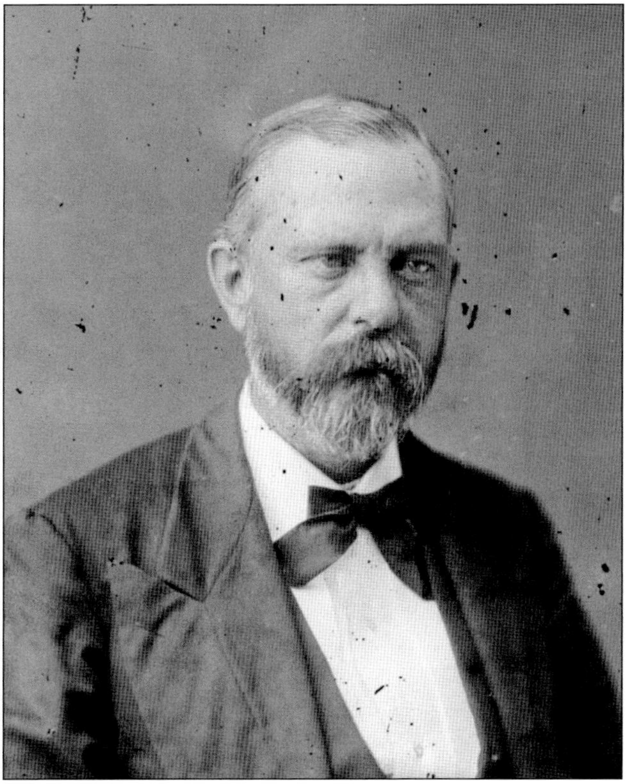

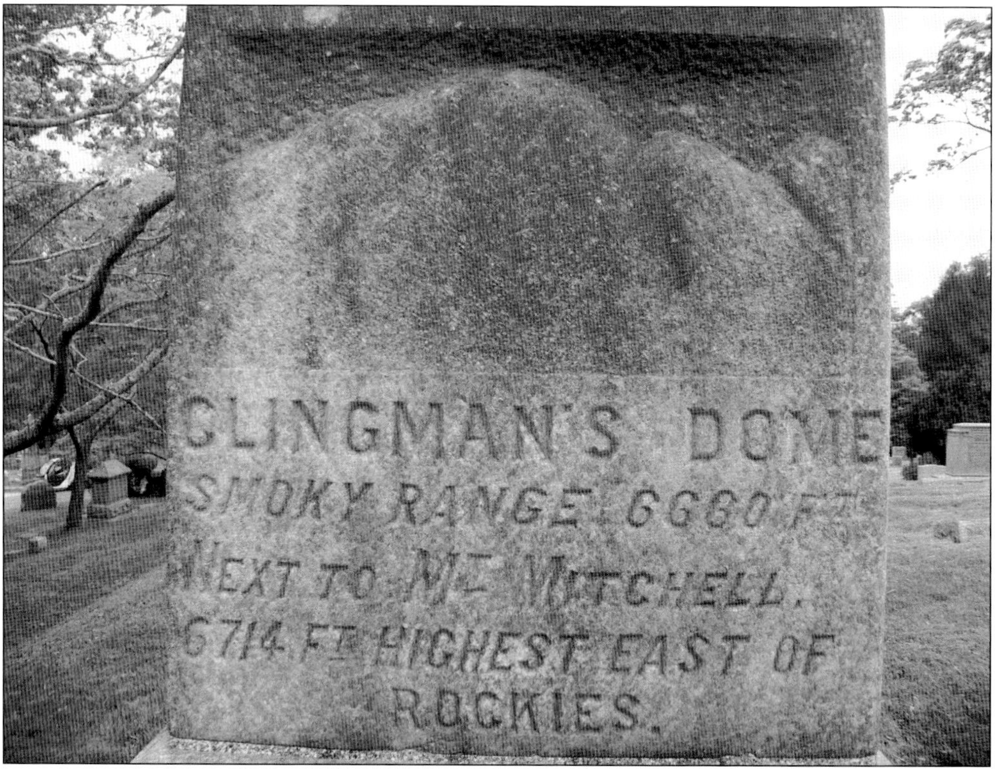

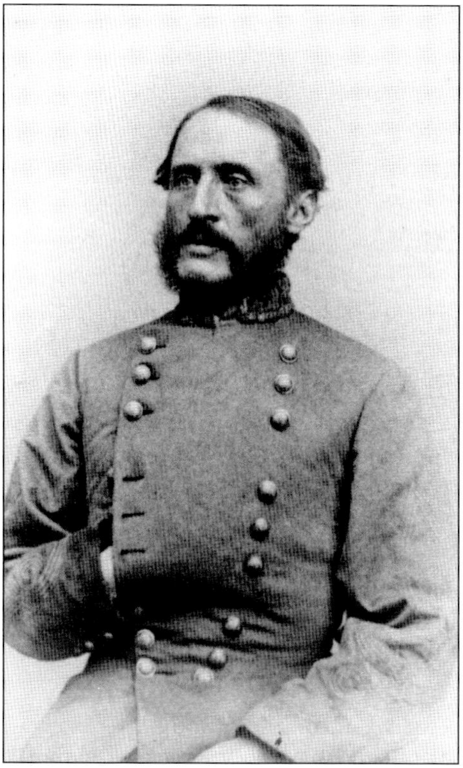

Thomas Lanier Clingman was a US senator from 1858 until 1861, when he was the last Southern senator to leave Congress. During his time there, he earned the nickname "the Prince of Politicians" as well as a reputation for hotheadedness that culminated in a duel with fellow congressman William Yancey. When he was expelled from Congress in 1861 in absentia, Clingman led the 25th North Carolina Regiment for the Confederacy as colonel and later brigadier general. He narrowly avoided death on several occasions during battle but managed to emerge from the war relatively unscathed. As he was prohibited from returning to politics, Clingman instead devoted his time to scientific studies of the Appalachian Mountains. The highest peak in the Great Smoky Mountains was named Clingman's Dome in his honor. (Left, LOC.)

Thomas Dillard Johnston entered the Confederate army in May 1861 as a part of Zebulon Vance's "Rough and Ready" 14th North Carolina Regiment. After being wounded thrice at the Battle of Malvern Hill and in the Shenandoah Valley Campaigns, Johnston left military service and retired to Asheville. There, he served as mayor, state representative, and twice in the US Senate. (NCC.)

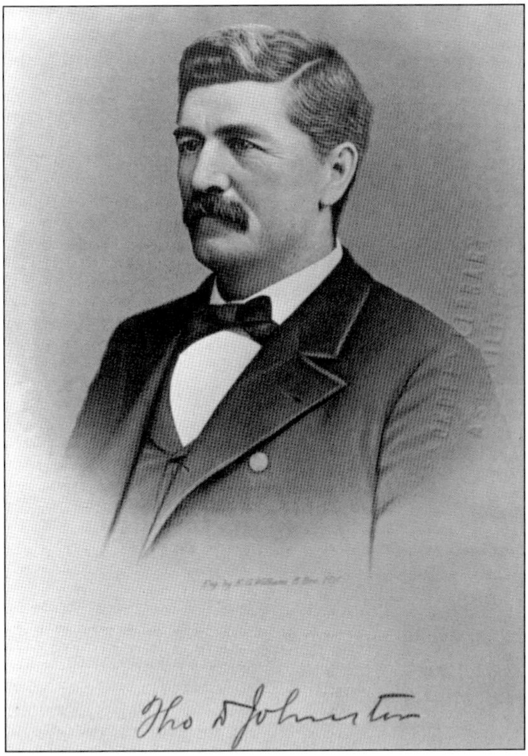

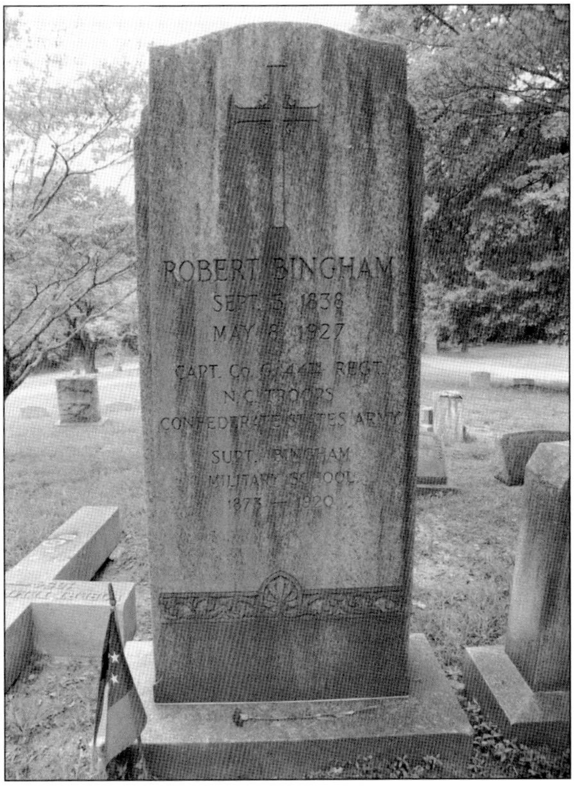

Robert Bingham was a well-known educator in Hillsborough, North Carolina, until 1862, when he joined the 44th North Carolina Infantry and was elected captain. He was captured in June 1863 and spent a great part of the war as a prisoner in Point Lookout, Maryland. After being released, Bingham rejoined his father's school and became headmaster in 1873. The Bingham School was moved to Asheville, where it gained national prominence under Bingham's direction.

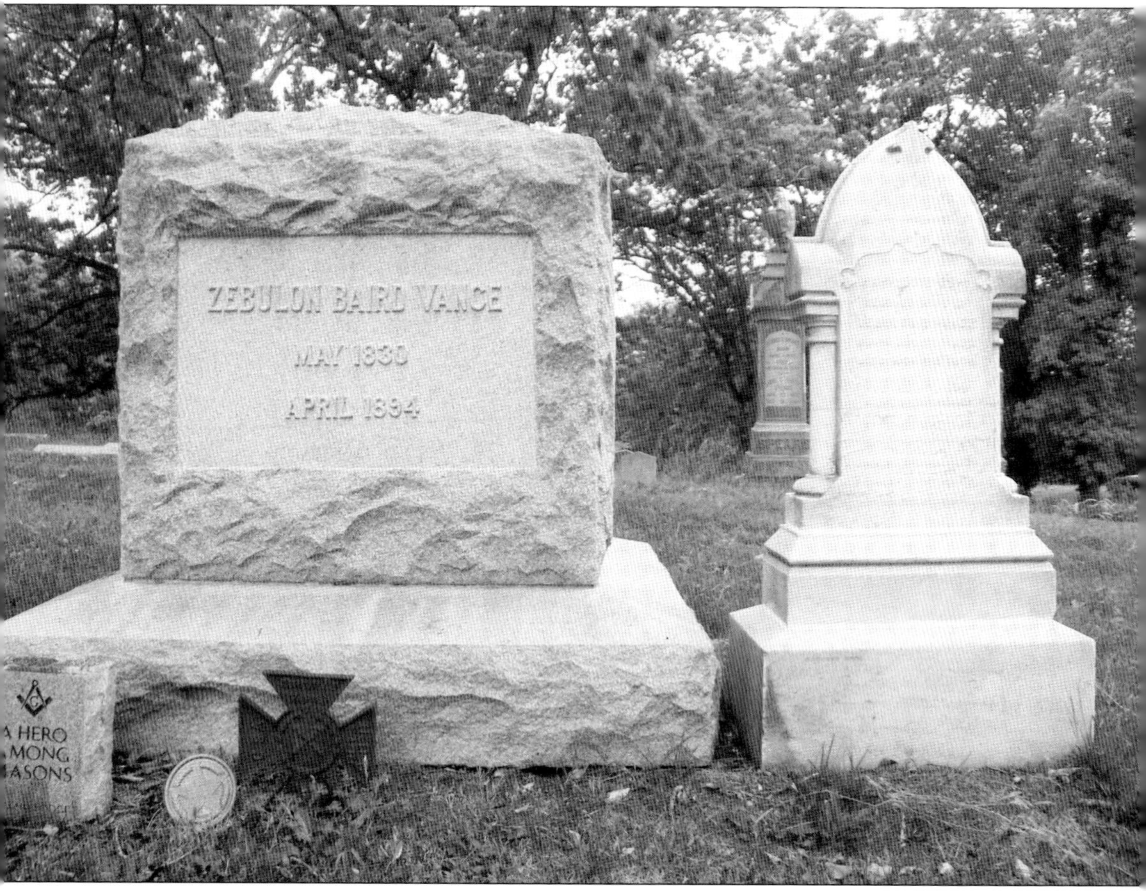

Zebulon Vance is arguably the most famous political figure in North Carolina history and has been for years been called "Mister North Carolina." Vance had reluctantly entered the Civil War upon hearing of President Lincoln's call for North Carolina troops to attack South Carolina. He said at the time, "If war is to come, I prefer to be with my own people." Vance commanded the "Rough and Ready Guards" 14th North Carolina Regiment and 26th North Carolina Regiment until he was called away to serve as governor of North Carolina in 1862. Vance earned the name "War Governor of the South" by continually being at odds with the Confederate government of Jefferson Davis. He was reelected in 1864 before being replaced by William Woods Holden after the surrender of the Confederacy. While under the political restrictions of the 14th Amendment, Vance practiced law in Charlotte. His most infamous client was murderer Tom Dula, a former Confederate soldier about whom the song "Tom Dooley" was written. After Dula's pardon in 1867, Vance was elected governor once again and US senator on four occasions.

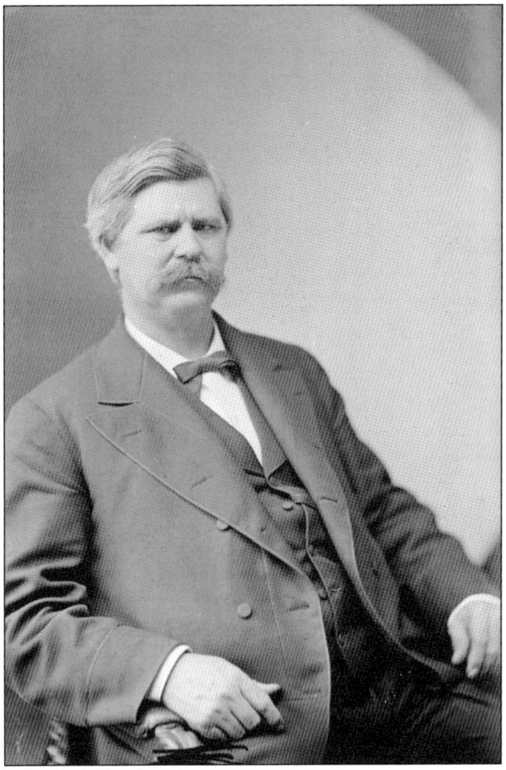

When Governor Vance passed away in April 1894, his burial became one of the largest events in Asheville's history, with thousands of mourners and flowers mounded on either side of the road for a mile. After the service, a strange wrangle among Vance's family played out in Riverside. He had originally been interred in his family plot with the intention of moving his first wife, Henriette, beside him. His second wife, Florence Steele Martin, had his remains removed to what she deemed a more appropriate spot for a man of his stature. Vance's son Charles learned of the removal and had his father disinterred and moved back to the original spot. The two family members argued through a series of letters in the *Asheville Citizen* before it was decided to let the governor remain at his original site. (Right, LOC.)

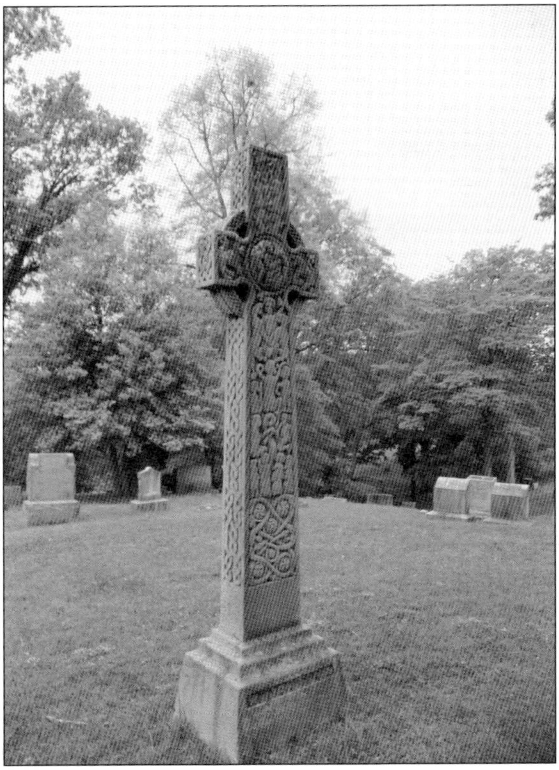

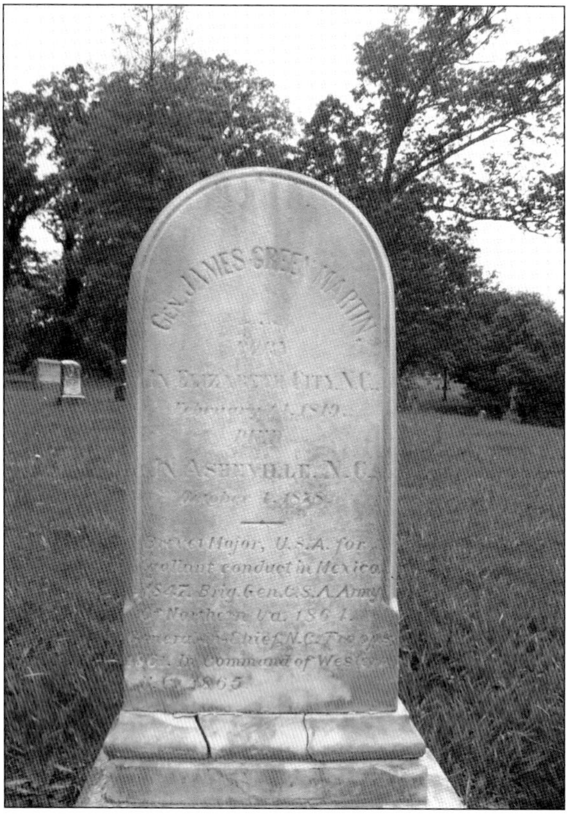

Gen. James Green Martin was affectionately known by his troops as "Ole One Wing" after losing an arm while serving alongside Stonewall Jackson during the Mexican-American War. Martin went on to become one of the best-known generals of the Civil War. In 1861, Martin was appointed adjutant general and was given all military power in the state to organize soldiers and equipment. Under his charge, North Carolina's troops were the most numerous and well equipped in the Confederate army. At the request of the Confederate government, Martin was commissioned as brigadier general and given command of the brigade at Kinston, North Carolina, tasked with holding Gen. Ambrose Burnside in check and protecting Richmond, Virginia. General Martin took command of the western troops in 1865 and was able to prevent the razing of Asheville with his stand at Swannanoa Gap. (Below, LOC.)

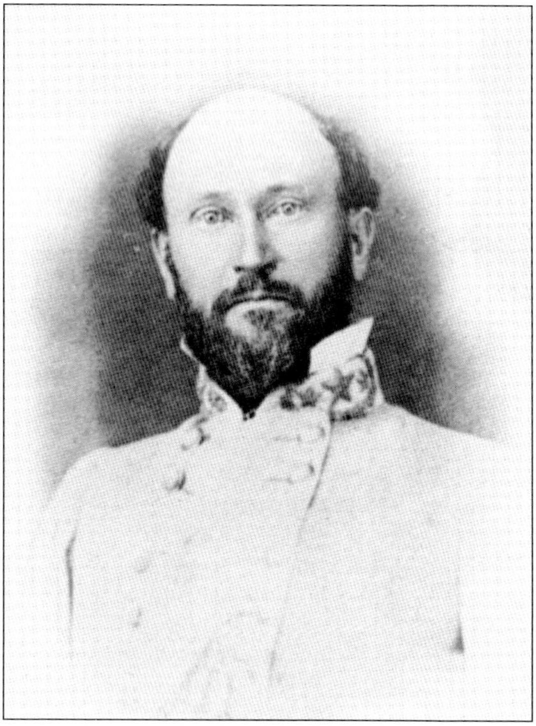

The Battle of Asheville, one of the last engagements of the Civil War, was fought on April 6, 1865, less than half a mile from the property that was to become Riverside Cemetery. The almost bloodless battle was fought between the 101st Ohio Infantry, comprising 1,100 men led by Col. Isaac B. Kirby, and the remnants of the 62nd North Carolina Infantry, led by General Martin. (NCC.)

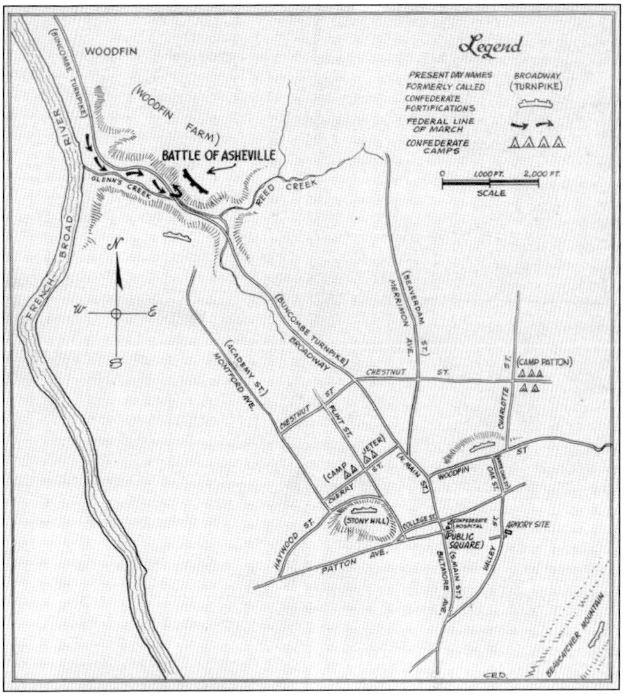

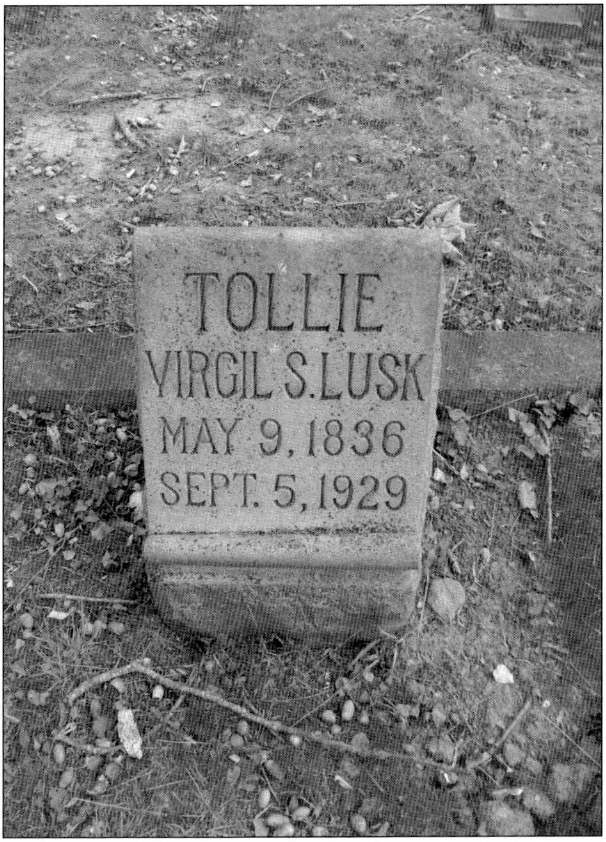

Col. Virgil S. Lusk spent a large part of the Civil War at Johnson's Island, a Union prison. After his release, Lusk became a fierce opponent of the Ku Klux Klan while serving as a US district attorney. He was ambushed by KKK leader and founder of the *Asheville Citizen* Randolph Shotwell at Pack Square. Lusk was able to escape by turning and firing two shots at Shotwell's legs, maiming him.

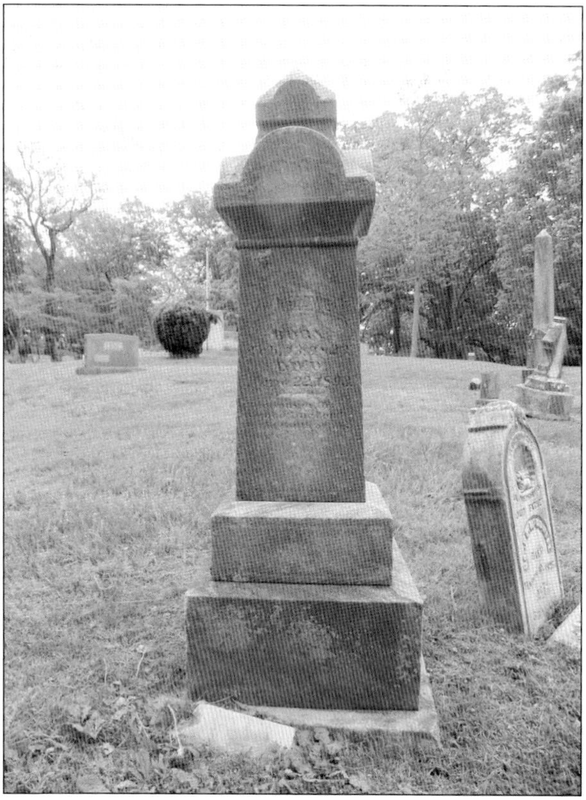

William Wallace McDowell was a Confederate major who organized the Buncombe Riflemen in 1861. He fought alongside them at the battles of Big Bethel, Chickamauga, and Bentonville. His home in Asheville, the Smith-McDowell House, is the oldest surviving house in Buncombe County and has been converted into a museum.

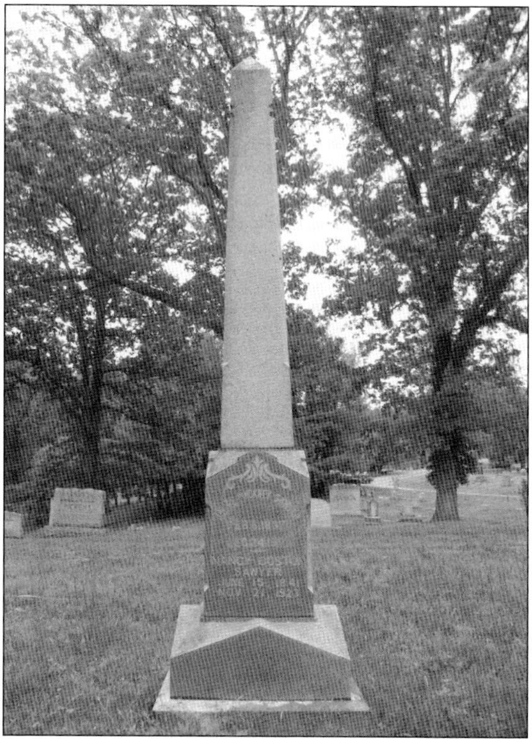

James Pinckney Sawyer was the son of Asheville's first mayor, Isaac B. Sawyer. He enlisted in Company A of the 25th North Carolina Infantry and was quickly named captain. He remained in the Confederate army until he was mustered out at Appomattox Court House when General Lee surrendered. Sawyer became the president of the Battery Park Bank as well as Asheville's fire chief following the war.

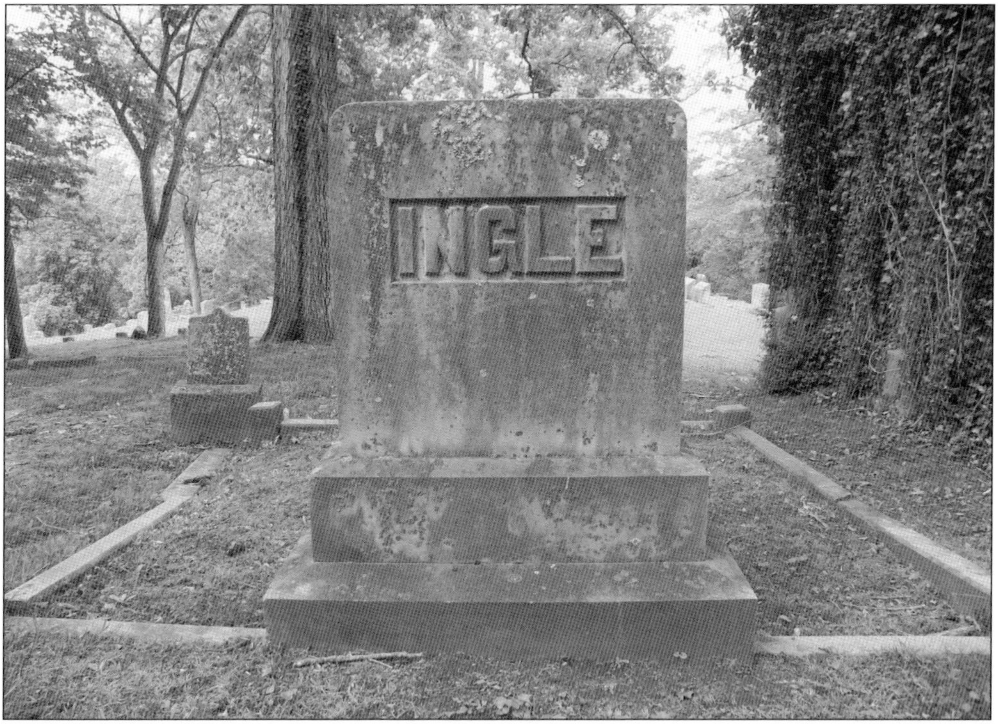

Lt. James M. Ingle's service in the Civil War is remarkable for both its length and patriotic devotion. Ingle participated in almost every major engagement from Manassas to Appomattox and was one of only three soldiers to escape General Grant's army at Petersburg. He was commended for heroism at both Gettysburg and Chancellorsville as he was among the last to retreat before overwhelming forces.

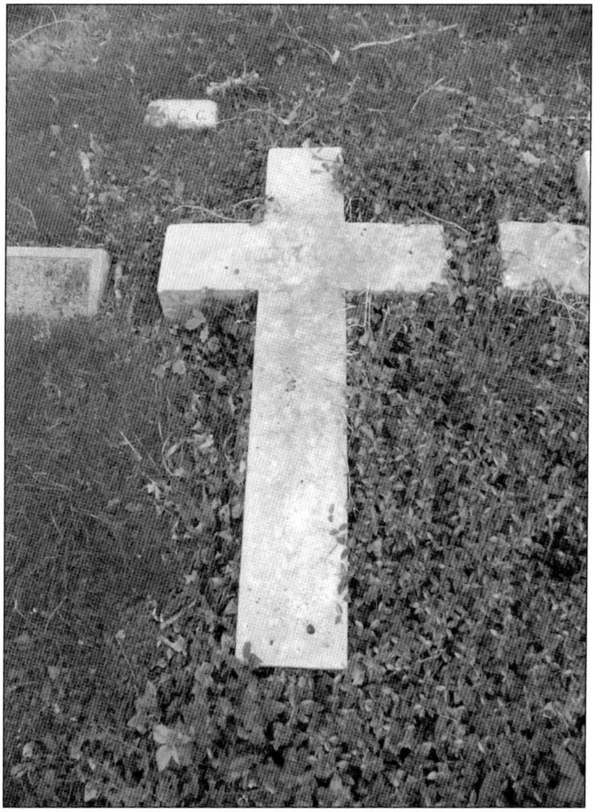

Lt. Col. John Kerr Connally became a military legend after leading the charge on Reynold's Brigade at Gettysburg. He was wounded twice bearing the Confederate flag after the color bearers were shot as his company fought its way to Gen. Stonewall Jackson on Cemetery Ridge. Connally was awarded the Cross of Honor in 1904 for his actions. His home after the war, Fernihurst, became the social center for Asheville's elite.

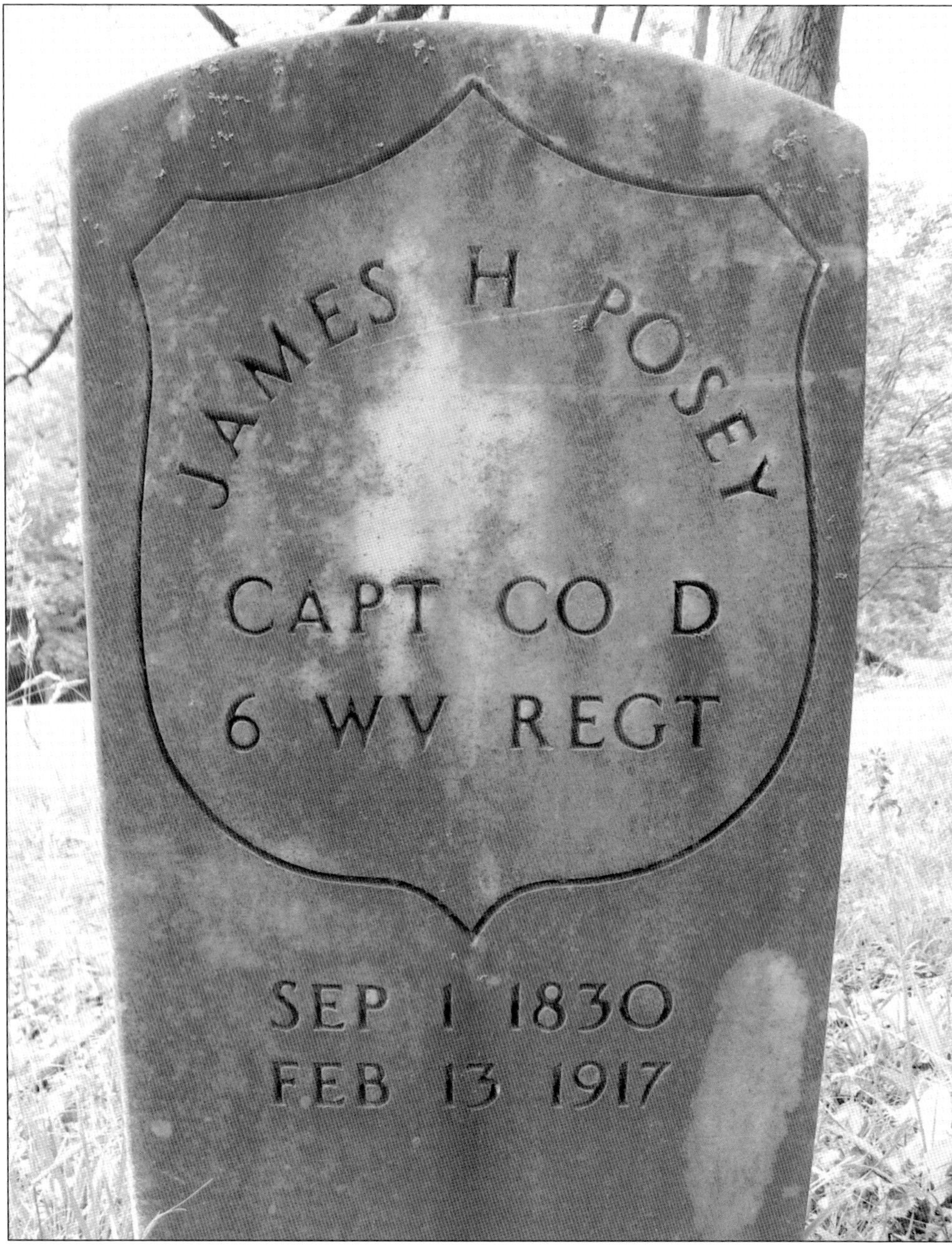

Capt. James Posey was a well-known Asheville character whose eccentricities endeared him to many. Though he was of an advanced age, on clear days he could be found in his chair in front of the Asheville fire station on the square handing out cards upon which he had printed "Do not Swear" or admonishing boys who he caught spitting on the sidewalks. In 1917, Posey was hit by a wagon crossing Patton Avenue and passed away from the injuries he sustained. Only after his death did many of the people of Asheville learn of his stellar military career. Posey had joined the Union army in the 6th West Virginia Regiment and was elected captain of the unit. After two years of service, he was chosen to be the personal bodyguard of Pres. Abraham Lincoln. He acted in this capacity until Lincoln's death in 1865 and then retired to Asheville for his health.

Three

Authors, Artists, and Architects

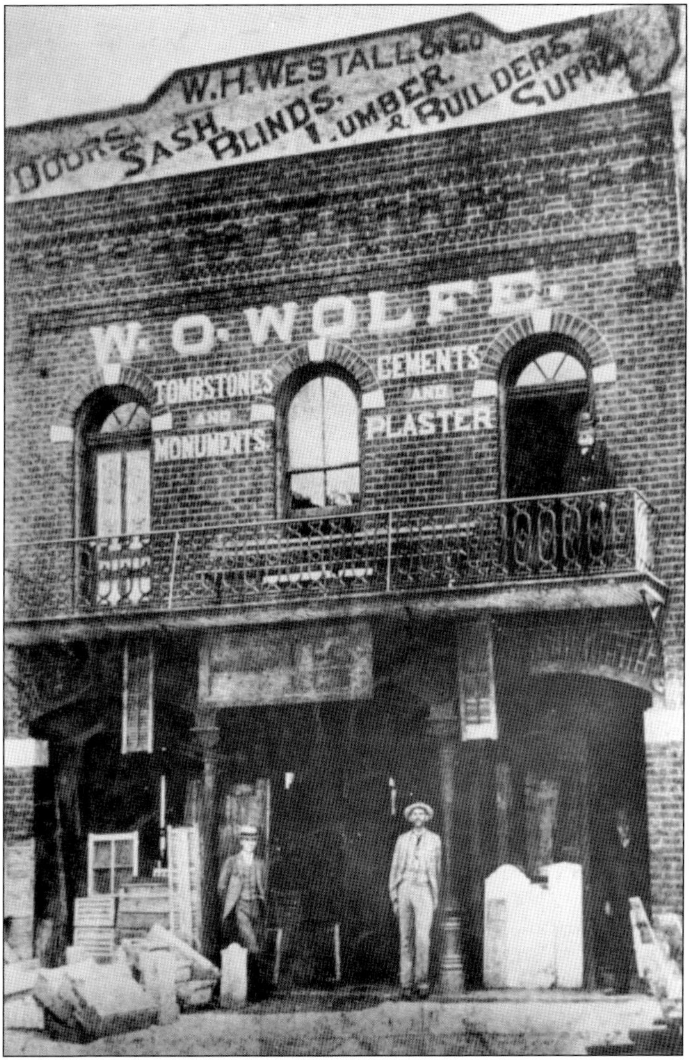

Asheville has long attracted artisans of all types, and perhaps no place has benefitted from this more than Riverside. Many of the monuments in the cemetery were crafted by master stonemasons drawn in by the allure of the booming mountain resort. Pictured here is the monument shop of W.O. Wolfe, one of the best-known monument masons in American history due to his son Thomas's writings. (TWC.)

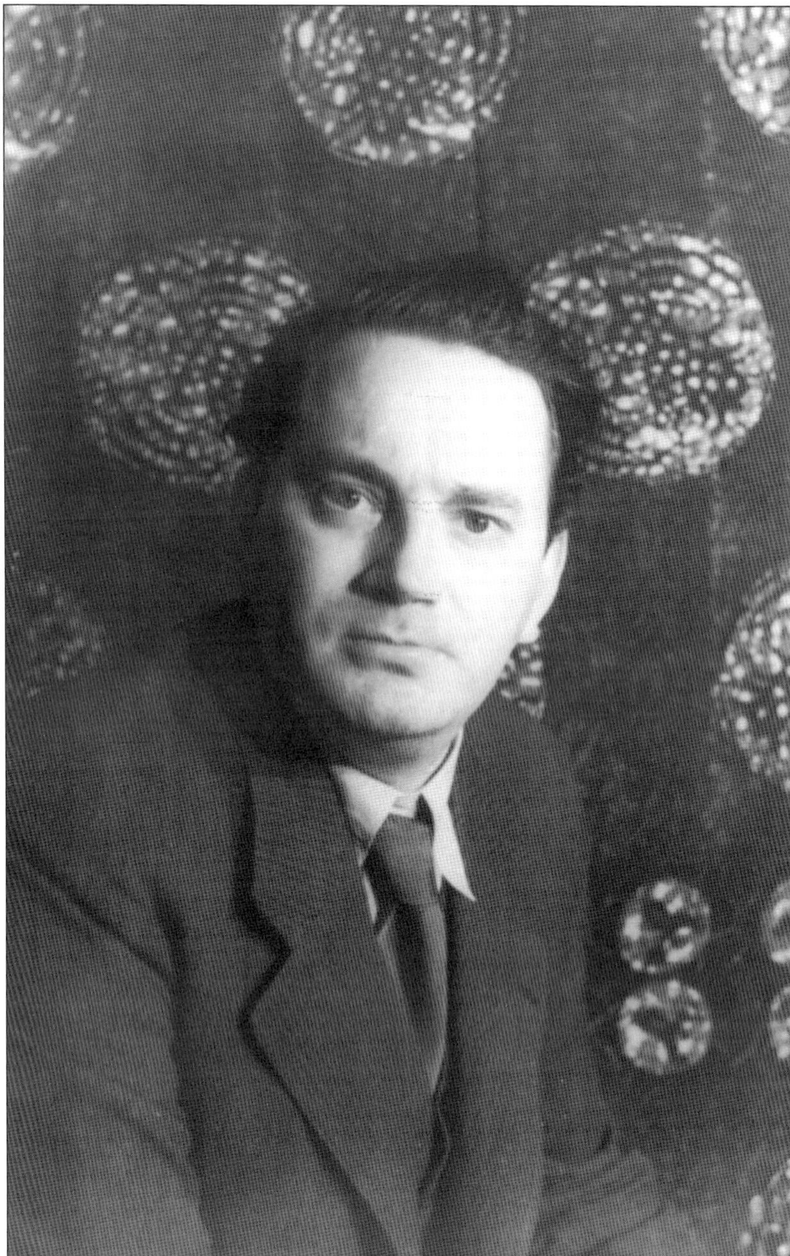

The most famous of North Carolina's authors, Thomas Clayton Wolfe was laid to his final rest at the highest point in Riverside, near his beloved brother Ben. He describes the cemetery as "a good place, on top of a hill" in his writings. Wolfe was born in Asheville in 1900, the youngest of eight children. His experiences growing up in Asheville at his mother's boardinghouse Old Kentucky Home were the basis for his first and best-known novel, *Look Homeward, Angel*. Wolfe became internationally known for his work and became a bestseller in Great Britain and Germany, where he is still held in great reverence. In all, Wolfe had 26 works published, many of them posthumously. He is considered one of the best writers of the golden age of American literature and by some its most talented. (LOC.)

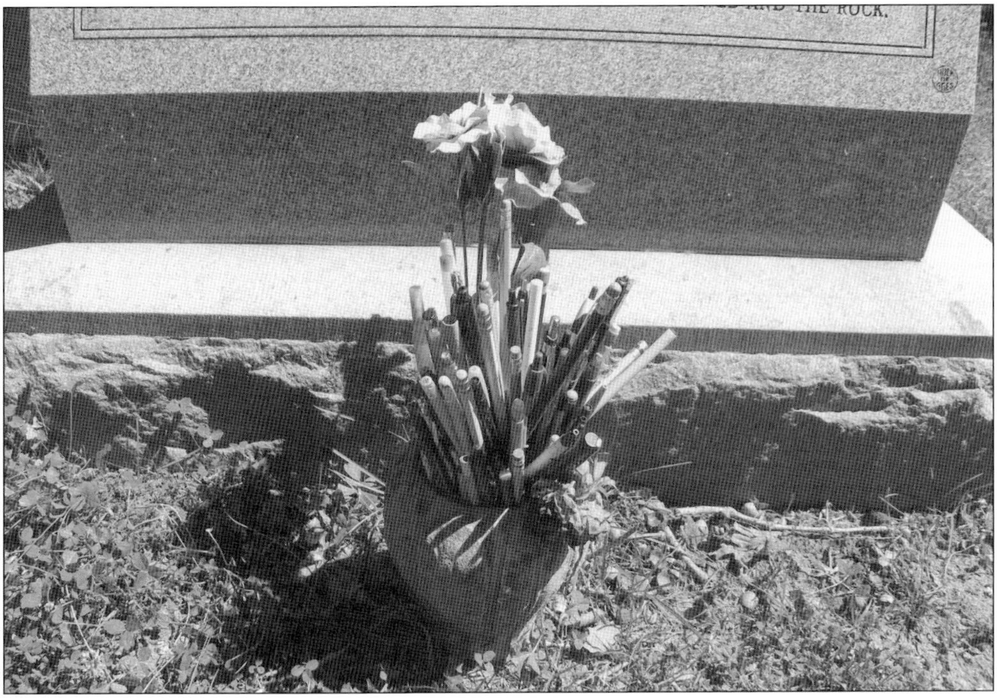

Two traditions have arisen around Thomas Wolfe's gravesite. Pencils and pens are left in the vase at Wolfe's grave along with notes by aspiring authors looking for a cure for writer's block. The other tradition takes place on September 15 each year, the anniversary of Wolfe's death. In his honor, visitors gather at his grave to share a bottle of scotch while reading passages from his works.

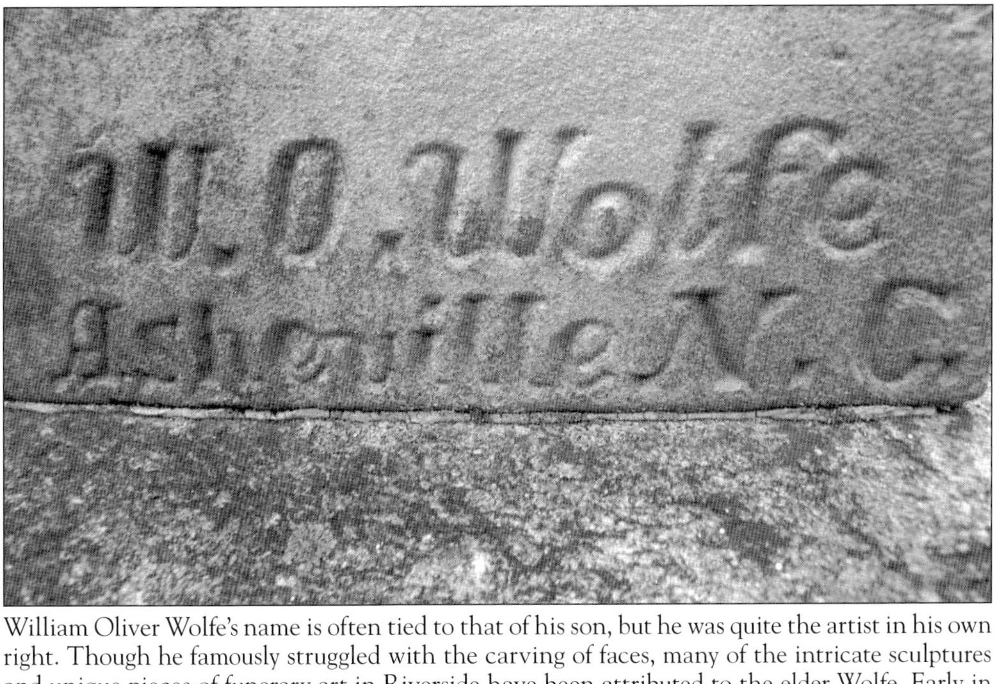

William Oliver Wolfe's name is often tied to that of his son, but he was quite the artist in his own right. Though he famously struggled with the carving of faces, many of the intricate sculptures and unique pieces of funerary art in Riverside have been attributed to the elder Wolfe. Early in his career as a monument mason, he inscribed his name in his finished pieces, as seen here.

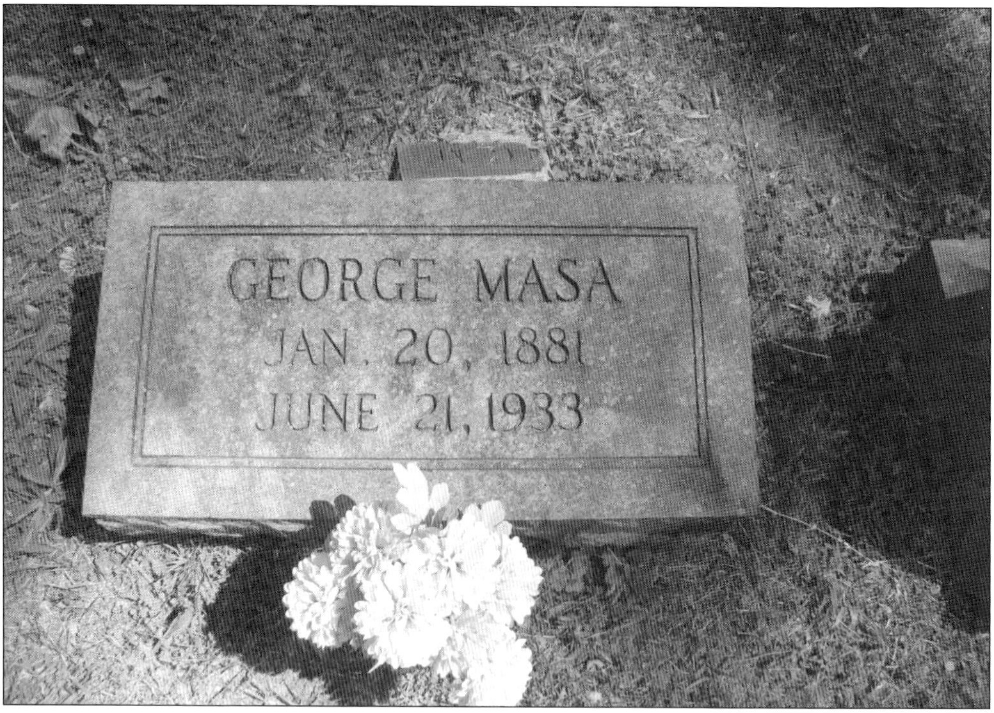

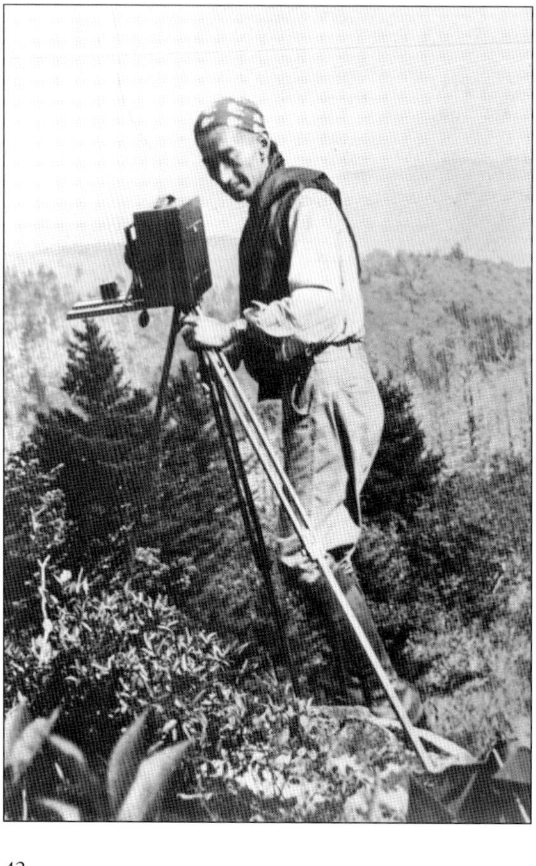

The headstone marking the grave of George Masa is a simple one, at odds with the enormous influence the man himself had on the world around him but also fitting for a man who believed in living simply. Masa was born Masahara Iizuka in 1881 in Japan and made his way to the United States with his parents after attending university. He worked at the Grove Park Inn as a valet before establishing his business as a large-format photographer. Masa loved the mountains of the Southern Highlands and was instrumental in establishing the Great Smoky Mountains National Park. When Masa passed away from influenza in 1933 almost penniless, members of the Carolina Mountain Club paid for the expense of his burial and for the monument that marks his passing. (Left, NCC.)

Vadim Bora was a master sculptor and painter whose works can be seen from his hometown in Russia to the Biltmore Estate. Bora was a founder of Asheville's booming art scene whose unique grave marker draws scores of visitors to Riverside. Bora chose the natural stone monument as one that never needed to be carved—its two embracing figures were sculpted by nature herself.

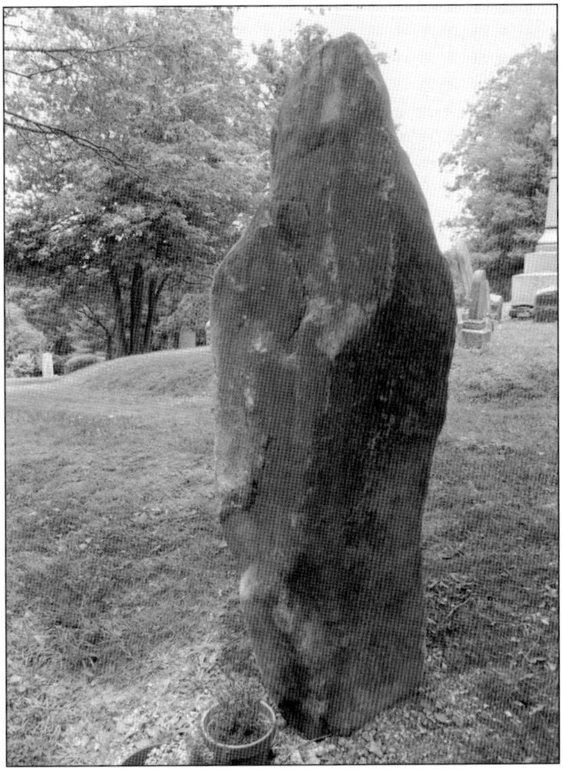

The Noland mausoleum is an eye-catching work of funerary art whose polished surface reflects the mountains surrounding it. This is fitting considering that the man entombed within, Kenneth Noland, was a leader of the color-field movement whose work has been featured from the Guggenheim to the Museum of Modern Art. The back window of the mausoleum contains a stained-glass reproduction of one his most famous pieces.

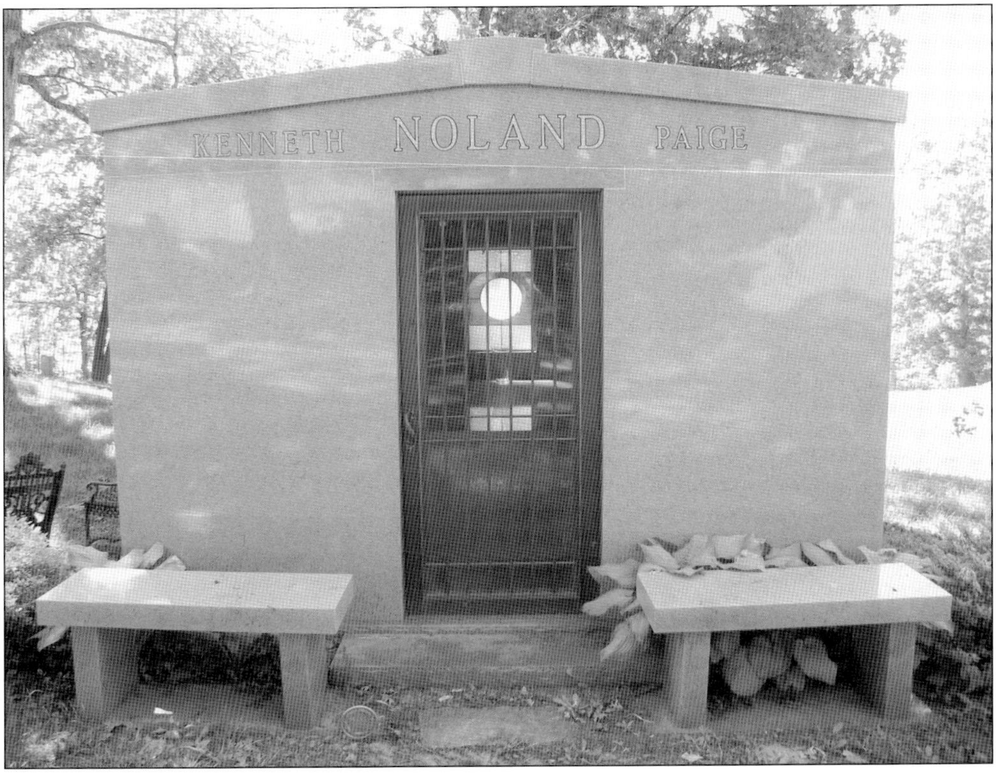

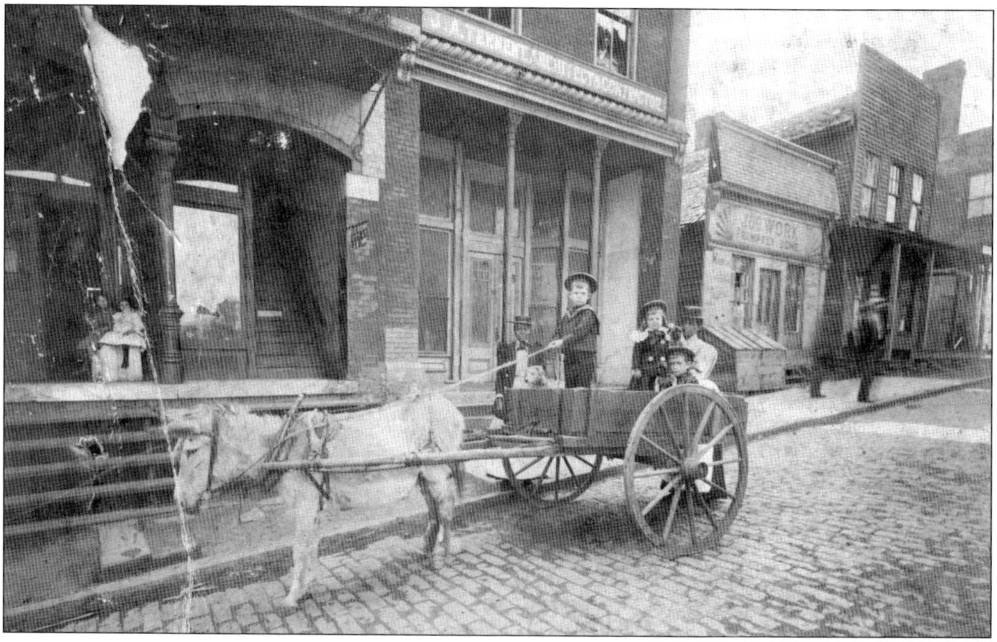

James Albert Tennent was a prominent builder and architect in the late 19th century who was responsible for some of Asheville's most iconic buildings, including the 1876 Buncombe County Courthouse and 1892 Asheville City Hall. Tennent owned the premises bordering the Wolfe building just off the square in downtown Asheville. (NCC.)

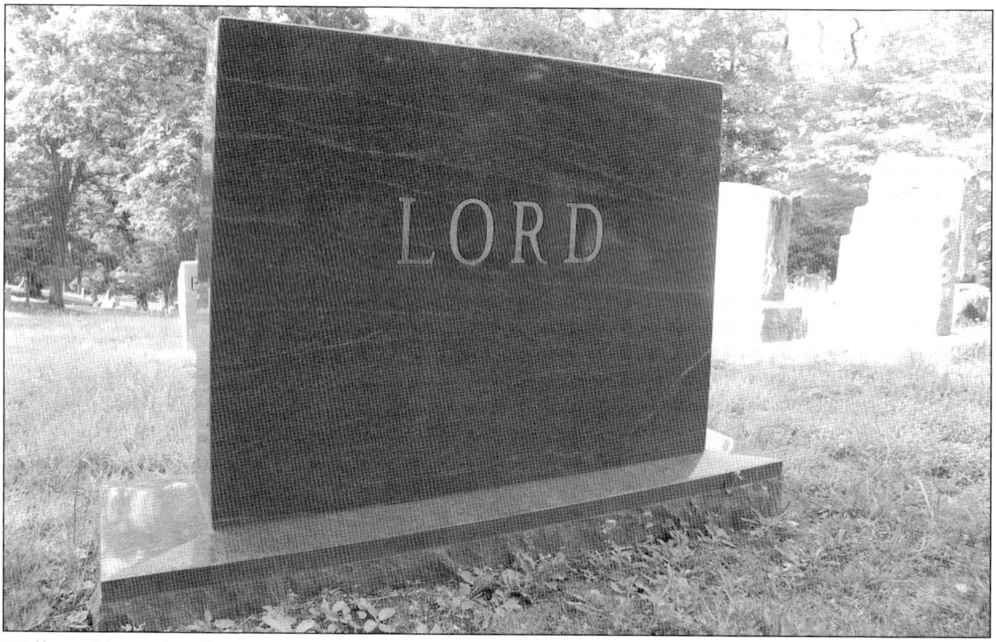

William Henry Lord was a prominent New York architect who moved to Asheville in 1899 at the urging of Richard Sharpe Smith. Lord was a devout classicist whose simple, utilitarian designs were in high demand for schools, hospitals, and offices throughout Western North Carolina. Lord was the first North Carolina architect to be named an American Institute of Architects (AIA) Fellow and served as president of the North Carolina chapter of the AIA until his death.

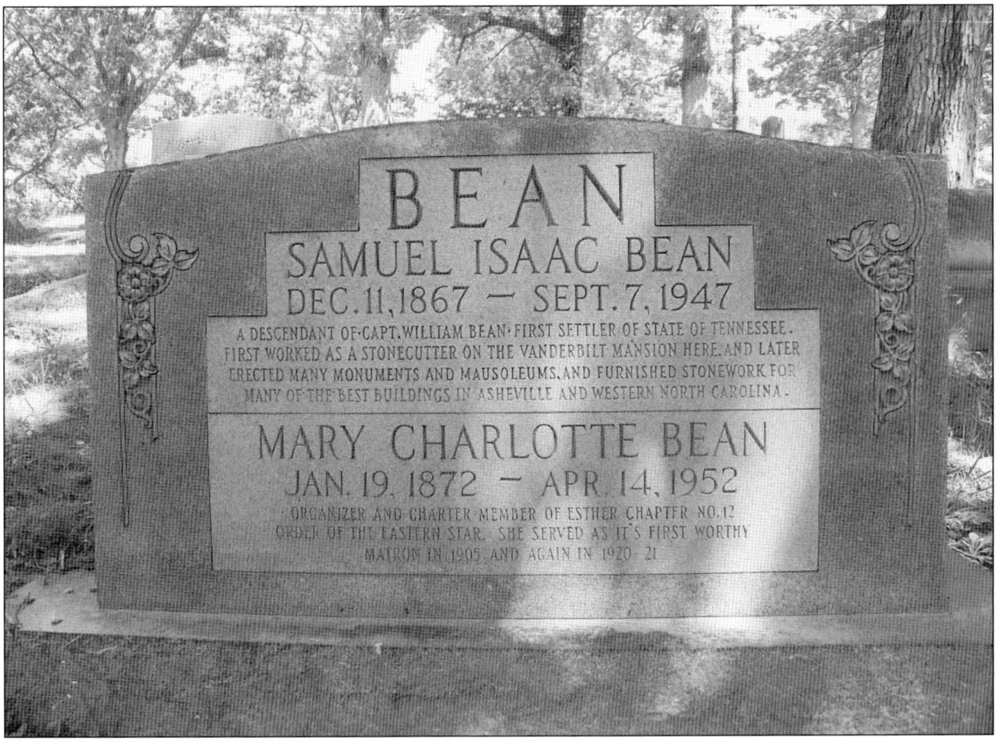

Many of the early monuments in Riverside came from the shop of stonecutter Samuel Isaac Bean. Bean had come to Asheville in 1891 to work on the construction of the Biltmore Estate as a stonecutter alongside Fred Miles. He worked for the Biltmore Estate for 12 years and then received the tile left over at the site from George Vanderbilt, of whom he was a favorite, in order to start his own monument business. His skill quickly made him the foremost monument mason in Asheville, much to the dismay of his professional rival, W.O. Wolfe. Many of the most recognizable buildings in Asheville from the early 20th century have elements from the S.I. Bean Tile and Marble Company. (Below, NCC.)

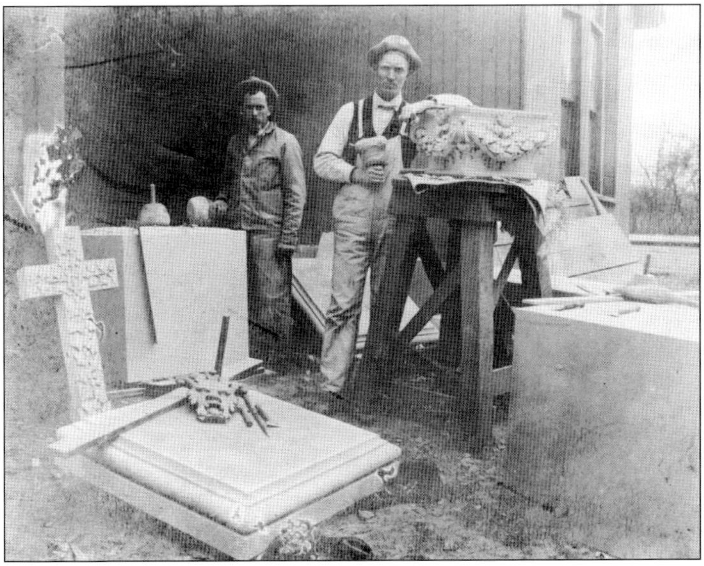

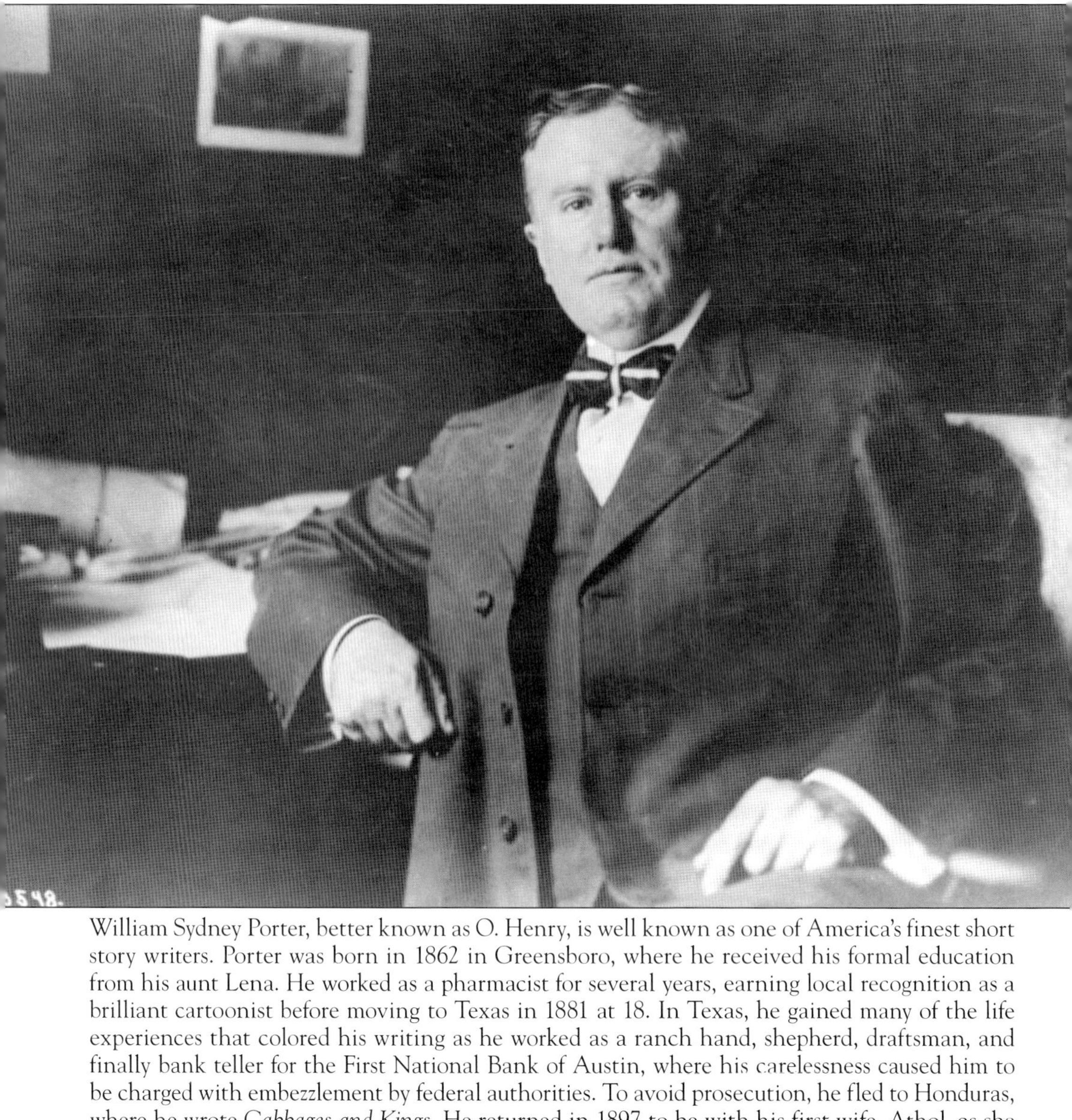

William Sydney Porter, better known as O. Henry, is well known as one of America's finest short story writers. Porter was born in 1862 in Greensboro, where he received his formal education from his aunt Lena. He worked as a pharmacist for several years, earning local recognition as a brilliant cartoonist before moving to Texas in 1881 at 18. In Texas, he gained many of the life experiences that colored his writing as he worked as a ranch hand, shepherd, draftsman, and finally bank teller for the First National Bank of Austin, where his carelessness caused him to be charged with embezzlement by federal authorities. To avoid prosecution, he fled to Honduras, where he wrote *Cabbages and Kings*. He returned in 1897 to be with his first wife, Athol, as she succumbed to tuberculosis, and he was convicted and sentenced to five years in prison. This is where he adopted his pen name. After being released, he moved to New York and began the most prolific part of his writing career, writing 381 short stories. (NCC.)

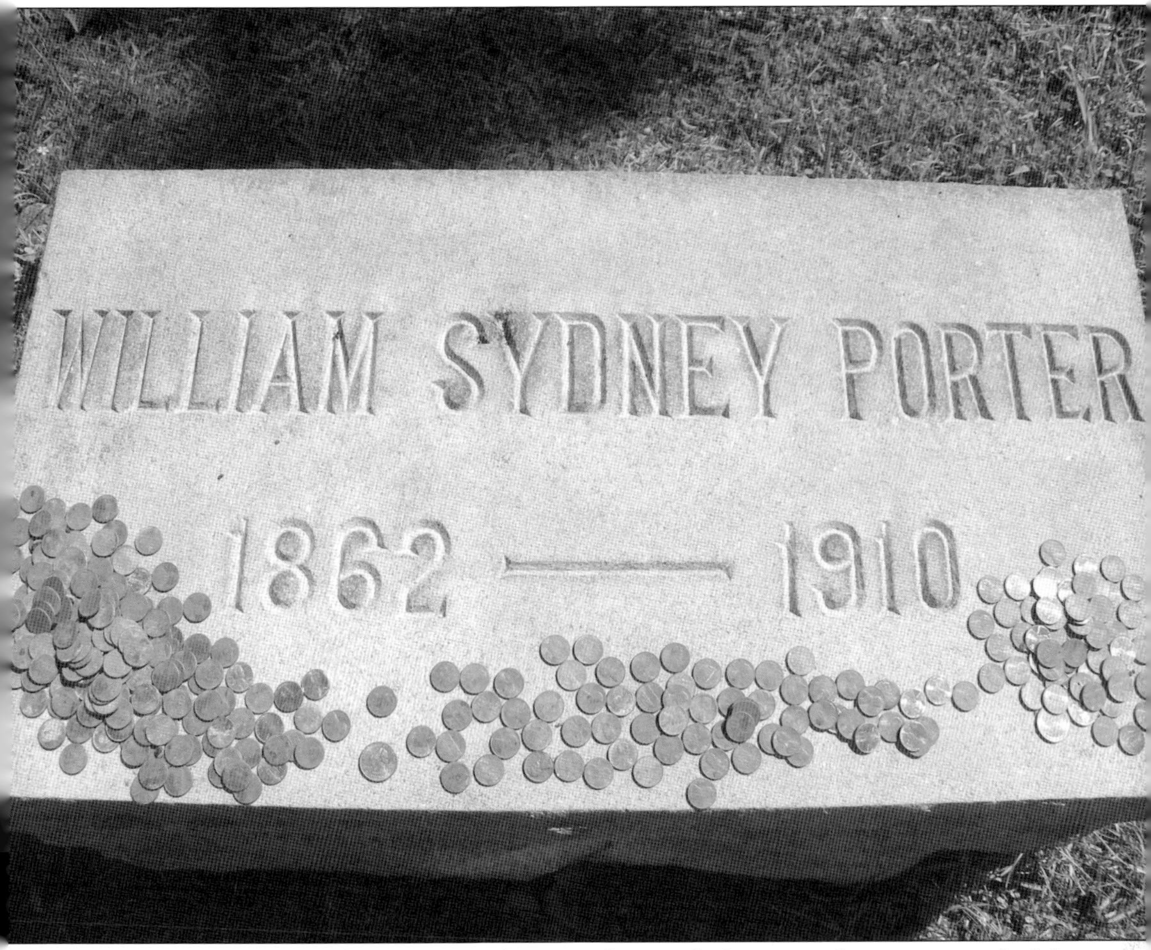

O Henry, the master of the surprise ending, was known for his witty short stories, colorful descriptions, and masterful wordplay, including the invention of the term *banana republic.*" O. Henry stories "The Ransom of Red Chief," "The Caballero's Way," and "The Cop and the Anthem" continue to be required reading in schools to this day. The best known of his works is undoubtedly "The Gift of the Magi," a tale of a poor young couple who part with their most precious possessions in order to buy Christmas presents for each other only to find that the gifts they bought were for the very thing the other sacrificed. The opening line of the story is "One dollar and eighty-seven cents. That was all." Ever since his untimely death in 1910 from cirrhosis of the liver, visitors to his gravesite have counted out that amount in pennies on his headstone in his honor.

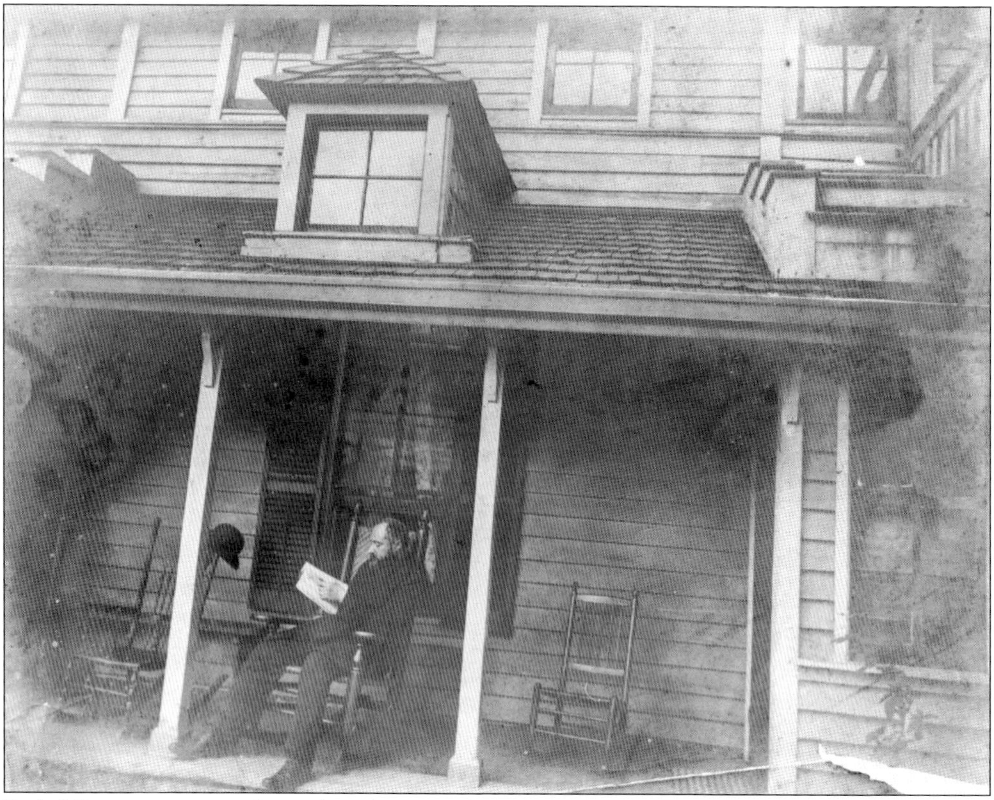

Rafael Guastavino was a Spanish architect and builder who became famous for his invention of the Guastavino tile, a system that allowed for the creation of self-supporting arches and architectural vaults. In 1881, Guastavino moved from Barcelona to New York City and was responsible for the tile work in hundreds of US landmarks, including Grand Central Terminal, Grant's Tomb, Carnegie Hall, the US Supreme Court Building, and the National Museum of Natural History. In 1890, George Vanderbilt hired Guastavino to construct the arches for his grand estate in Asheville. After this project, Guastavino retired to the North Carolina mountains, where he built his own estate, Rhododendron. One of his last projects was the Basilica of St. Lawrence, where he was allowed to be entombed in the crypt as a mark of honor rather than in his family lot in Riverside. (Above, NCC.)

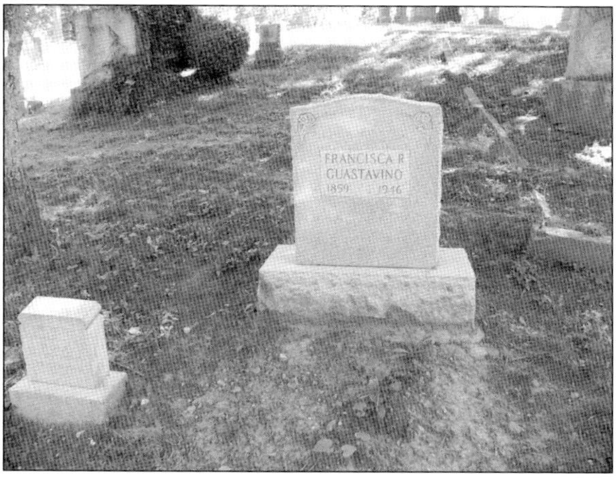

Caryl Florio was born as William James Robjohn in 1843. He was an English composer, organist, and choirmaster in New York before being brought to Asheville at the request of George Vanderbilt to lead music at Biltmore. He stayed at Biltmore until 1901 and then remained in Asheville, where he was organist, choirmaster, and music teacher at All Souls Church in Biltmore Village. (NCC.)

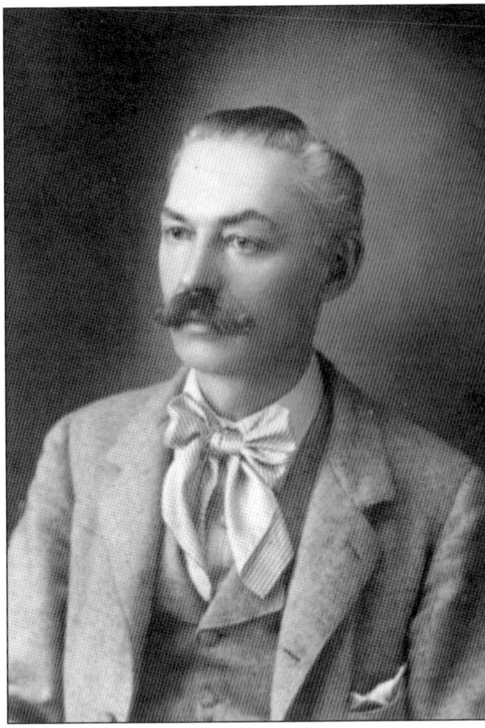

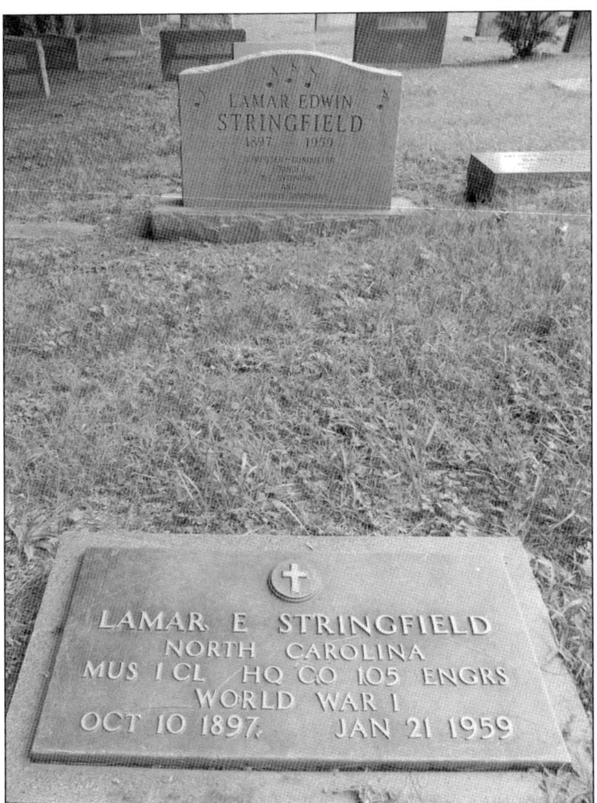

Lamar Stringfield was a highly respected composer, conductor, and musician who founded the North Carolina Symphony and served as conductor for the National Symphony Orchestra, US Navy Band, and Radio City Music Hall. He was also founder of the Asheville Symphony Orchestra and the Institute of Folk Music at the University of North Carolina–Chapel Hill.

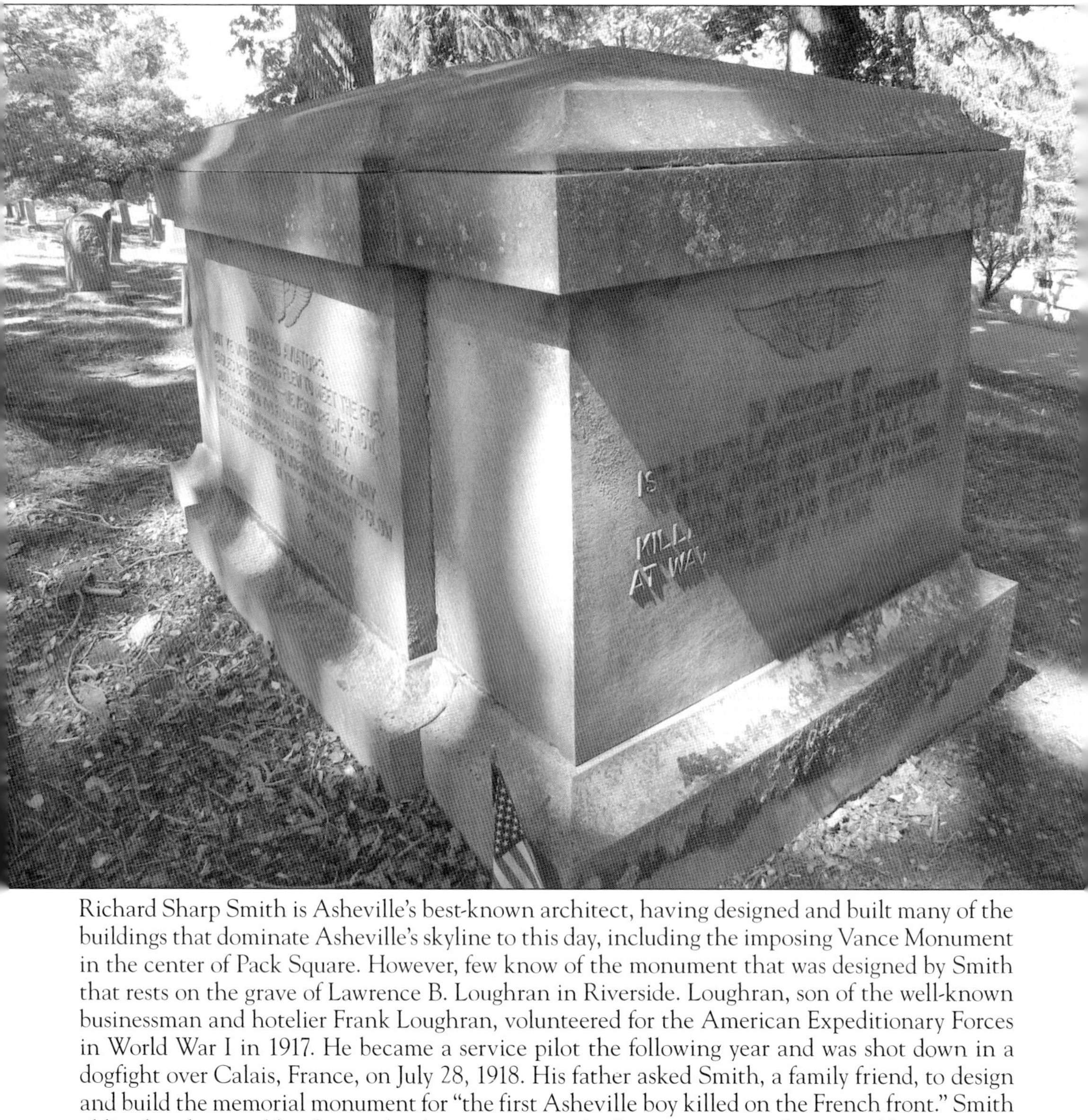

Richard Sharp Smith is Asheville's best-known architect, having designed and built many of the buildings that dominate Asheville's skyline to this day, including the imposing Vance Monument in the center of Pack Square. However, few know of the monument that was designed by Smith that rests on the grave of Lawrence B. Loughran in Riverside. Loughran, son of the well-known businessman and hotelier Frank Loughran, volunteered for the American Expeditionary Forces in World War I in 1917. He became a service pilot the following year and was shot down in a dogfight over Calais, France, on July 28, 1918. His father asked Smith, a family friend, to design and build the memorial monument for "the first Asheville boy killed on the French front." Smith obliged and created his first and only gravestone—the large granite tomb pictured here.

Four

Asheville's Movers and Shakers

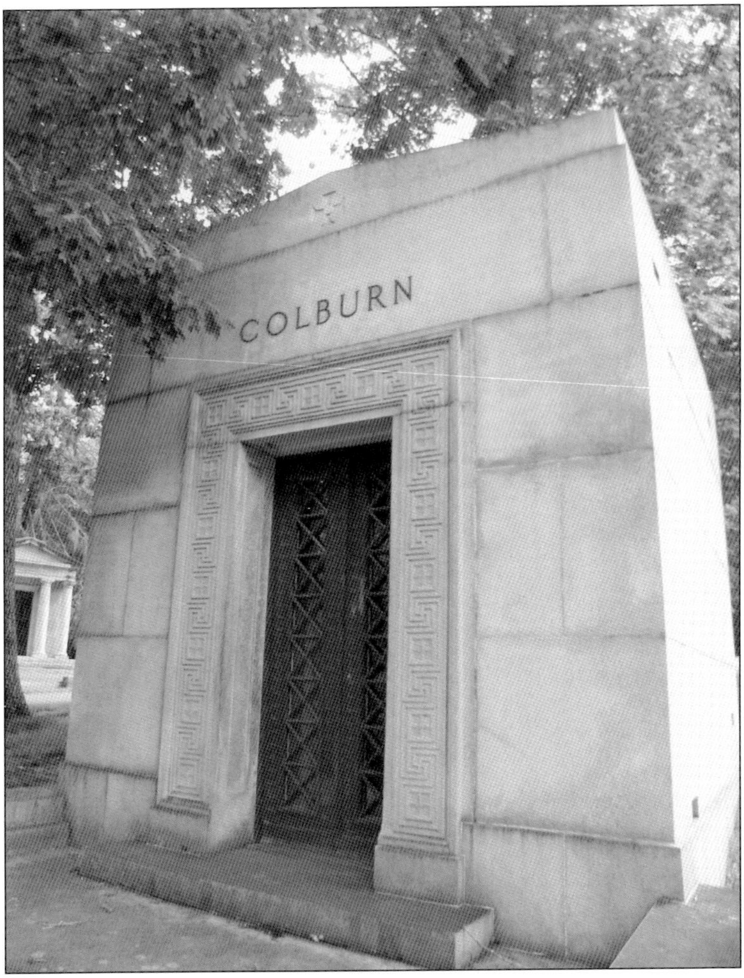

Almost every street or building in Asheville owes its name to someone who now rests within Riverside's hallowed grounds. Pictured here is the Colburn mausoleum. The interior of the mausoleum contains marble and turquoise mosaics, a nod to Burnham Standish Colburn, whose collection of North Carolina minerals made possible the Burnham S. Colburn Memorial Mineral Museum.

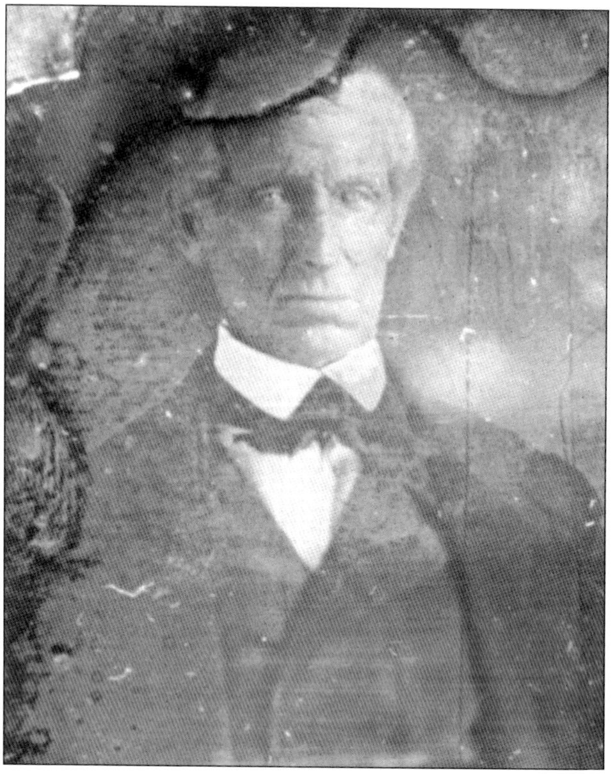

Isaac B. Sawyer was born in 1810 and acted for years as one of the magistrates for the Buncombe County Court. He later became the first person elected mayor of the city of Asheville. He was given a place of honor in Riverside overlooking the French Broad River. (NCC.)

Former sugar plantation manager Leicester Chapman moved to an area just north of Asheville named Turkey Creek at the urging of Thomas Lanier Clingman. He purchased property there and became postmaster in 1852. The township was renamed Leicester in 1859 to honor Chapman's godfather, the Earl of Leicester, at his request.

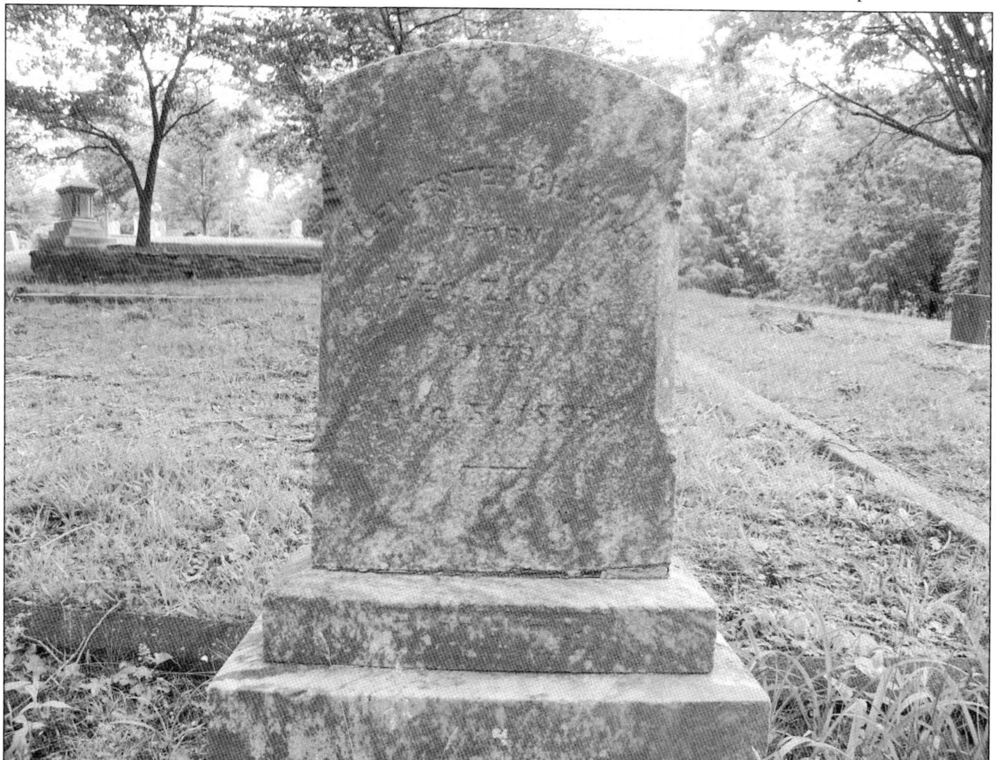

Gay Green was a noted Asheville financier who was Asheville's largest property holder at the time of his death in 1951. The white marble mausoleum in which he is entombed was crafted by stonemasons who had been brought in by George Vanderbilt during the construction of the Biltmore Estate.

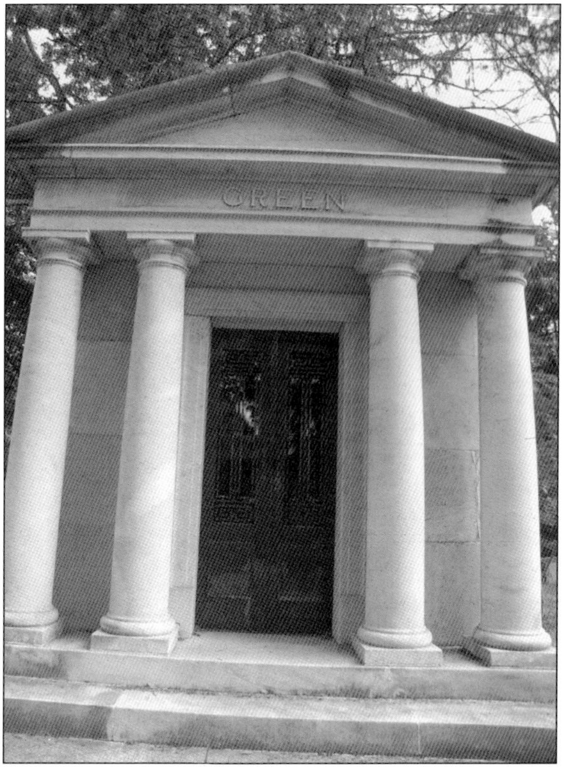

Of all of the public servants to the city of Asheville and Buncombe County, none can claim more dedication than James Eugene Rankin. Rankin served for the majority of his life and was said to have held more than 50 public offices, including mayor for five terms.

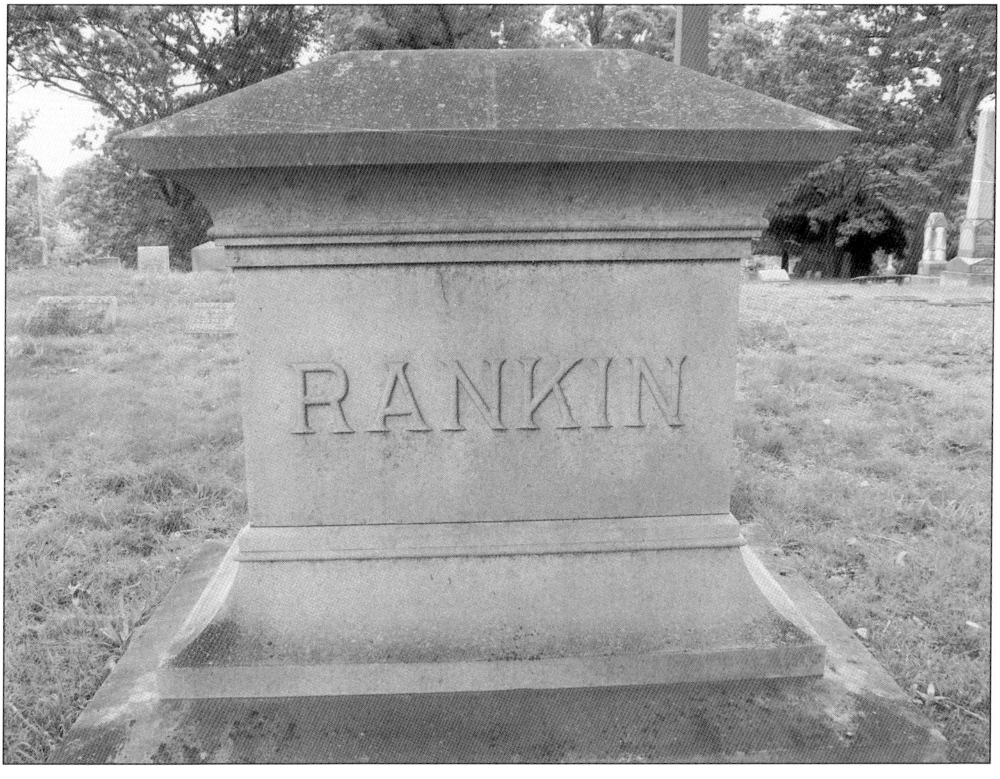

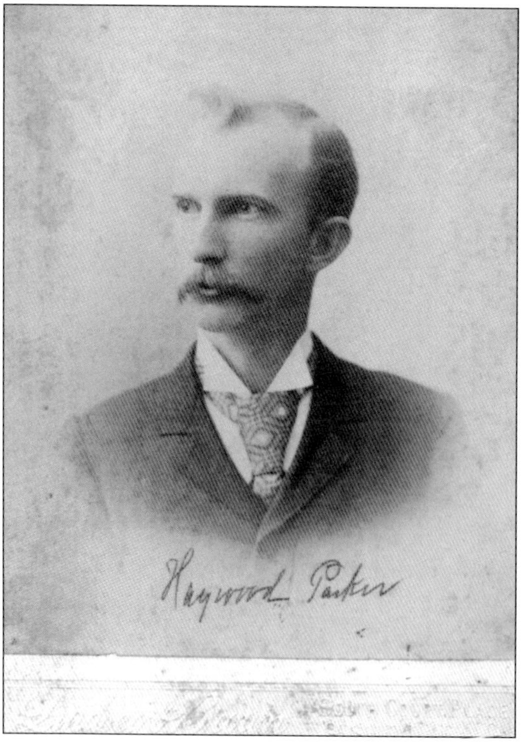

Haywood Parker, son-in-law to Thomas Walton Patton, was a prominent Asheville attorney who was very involved in civic affairs and promoting a better relationship between races. He served as secretary and then president of the Asheville Cemetery Company, and it was through his efforts that many of the early cemetery records survived the fire that destroyed the cemetery office in 1918. (NCC.)

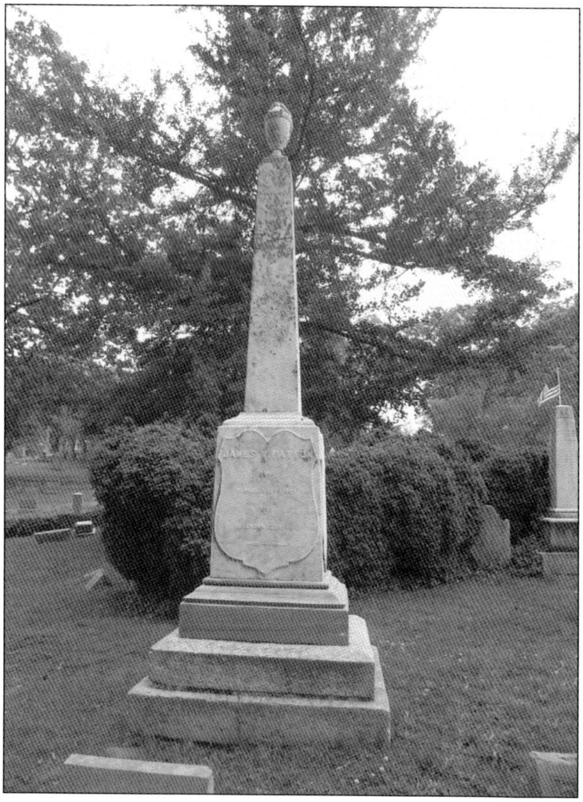

The Patton family is considered by many to be Asheville royalty. From James, an Irish immigrant who used his business acumen to amass a small fortune, to his great-great-granddaughter Mary Toole Parker, founder of the League of Women Voters in Asheville, the Pattons have always been known for their devotion to the greater good through large donations of land and money and decades of public service.

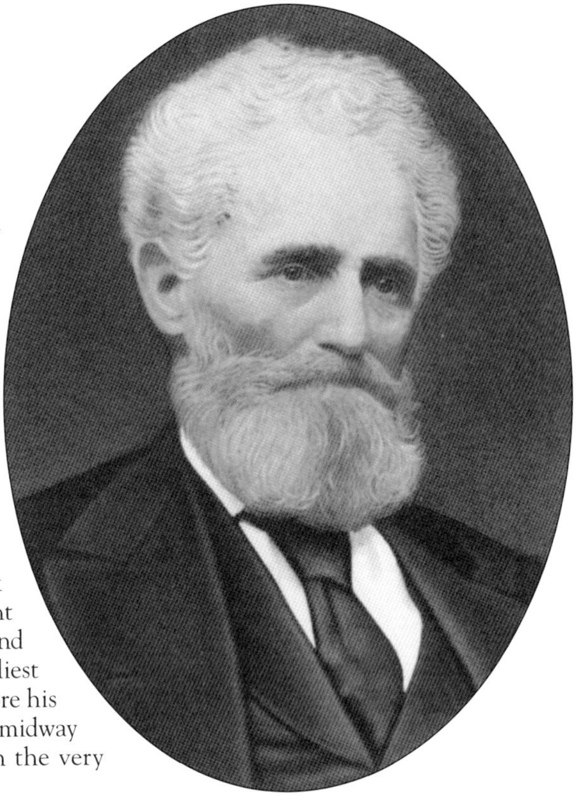

Though Nicholas Woodfin passed away nine years before the formation of the Asheville Cemetery Company, he remains one of the most important figures in Riverside's history. Woodfin was a legislator, lawyer, and farmer who amassed extensive land in Buncombe County before the Civil War and was the region's largest slaveholder. After the war, he bequeathed large amounts of land to his former slaves and donated the property that was to become Riverside Cemetery. Woodfin founded the Elk Mountain Cheese Factory, which brought together T.W. Patton and W.S. Cornell, and was involved with these two in the earliest stages of planning for the cemetery before his death in 1876. His cemetery lot stands midway between those of his former friends in the very center of the cemetery. (Right, NCC.)

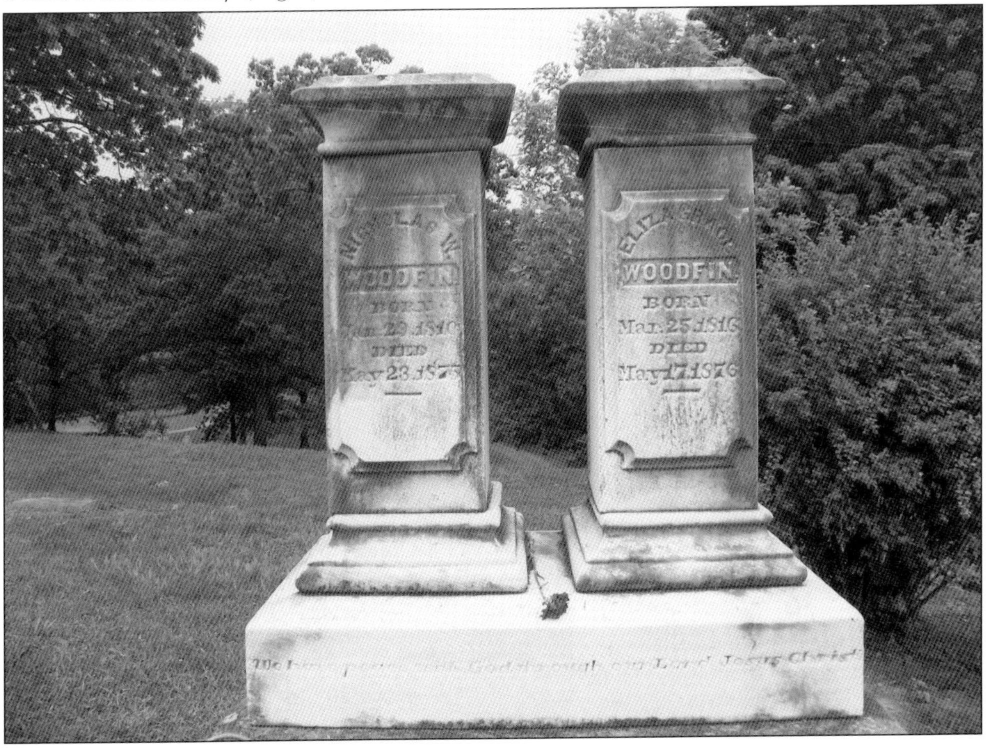

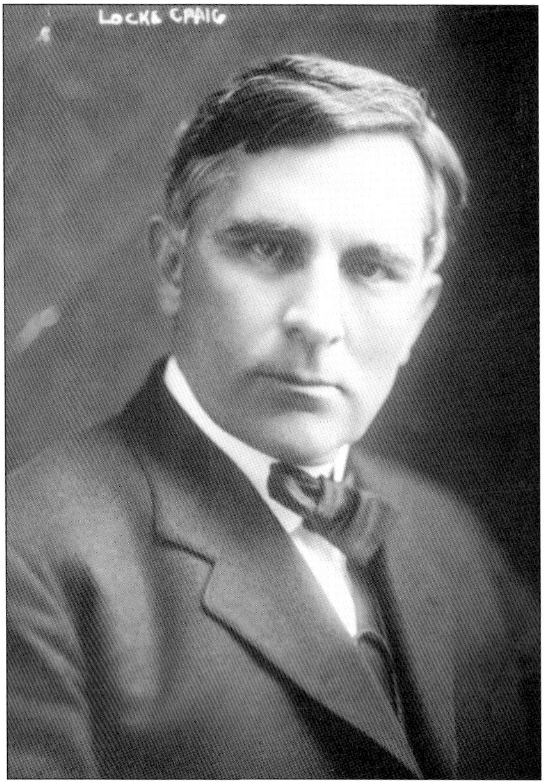

A man who would come to be known as the "Little Giant of the West" for his short stature and commanding words, Locke Craig began his path towards a political career as an eloquent student leader at the University of North Carolina, where he became the youngest graduate at just 19. Craig moved to Asheville in 1889 to practice law and became an active member of the Democratic Party. His fiery speeches and sharp political acumen led to his election to the state legislature and eventually as the 53rd governor of North Carolina in 1913. His administration was noted for the creation of the first highway commission, educational reforms, and the advancement of state parks in the western part of the state. (Left, LOC.)

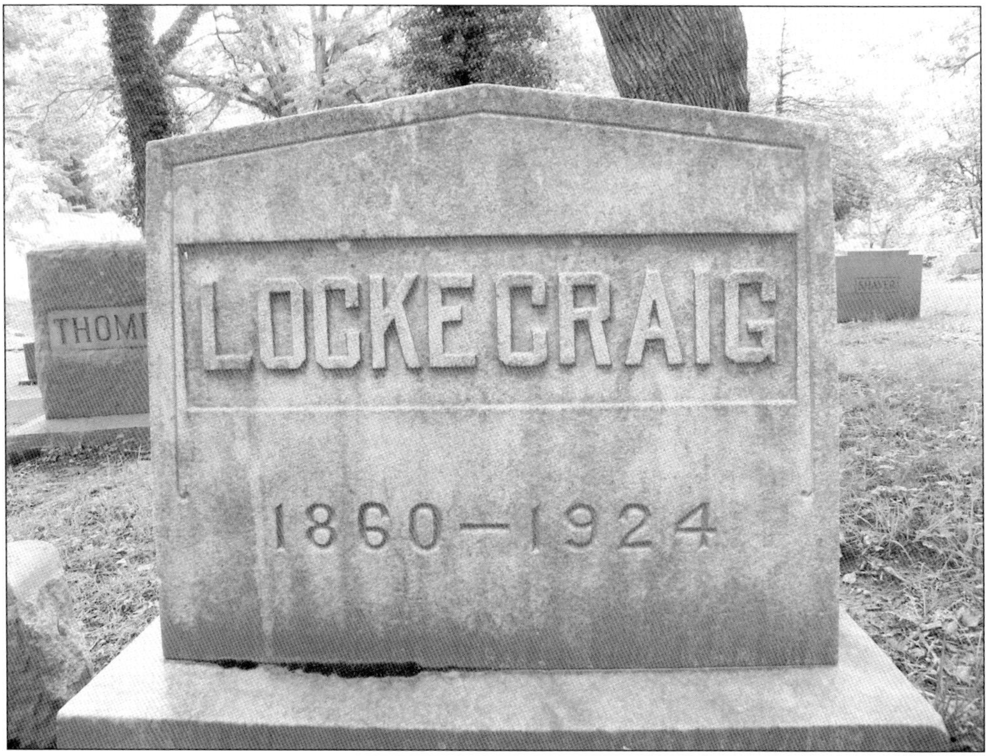

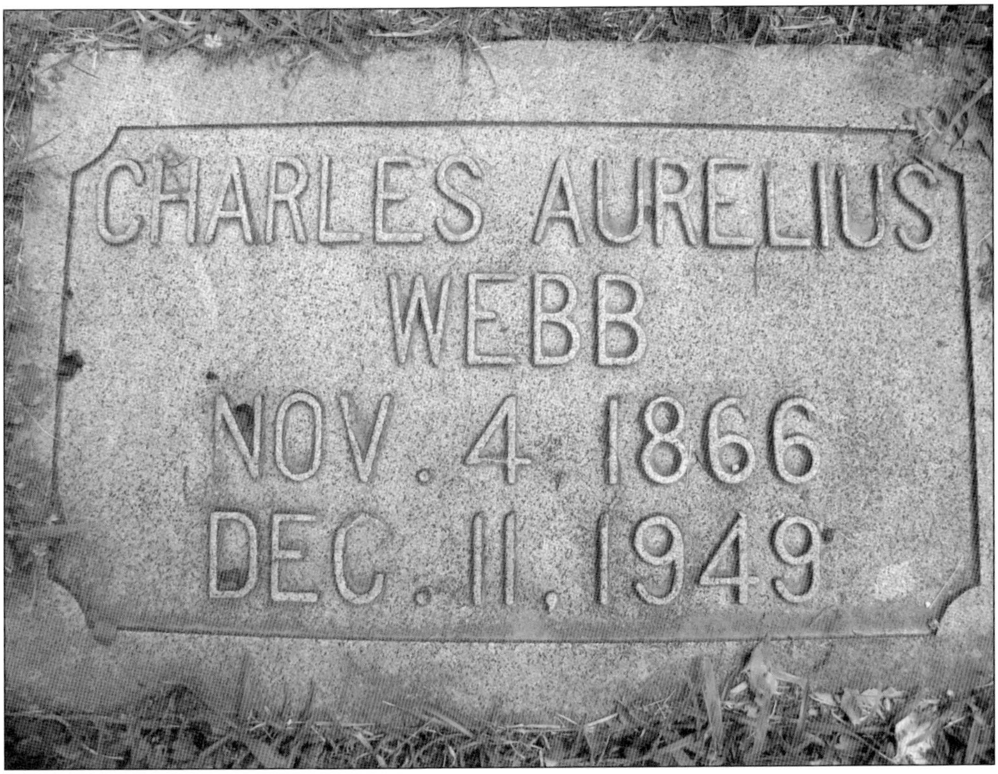

Charles Aurelius Webb was a successful attorney, US marshal, and legislator who turned his attention towards the world of newspapers in 1919 with the purchase of the *Asheville Citizen*. He directed publication of the *Citizen* until 1930, when he and Don S. Elias, owner of Asheville's other leading newspaper, the *Asheville Times*, merged the two papers to form the Asheville Citizen-Times Company. Webb became president of the new company, and Elias stayed on as vice president. They used the considerable influence of the papers to push for the establishment of a national park in the southern Appalachians and for securing the Blue Ridge Parkway.

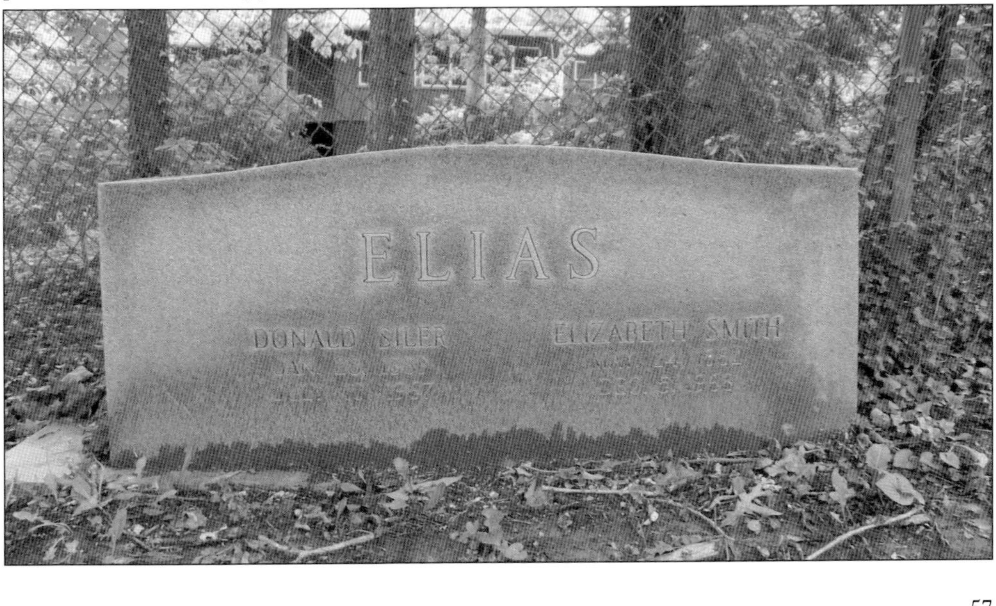

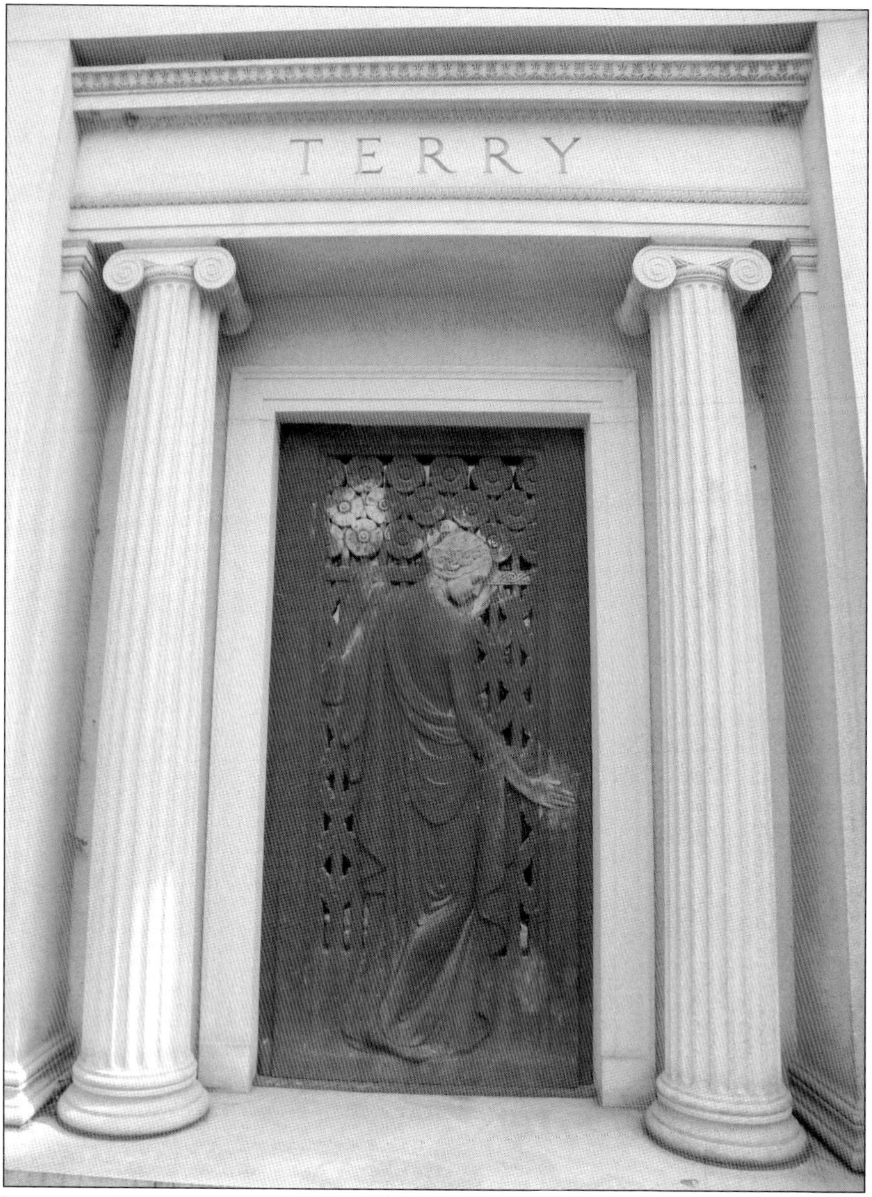

The Terry mausoleum stands out as one of the most recognizable in Riverside with its distinctive bronze art deco door. Franklin Terry, interred inside, worked as an office boy for an electrical company, where he met Thomas Edison. Edison set him on the path to becoming one of the most important men in the new industry. Terry managed a small electric lighting company in Chicago for a time before establishing the National Electric Lamp Company. Terry became known as an inspired inventor in his own right, most notably inventing a longer-burning incandescent lightbulb. His company merged with General Electric in 1912, and Terry was named its first vice president. In 1923, Terry and his wife, Lillian, moved permanently to Black Mountain, North Carolina, to oversee the construction of their grand estate, Intheoaks. With 80 acres, 67 rooms, a golf course, indoor bowling alleys, a swimming pool, and a hidden wine cellar, the estate rivaled Biltmore. Terry was only able to enjoy living here for three years before he died unexpectedly in 1926. Intheoaks was purchased by Montreat College in 2001.

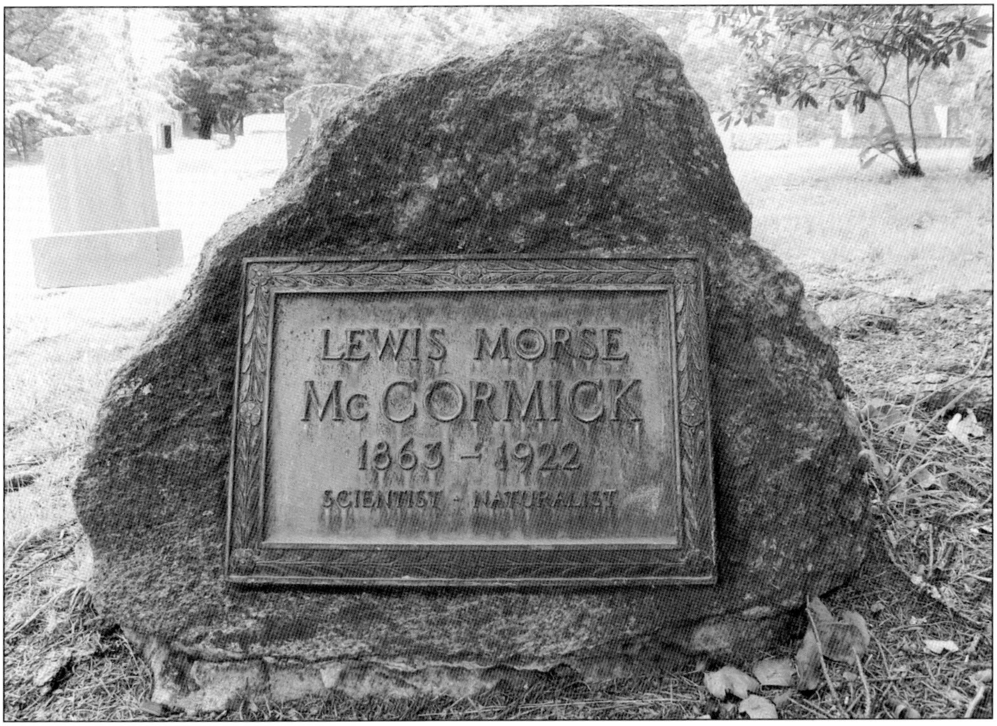

Dr. Lewis McCormick was a leading bacteriologist who spearheaded the local Swat That Fly! campaign and was known to offer a bounty of 5¢ to any child who could bring him a dead fly. The campaign was wildly successful in preventing the spread of illness, and McCormick was recognized for his contributions when Asheville's minor-league baseball stadium was named McCormick Field in his honor.

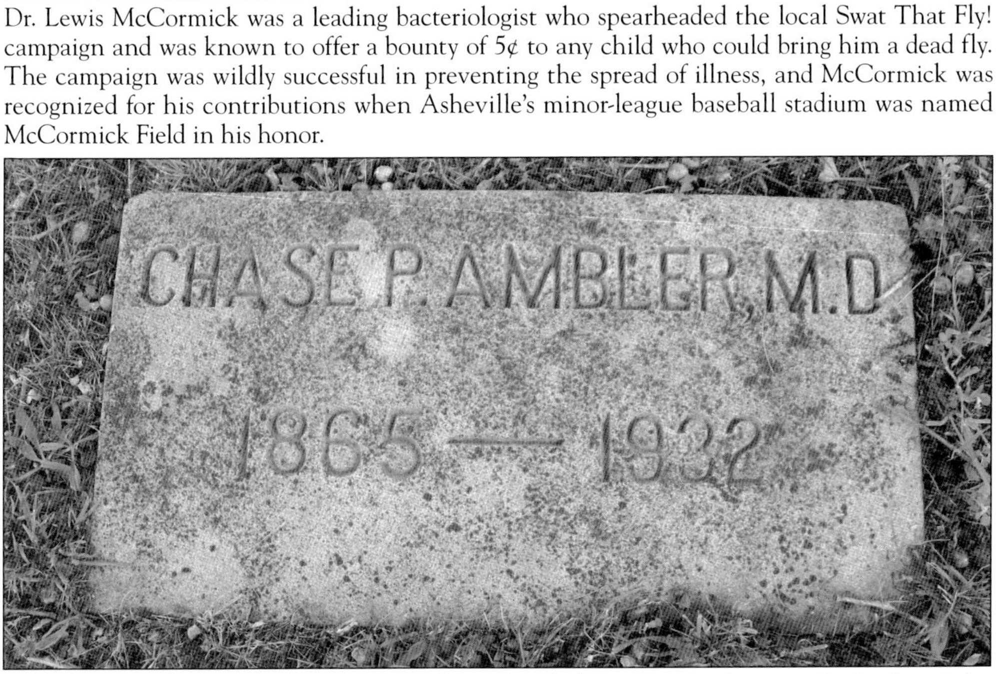

Dr. Chase Ambler was a well-known and respected physician who became the leader of the movement to conserve natural resources in Western North Carolina and establish a national park here. He was the driving force behind the Appalachian National Park Association and the push to pass the Weeks Bill of 1911, which resulted in the first purchase of land to be established as a national park in the region.

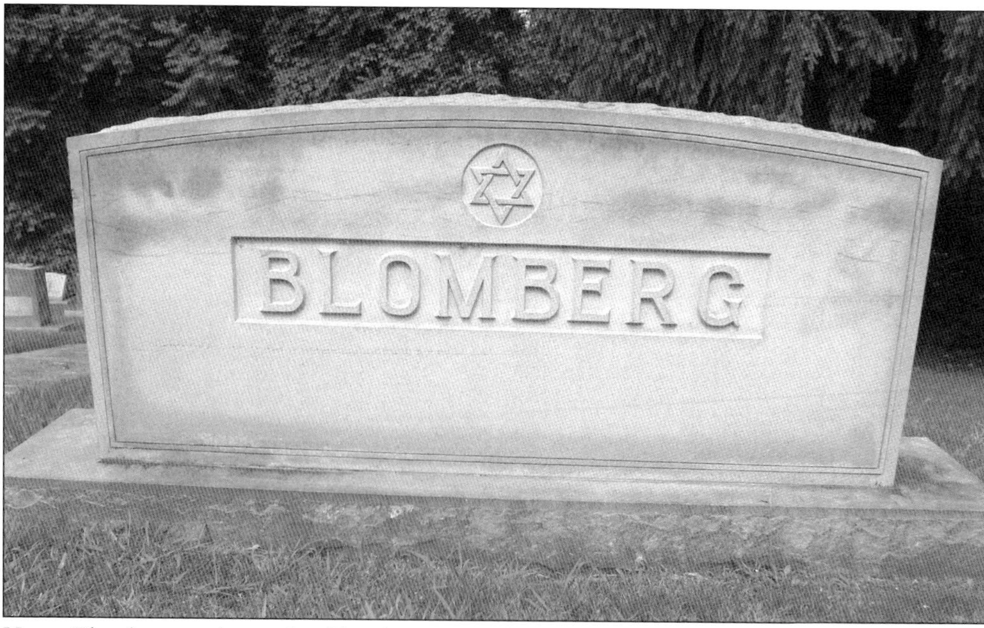

Harry Blomberg made much of his fortune in the automobile business with a service station, car dealerships, and two motor inns. Blomberg put his money to good purpose. He saved the boardinghouse of Julia Wolfe from the bulldozer by buying it to sell back to the family at a loss, and he later bought and revitalized the failing Biltmore Industries, which had been started by Edith Vanderbilt.

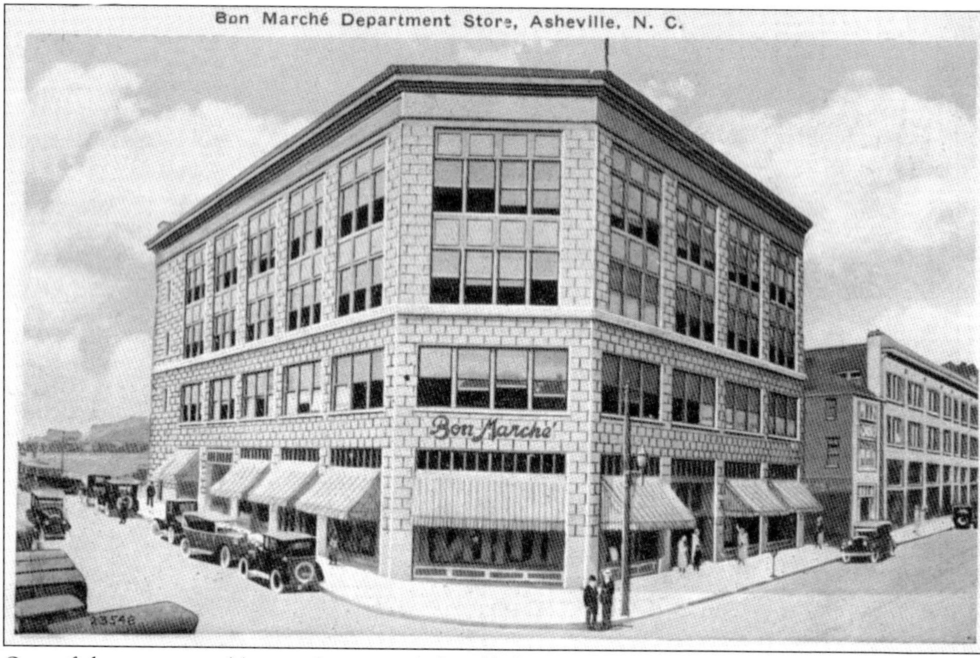

One of the most notable merchants in Asheville history, Solomon Lipinsky was the founder of Bon Marché in the 1890s. Bon Marché became the premier department store in the region and an Asheville landmark for over 90 years. Lipinsky was also a founding member of Temple Beth HaTephila and instrumental in the establishment of the Jewish cemetery within Riverside. (NCC.)

The Reverend Charles Dusenberry was a pioneering minister of the Presbyterian Church who founded the Calvary Church and School for African Americans in the East End community of Asheville. He was deeply invested in the betterment of his race through his ministry and teachings and made several addresses to the General Assembly of the Presbyterian Church that served to illuminate the struggles of African Americans to church leadership. (Black Highlanders Collection, Ramsey Library, University of North Carolina–Asheville.)

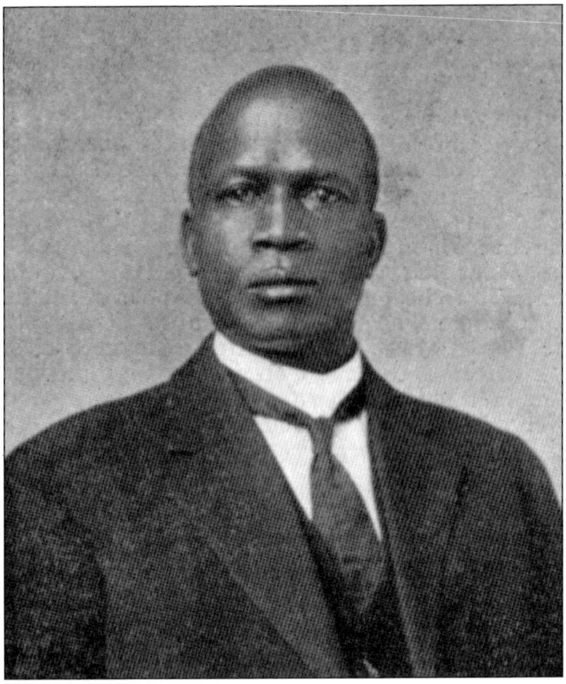

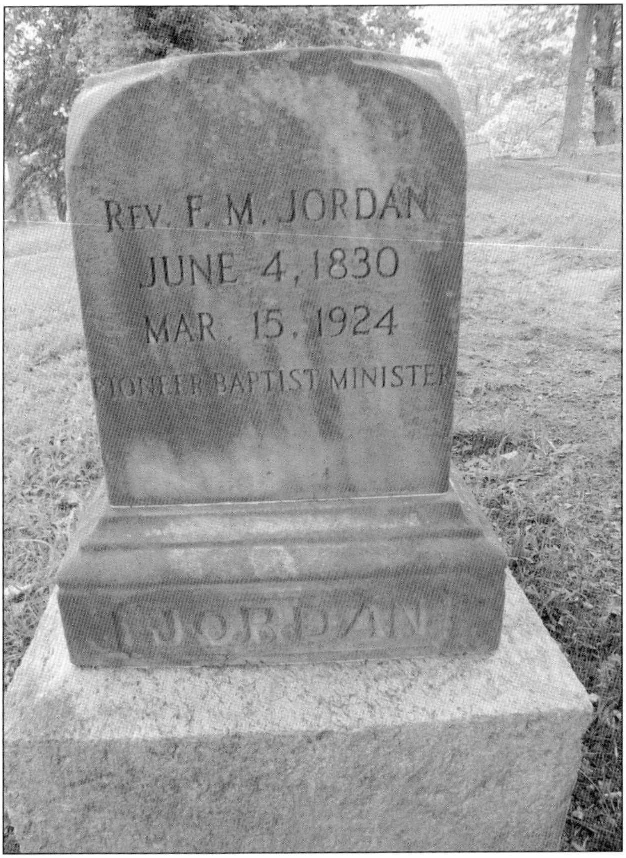

Frank M. Jordan was the best-known Baptist evangelist of his time, who in his own words baptized "believers in almost every river, creek, and pool in the state." An outspoken leader known for his fiery sermons and unmatched zeal, Jordan maintained his ministry in every corner of North Carolina for over 50 years.

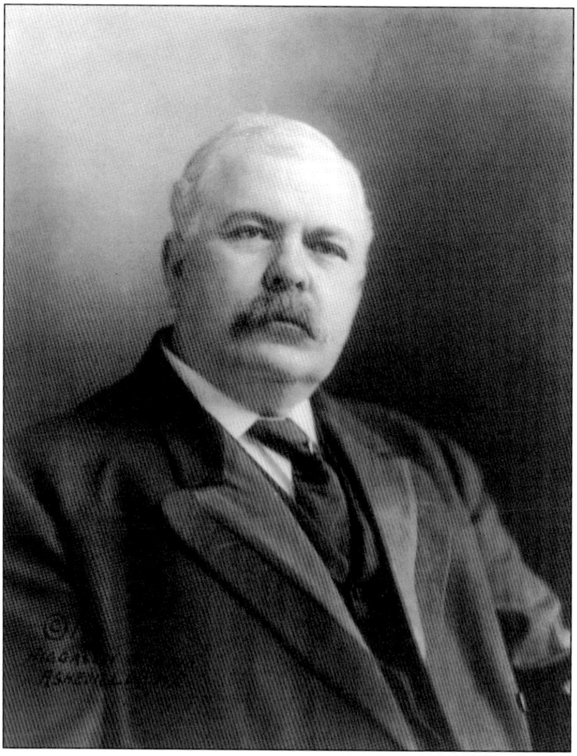

Known around Asheville simply as "the Judge," Jeter Conley Pritchard was an imposing figure. Pritchard lost his father at 12 years old to an illness contracted during the Civil War and supported himself as a newspaperman in Alabama. In 1877, Pritchard moved to North Carolina, where he began to study law and quickly made a name for himself. He became a US senator in 1895 and was the first Southern republican elected to the US Senate since 1875. He remained a senator until 1901 before quitting partisan politics. In 1903, Pritchard was appointed by Pres. Theodore Roosevelt as an associate justice of the Supreme Court of the District of Columbia and then to the Circuit Court of Appeals for the Fourth District. He served in this capacity for the remainder of his years. (Left, LOC.)

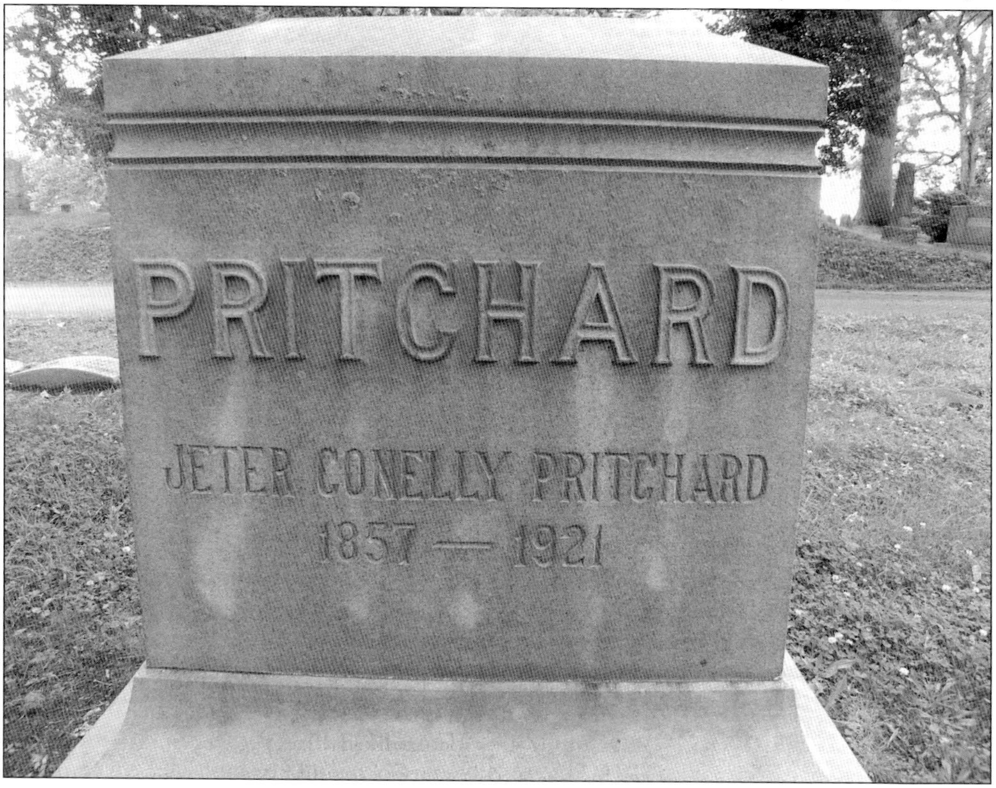

George Tayloe Winston started down his path as North Carolina's leading educator at an early age, distinguishing himself as the top of his class at the University of North Carolina at just 14 years old. He continued in education and eventually became president of the university. He later was the first president of the University of Texas and then served as president of North Carolina State University.

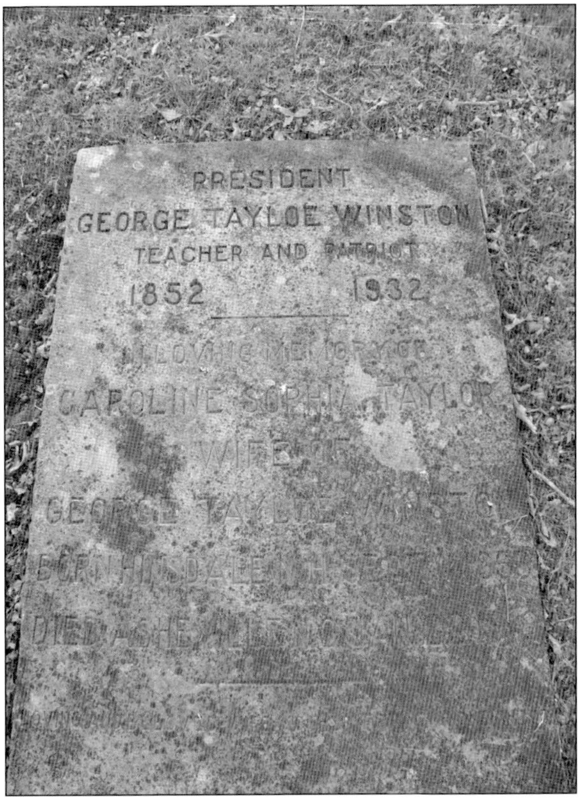

Hall Fletcher Junior High School was named after beloved Asheville physician and surgeon Marshall Hall Fletcher in 1925, the same year as his death. Fletcher had served in the US Medical Corps during World War I despite being in his mid-60s and as the first chief of staff for Mission Hospital.

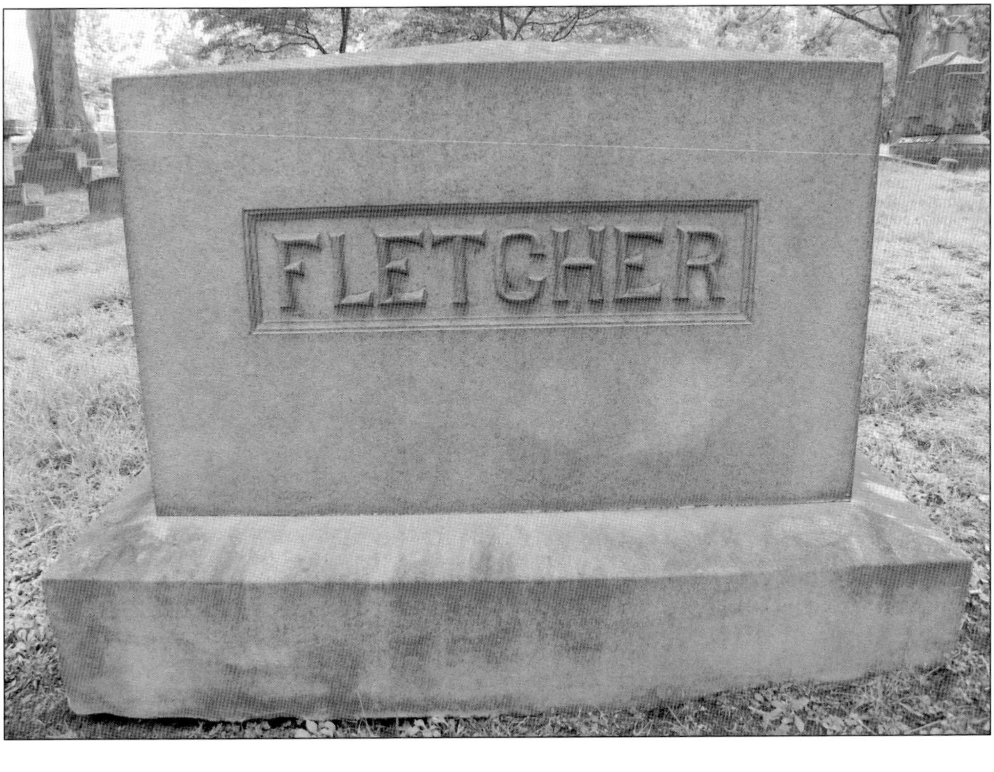

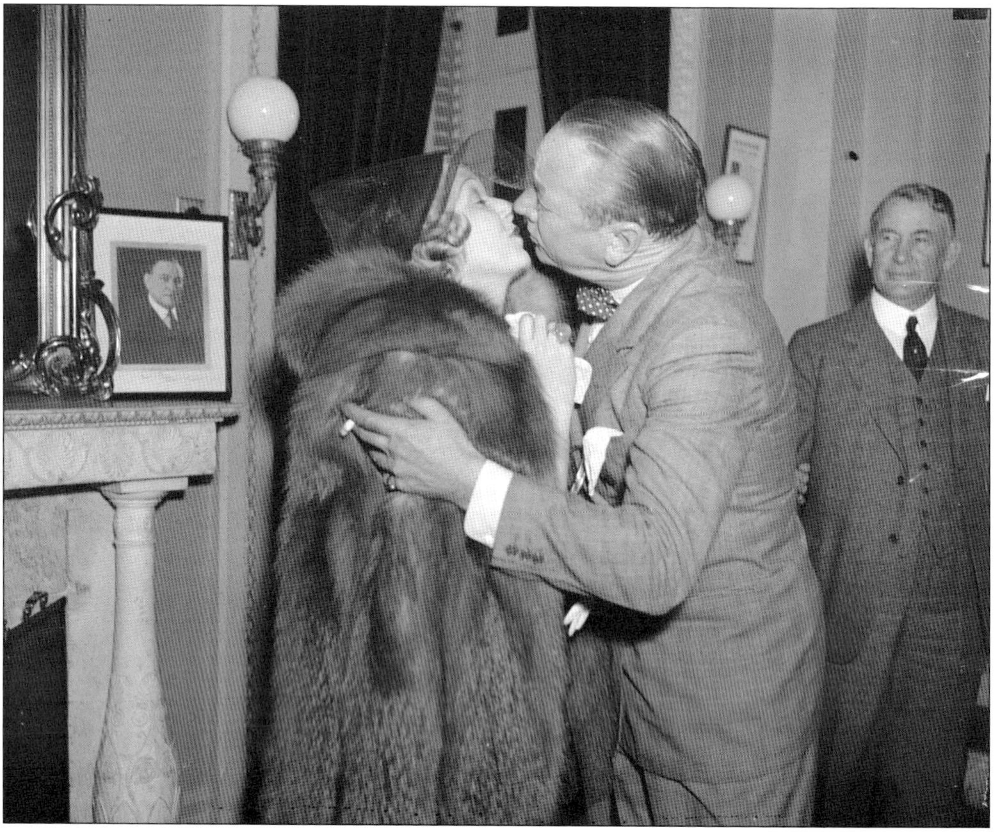

US senator Robert Rice Reynolds was a character far larger than life. Never one to shy away from controversy, the senator affectionately nicknamed "Our Bob" was the lone Southern senator to support FDR's New Deal, a strong isolationist, and had a reputation for being a womanizer. Reynolds was married five times, the last of which was to Evalyn Walsh McLean, whose mother was the last private owner of the Hope Diamond. Reynolds was 57 when he married the 19-year-old socialite, a scandal that shook Washington, DC. Many consider Evalyn to be the last victim of the "Hope Diamond Curse," as she died from an overdose of sleeping pills just a few years into their marriage. Reynolds retired back to Asheville after this to raise their young daughter, Mamie. He passed away in 1963. (Above, LOC.)

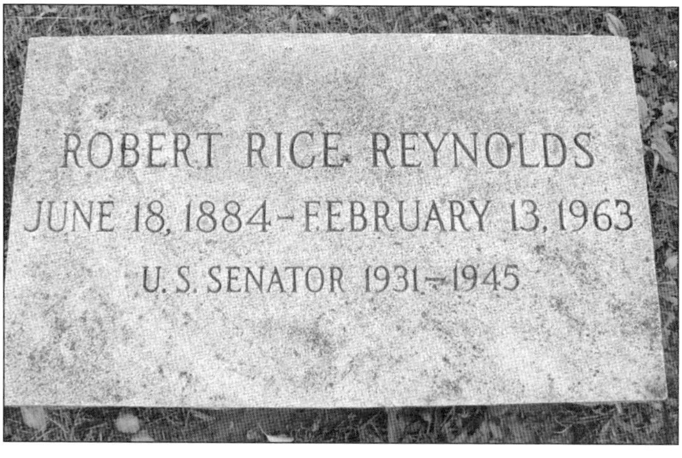

E.J. Aston was a realtor who billed Asheville nationally as a health destination. His pamphlets claimed the Asheville air pressure and climate were the best cures for the tuberculosis ravaging the nation. Aston's promotions worked; sanatoriums were built all over the city and people flocked to the mountains. After he served a term as mayor of the city, Aston Park was named for him.

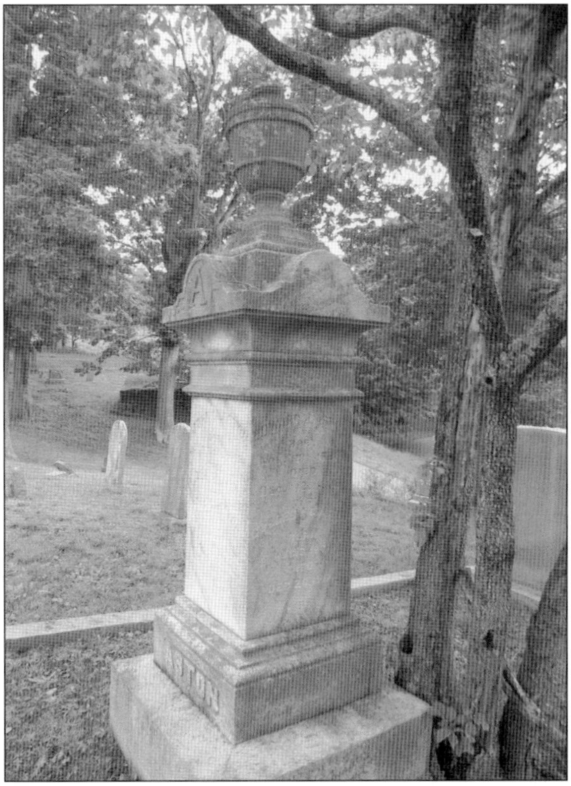

Theodore Summey Morrison was an Asheville merchant best known for founding one of the oldest and longest-running mercantile firms in the city, T.S. Morrison & Company. The store opened in 1895 and closed in the early 2000s. The building now houses the Lexington Avenue Brewery and is the starting point for haunted cemetery tours of Riverside.

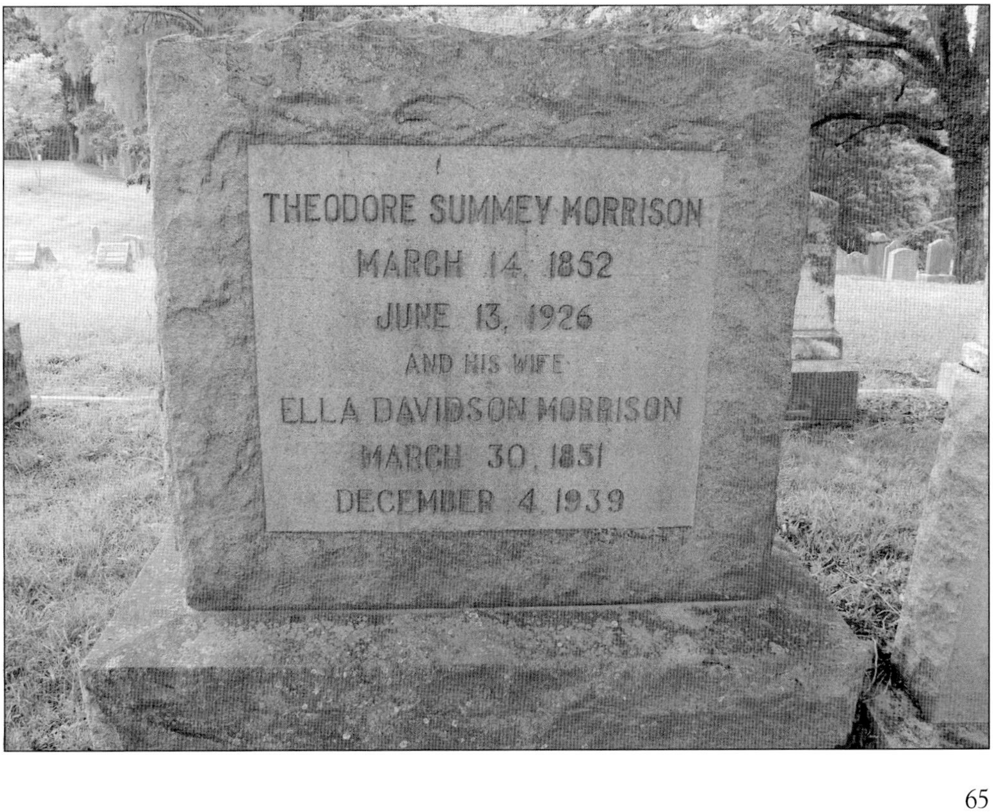

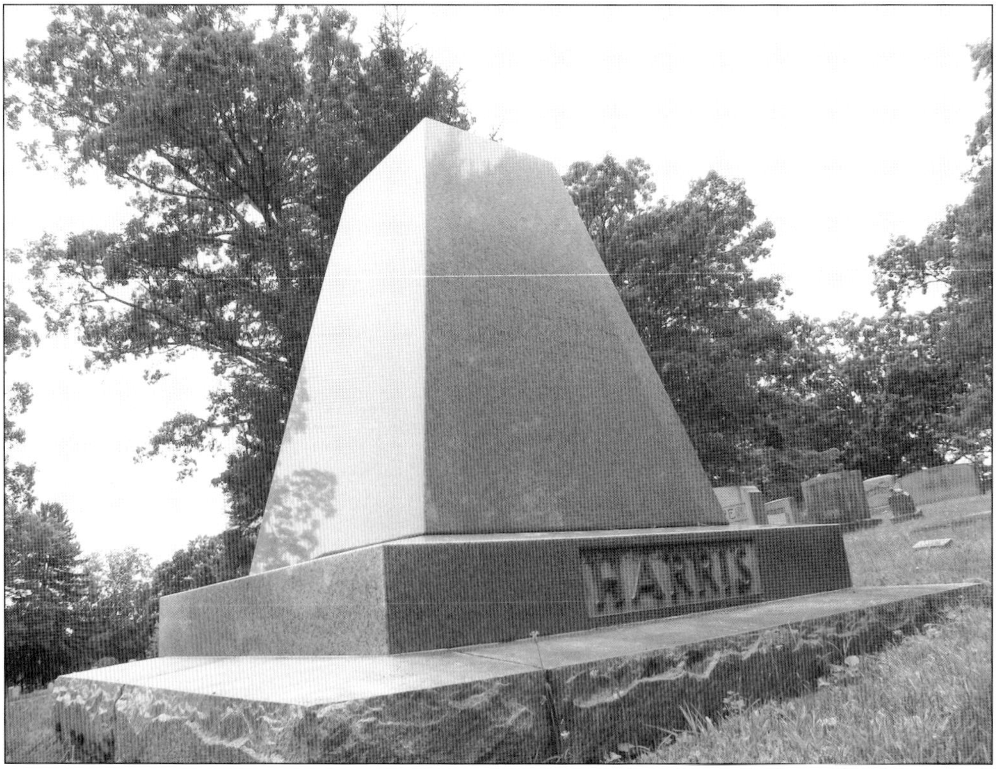

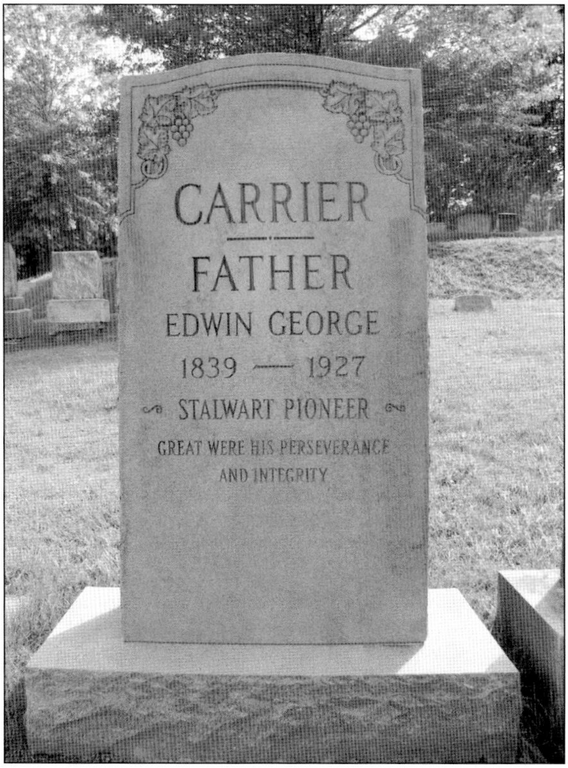

This large and imposing obelisk is one of the first markers to be seen upon entering Riverside. It was erected to the memory of the "Kaolin King of North Carolina" and former candidate for governor, Charles J. Harris. Harris was a Connecticut-born industrialist who owned the highly successful Harris Clay Company in Webster, North Carolina.

West Asheville, the eclectic neighborhood just across the river from downtown, owes much of its development to hotelier Edwin Carrier. Carrier moved to Asheville in 1885 in order to revitalize the Sulphur Springs Hotel. He renamed the hotel the Carrier Springs and built an electric railway line powered by the first hydroelectric dam in the area, a racetrack, and fairgrounds to entice visitors.

Richmond Mumford Pearson Jr., son of the North Carolina Supreme Court justice whose name he bore, was a US congressman and diplomat who developed and named the Montford community and was one of the original stockholders of the Asheville Cemetery Company. Pearson served in the US House of Representatives as both a Republican and a Democrat and was US consul to Italy, Persia, Greece, and Montenegro. After retiring, Pearson moved back to his home in Asheville, named Richmond Hill. The Richmond Hill Inn, as it was later known, sits just across the French Broad River from Riverside and could be seen clearly from the cemetery grounds until in burned down in recent years. The large natural stone marking Pearson's grave was hauled into Riverside by a mule team after his death in 1923. (Right, NCC.)

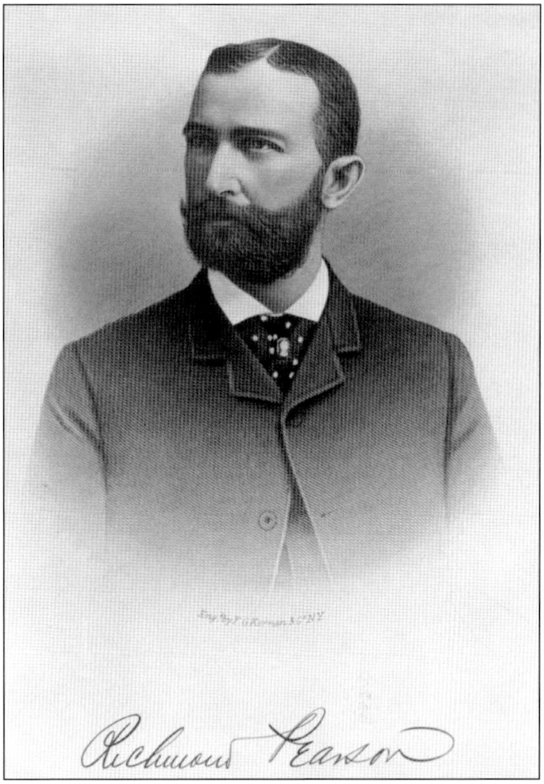

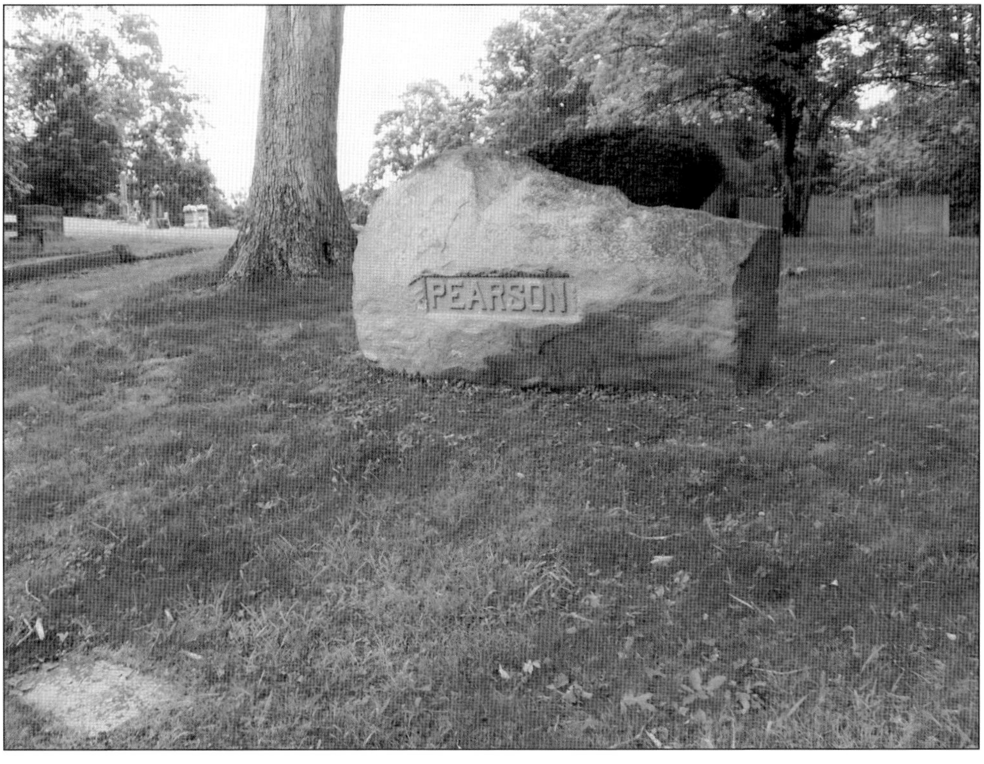

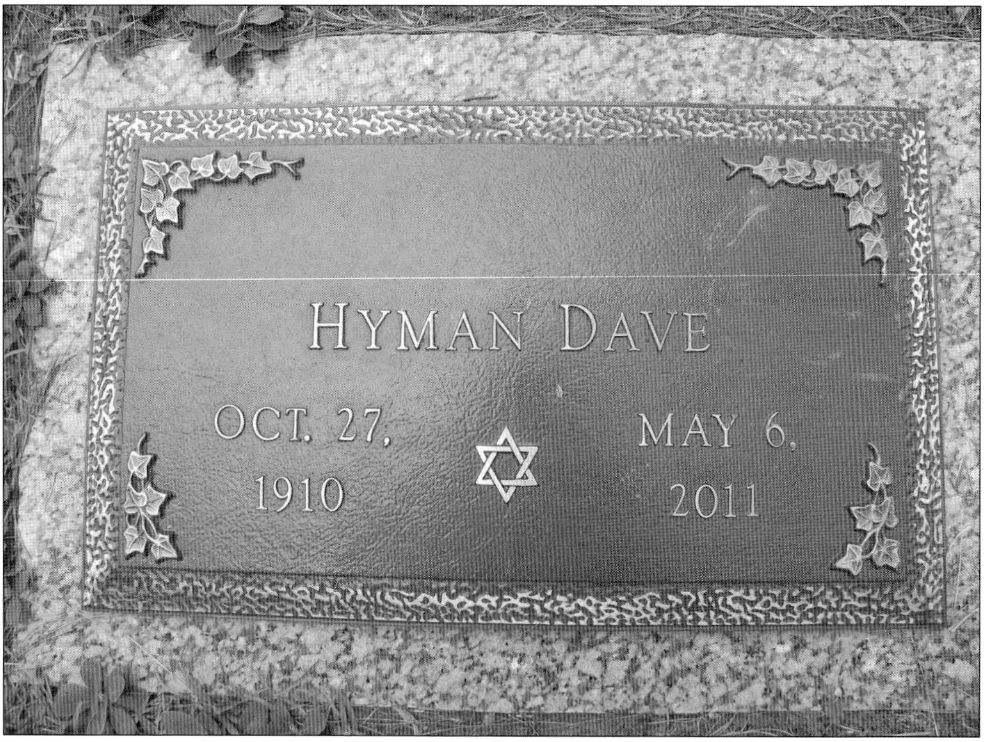

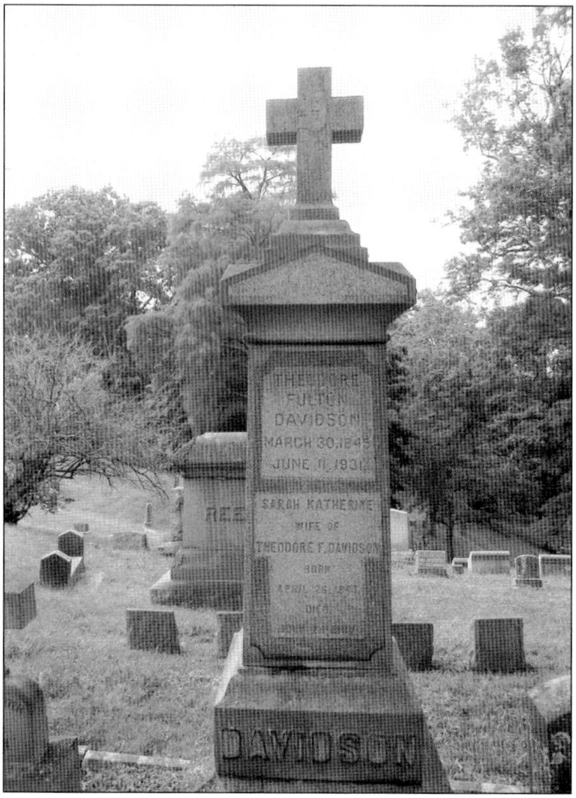

Hyman Dave, who lived for over a century, was one of the best-known figures in Asheville. He served as president of the Dave Steel Company until his retirement in 1976, then as manager of the Asheville Downtown City Club and Asheville Country Club and as president of Congregation Beth HaTephila. For many years, Dave was also manager of the cemetery for the temple.

Theodore Fulton Davidson, son of Allen Turner Davidson, was a successful legislator and lifelong politician who served as North Carolina attorney general, mayor of Asheville, state senator, and Buncombe County judge. Davidson studied under Col. Stephen Lee and was one of the youngest members of the Confederate army at 16. He was appointed adjutant general under Gen. James Martin.

Gilbert Sleigh Sr. is buried in Section HH of Riverside. Sleigh was a well-respected and upstanding member of the community who became the first African American police officer to join the City of Asheville police force. This 1946 photograph shows Sleigh (right) posing with an unidentified officer. (Young Men's Institute Cultural Center.)

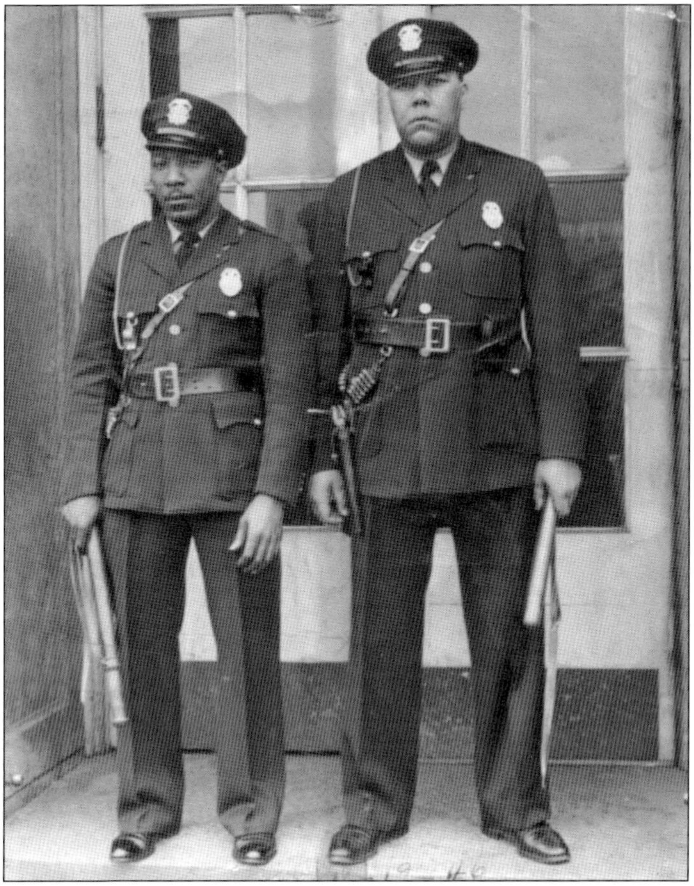

William Randolph was a public servant and education advocate who served as vice mayor, fire chief, city alderman, and the first secretary of the Asheville City School Board. Fifteen years after his death, the Montford Avenue School was renamed William Randolph Elementary in honor of his contributions to the city.

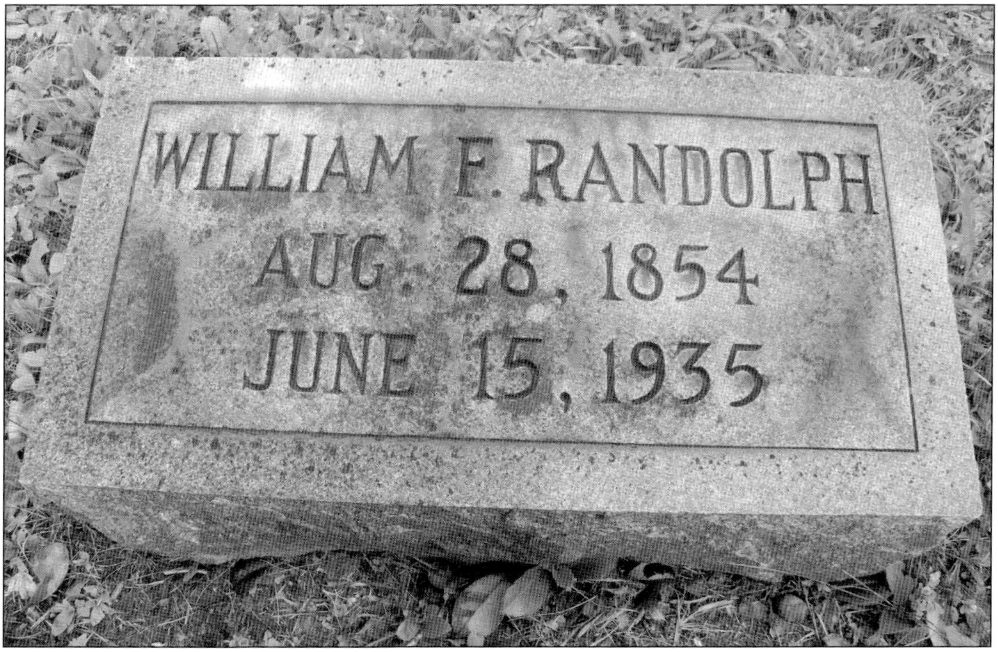

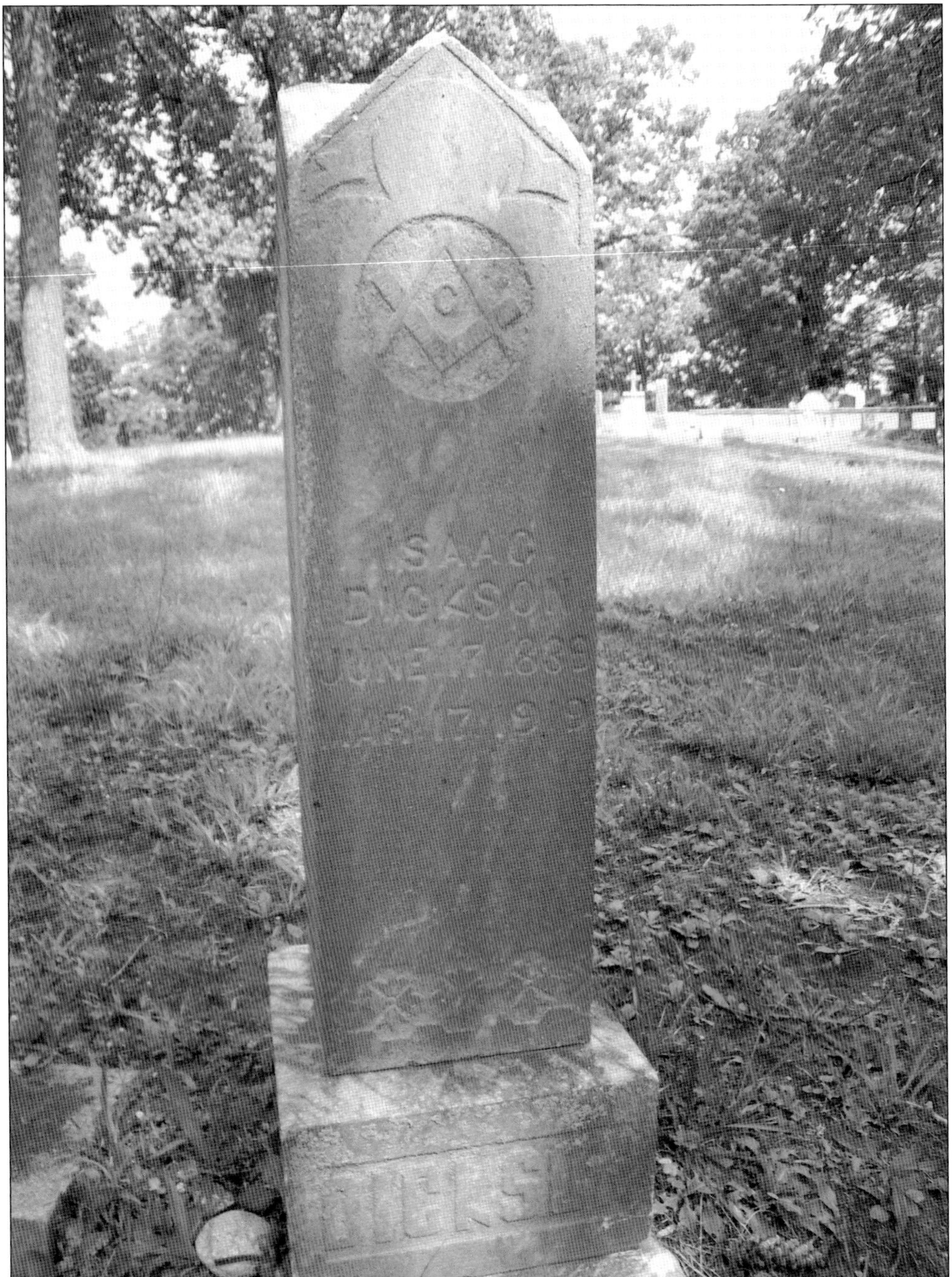

Isaac Dickson was born a slave in 1839 in nearby Cleveland County, North Carolina. After being emancipated in 1856, Dickson moved to Asheville in search of better opportunities. He worked as a butler for the Reverend D.H. Buel and was able to save $275 to buy property on Valley Street, including the former Patton slave quarters. There, he established a community called Dicksontown. Dickson became one of the most well-known men in the community and garnered respect from those of all races. Dickson served on the first city school board and helped found the first public school for African Americans. The school board named Isaac Dickson Elementary after him.

Five

The Biltmore Connection

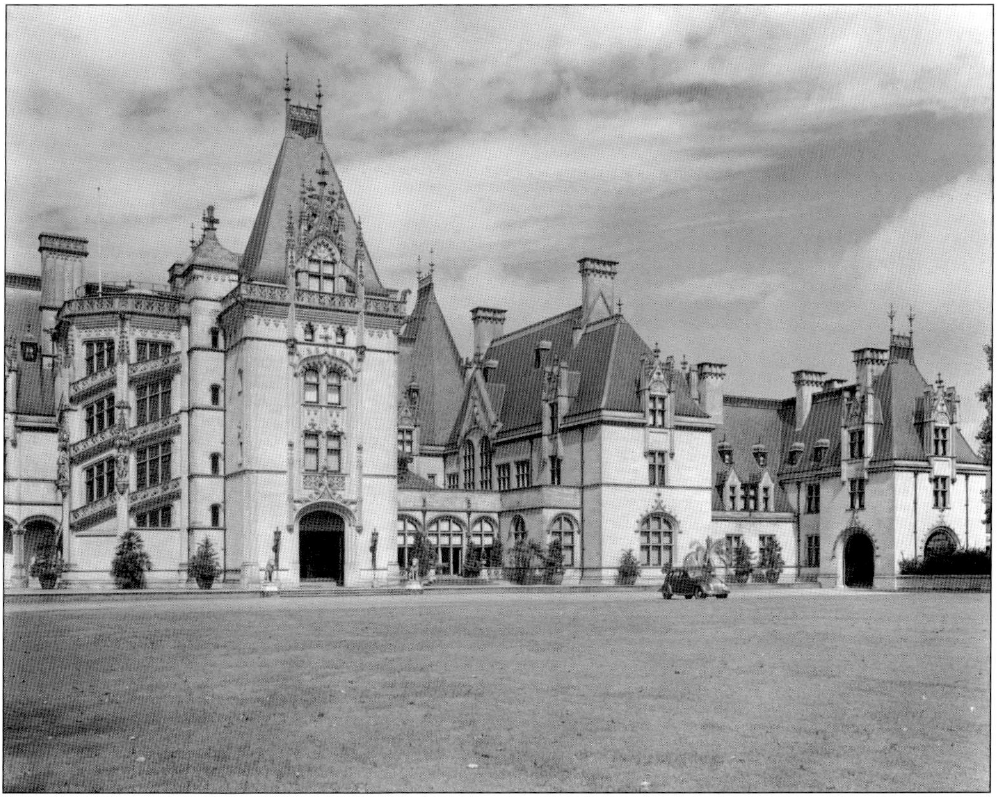

When George Vanderbilt chose Asheville as the location for his grand estate in 1889, he brought with him scientists, artists, stonemasons, and architects who were at the top of their respective fields. Many of these artisans stayed after the mansion's completion to make Asheville their new home. Much of the wonderful funerary art and stories that draw people to Riverside are connected to those drawn to Asheville by the Vanderbilts. (LOC.)

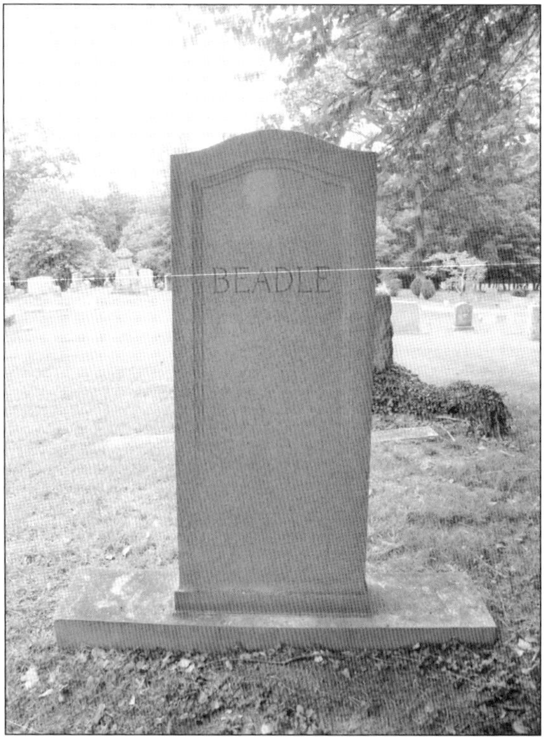

One of the best-loved figures in the history of the Biltmore Estate is famed botanist and horticulturalist Chauncey Delos Beadle. Beadle was hired by landscape architect Frederick Law Olmsted in 1890 to oversee the nursery at Biltmore. Beadle's business acumen and management skills quickly impressed the Vanderbilts, and he eventually became the superintendent of the entire estate. Beadle worked at Biltmore for 60 years and became known as one of the "Azalea Hunters" along with Frank Crayton, Sylvester Owens, and William Knight. His native azalea collection on his farm on the east side of Asheville was considered the most complete in the country and was moved to Biltmore in 1940 when he became too old to manage it. Until his death in 1950, Beadle was often called upon by the Asheville Cemetery Company to landscape the lots of Asheville's prominent citizens. (Below, Biltmore Estate Archives.)

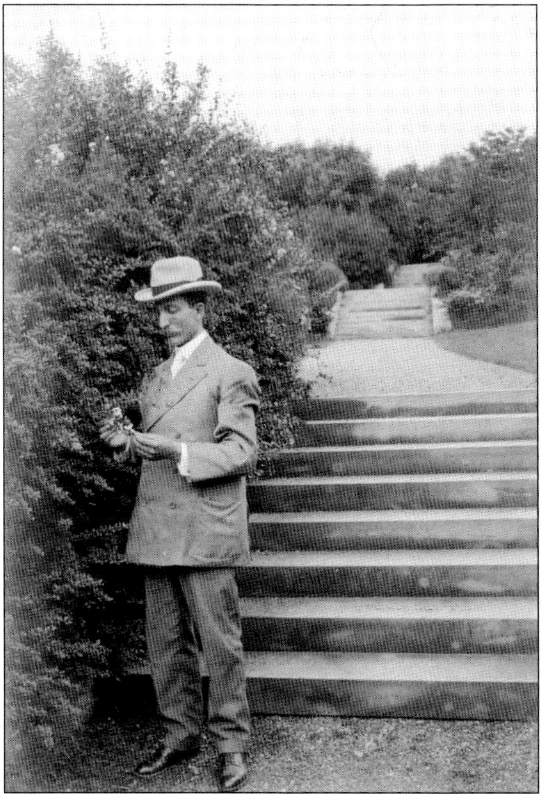

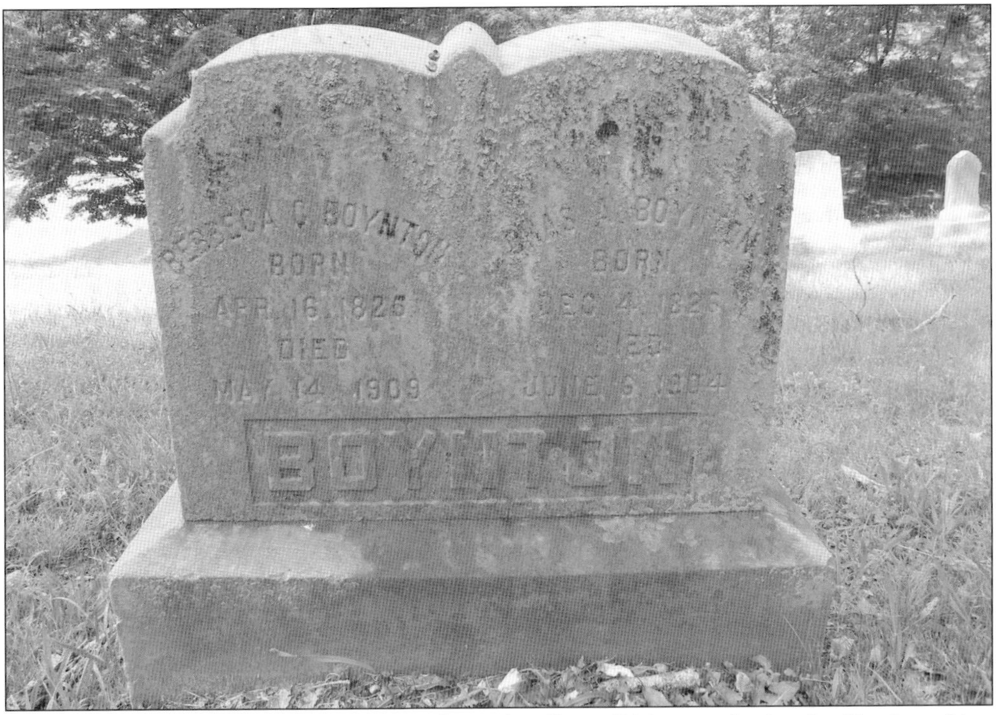

Charles Boynton was a botanist who moved to Asheville in 1896 to join his brother Frank working for the Biltmore Nursery and Herbarium. Within a year, Boynton was named chief collector for the nursery. Through the efforts of the Boynton brothers and Chauncey Beadle, Biltmore soon gained a reputation as having one of the best nurseries in the country.

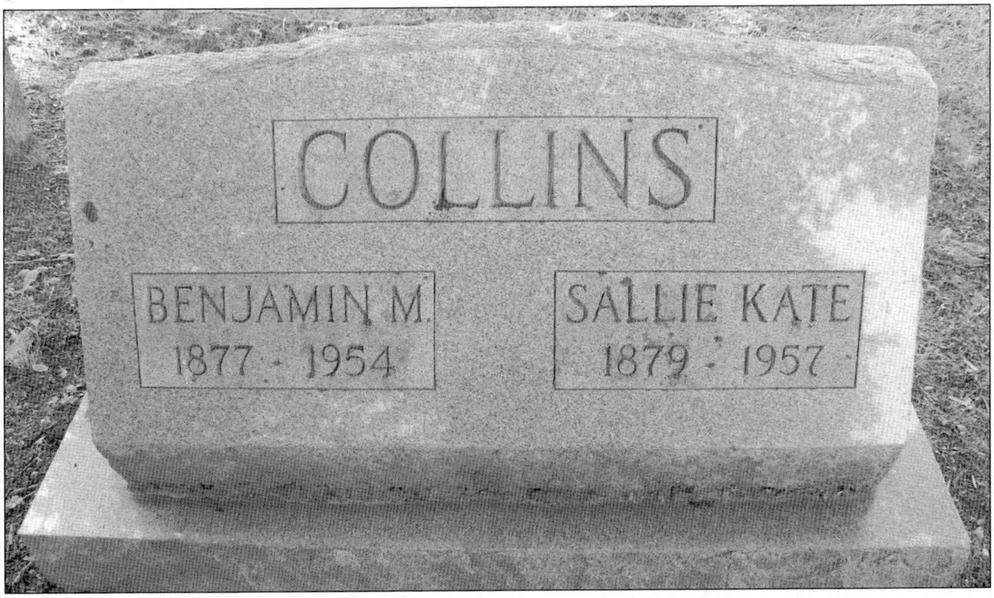

Benjamin M. Collins was an estate laborer who first worked for Chauncey Beadle as a printer. Two years later, Collins began as the keeper of the Swannanoa Gate Lodge for Dr. Carl Schenck, handling the firewood and lumber sales at that location and managing the teamsters. Collins left the estate in 1900 to become the postmaster of Balfour, North Carolina.

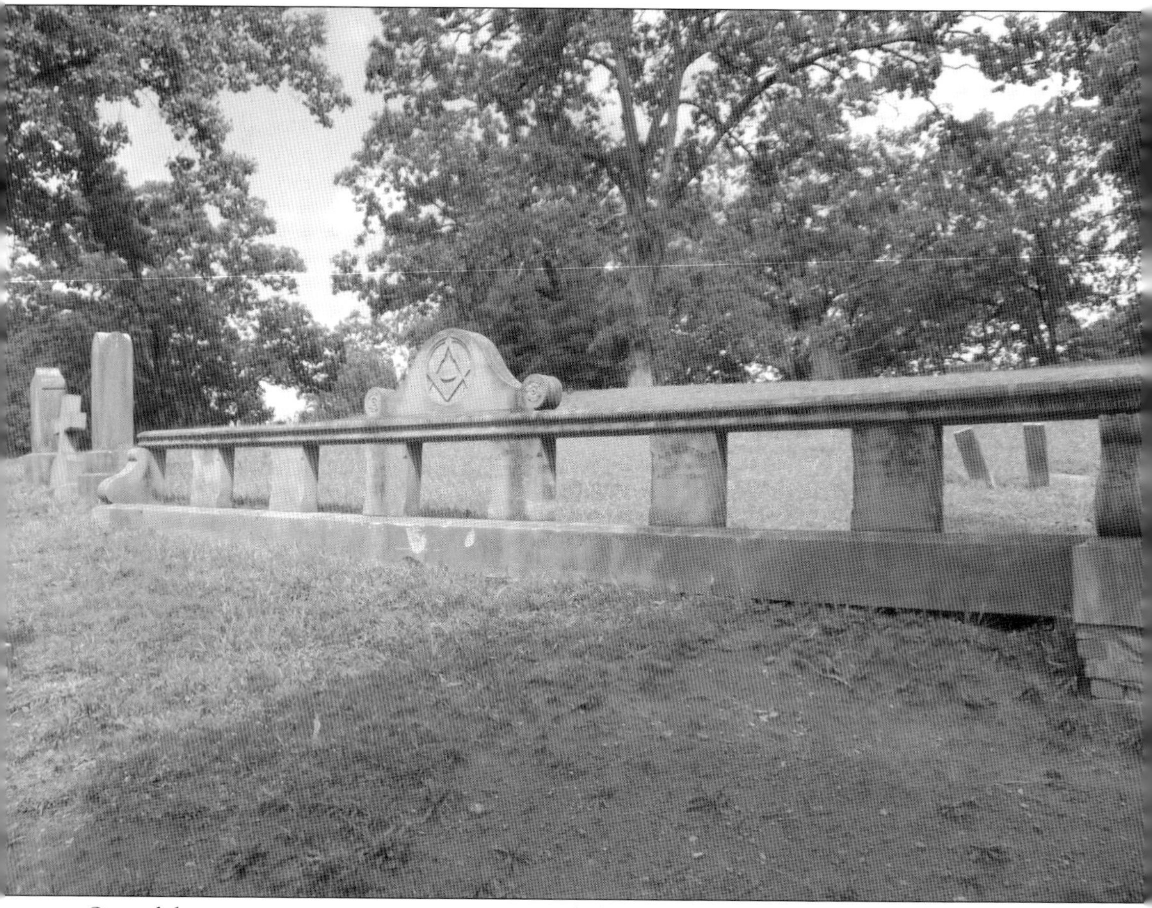

One of the most unique monuments in Riverside has the deepest connections to Biltmore. The monument, designed by master stonecutter Fred Miles, was built using limestone from the estate and paid for by the Vanderbilt family. It was erected in honor of the six stonecutters who had been hired by D.C. Weeks and Son of New York and had passed away during the estate's construction. Contrary to stories at the time that the men had passed away in construction accidents, only Peter Smith was actually on the estate property at the time of his death from lung problems, a common ailment for masons at the time. Two others, Henry Clay and Patrick McKenna, died two days apart from drowning in the Tuckasegee River under suspicious circumstances. After their deaths, Miles constructed the 30-foot marker with the six men's names and had them buried together at Riverside.

Arguably the most famous of the Biltmore stonecutters was Fred Miles, an Englishman who came to work at Biltmore alongside S.I. Bean in 1891. Miles carved several monuments in Riverside, including the monument to the stonecutters who passed away during his time at Biltmore. He was also responsible for the elaborate frieze on the Drhumor Building in downtown Asheville and the ornamentation on Guastavino's Basilica of St. Lawrence. (NCC.)

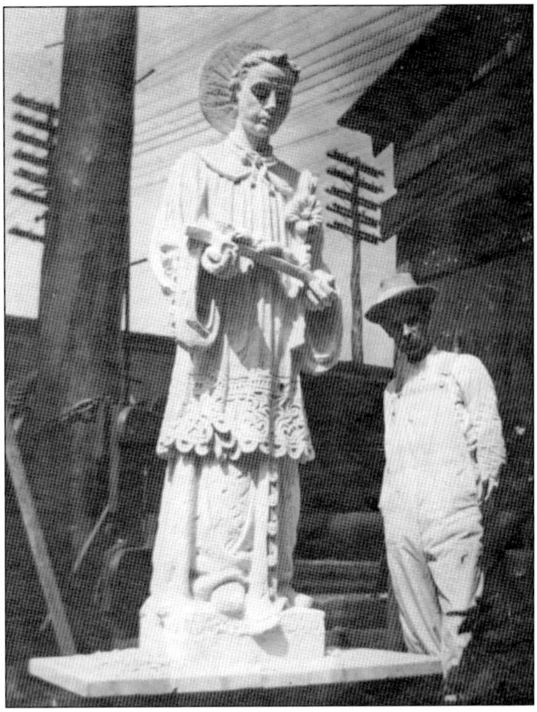

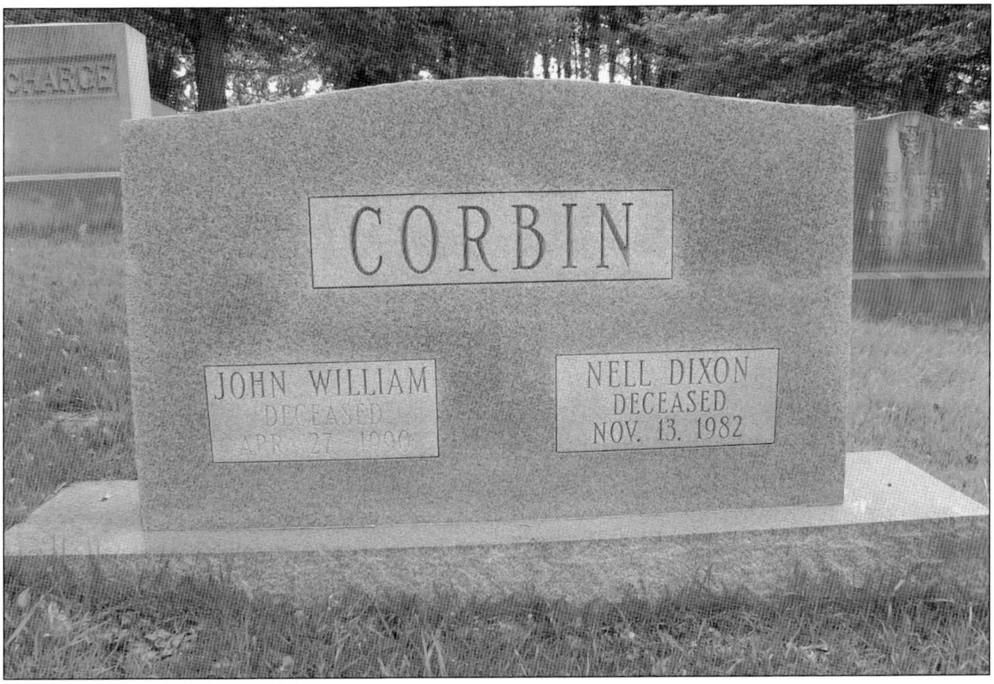

John Corbin began his work in Asheville as a stonecutter for the Biltmore Estate. After its completion, Corbin spent several years as the foreman at the Biltmore Nursery before going to work alongside S.I. Bean, with whom he worked at the estate. Corbin became a noted craftsman who sculpted stone at the Grove Park Inn, Masonic temple, and Central United Methodist Church, as well as erecting many monuments inside Riverside Cemetery.

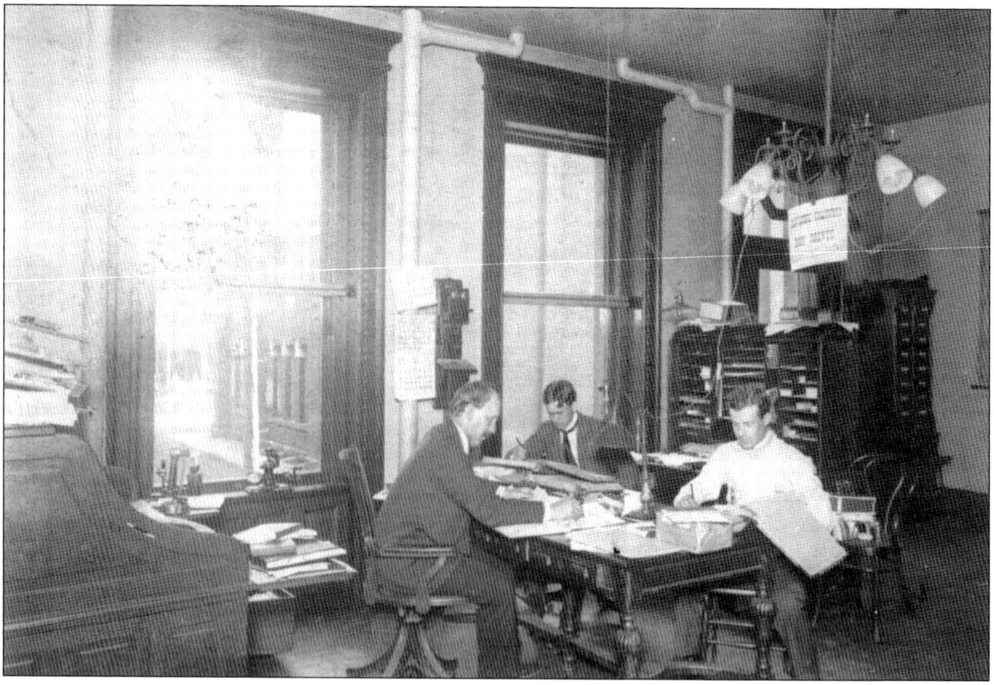

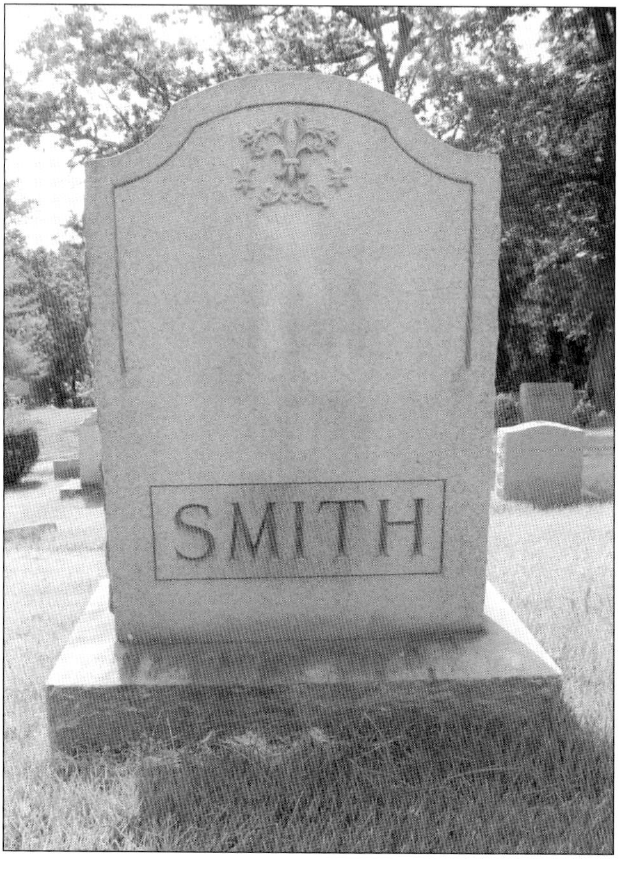

Richard Sharp Smith (left) changed the face of Asheville more than any other architect of his time, with over 700 projects attributed to his firm, which he owned with Albert Carrier. Smith came to Asheville in 1889 as the supervising architect of the Biltmore estate for Richard Morris Hunt. He married a member of Vanderbilt's house staff, Isabella Cameron. Though Smith primarily followed the plans drawn up by Hunt for the Biltmore House, he was sole designer for many of the other estate buildings as well as Biltmore Village, the idyllic town Vanderbilt had built near the estate's entrance. The English cottage style of Biltmore Village and of many of Asheville's buildings can be attributed to the Yorkshire-born Smith. His legacy and style have influenced and inspired many of the architects who came to Asheville after him. (Above, NCC.)

B.J. Alexander was an entrepreneur who sold land to George Vanderbilt comprising important parts of the estate, including the Bass Pond, pictured here, formerly the Alexander Mill Pond. His brick farmhouse located there served as Vanderbilt's headquarters during construction of the estate. Alexander was also known as the "man who owns the river" after he purchased a 12-mile tract of the French Broad's riverbed from the state in 1891. (Biltmore Estate Archives.)

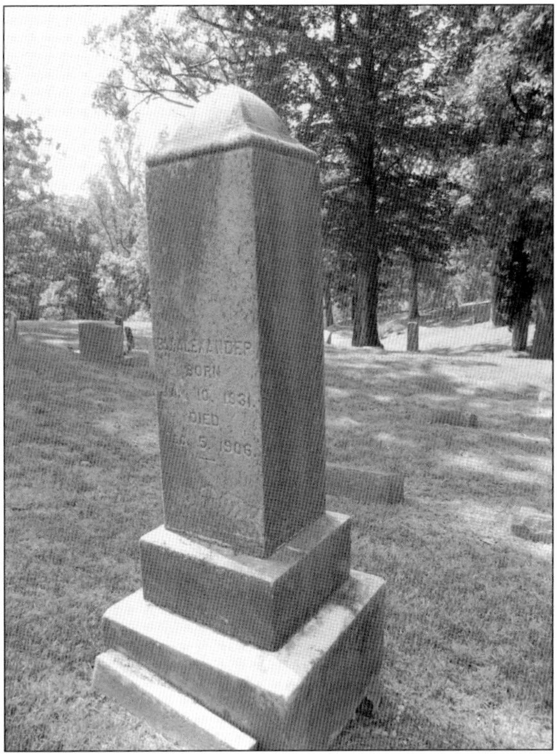

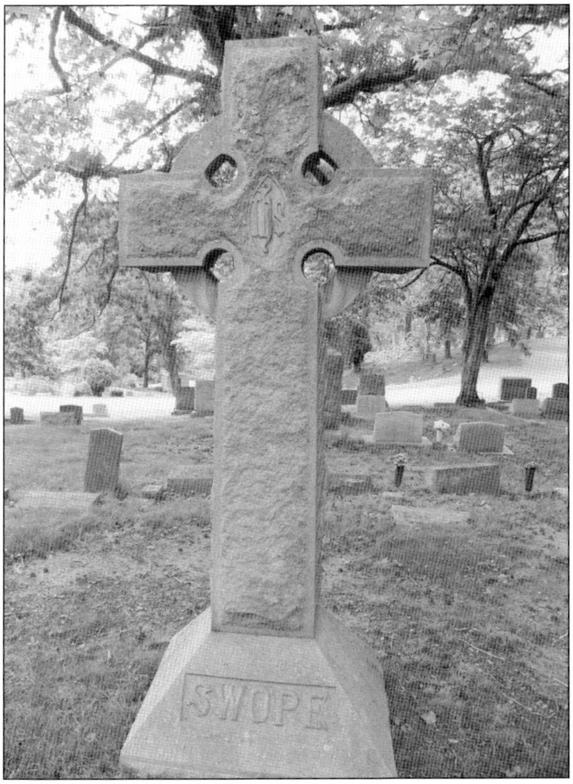

Dr. Rodney R. Swope became the rector of All Souls Church in Biltmore Village at the request of George Vanderbilt in 1897. Dr. Swope ran the church for the next 20 years, with George Vanderbilt paying both his salary and the churches expenses until Swope's death. Because of this, Dr. Swope was able to use all of the offerings made to the church by other parishioners for charitable purposes.

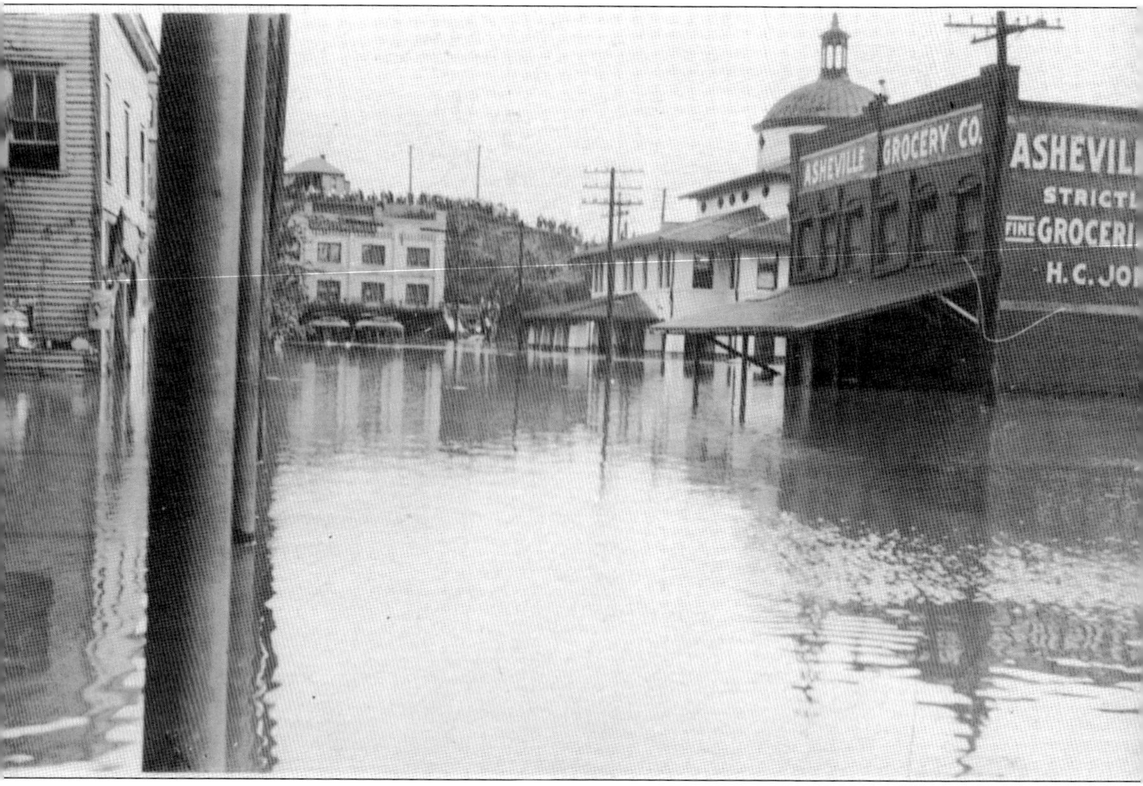

The 1916 flood had a devastating impact on North Carolina and on Biltmore in particular. On July 16, 1916, torrents of water from the Swannanoa and French Broad Rivers engulfed Biltmore Village without warning. Though many were able to escape their homes and find higher ground, the family of Capt. J.C. Lipe, along with Biltmore Hospital nurses Mabel Foister, Charlotte Walker, and Louise Walker, were not so fortunate. The floodwaters caught them as they left their house just outside the main entrance of the estate, the Lodge Gate. To save themselves, Lipe, his daughters Nellie and Katherine, and the nurses clung to a tree amid the rushing waters. The waters proved to be too strong, as one by one they were swept away, save for Captain Lipe's youngest, Katherine. Captain Lipe was buried in his family lot in Riverside, and the Biltmore nurses were held in the receiving vault until Edith Vanderbilt could arrange for them to be moved to Tabernacle Methodist Church, where their monument was paid for by the Vanderbilt family. (NCC.)

Capt. J.C. Lipe was a well-respected employee of the Vanderbilts who worked for 27 years as the estate carpenter before his death in the 1916 flood. Lipe's final act in life was an unselfish one, as he expended the last of his energy to hoist his daughter Katherine as high as he could into the branches of the tree they clung to before he was swept away.

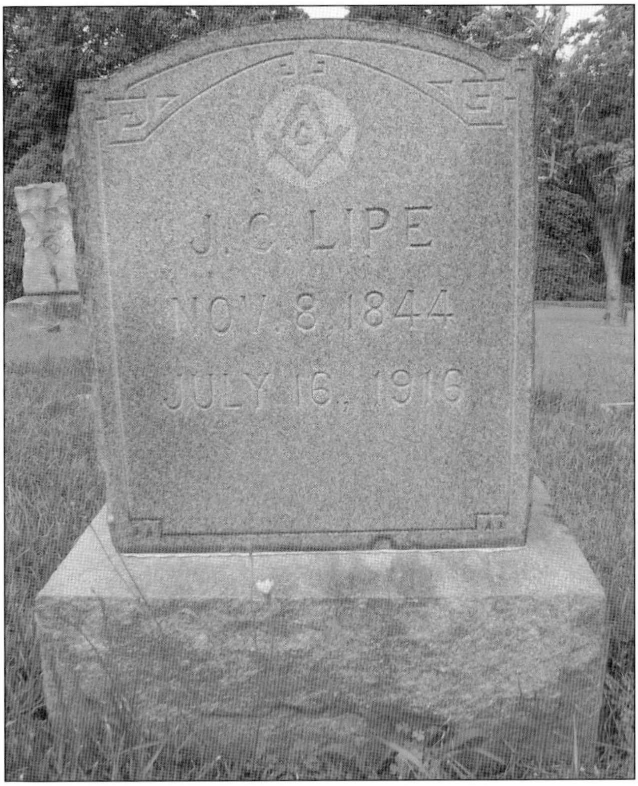

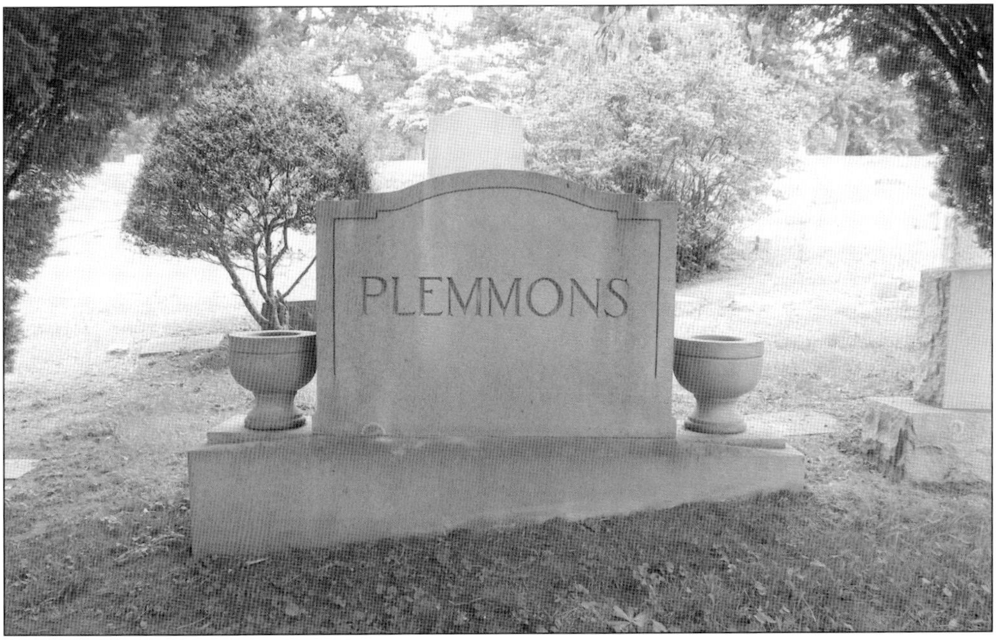

Raymond J. Plemmons was both the chauffeur and mechanic for the Biltmore Estate from 1909 until 1922, when he left the Vanderbilts' service to open up a luxury car dealership. Plemmons was one of the heroes of the 1916 flood, as he was able to get a boat through the floodwaters at his own peril to rescue Katherine Lipe after the rest of her party had perished.

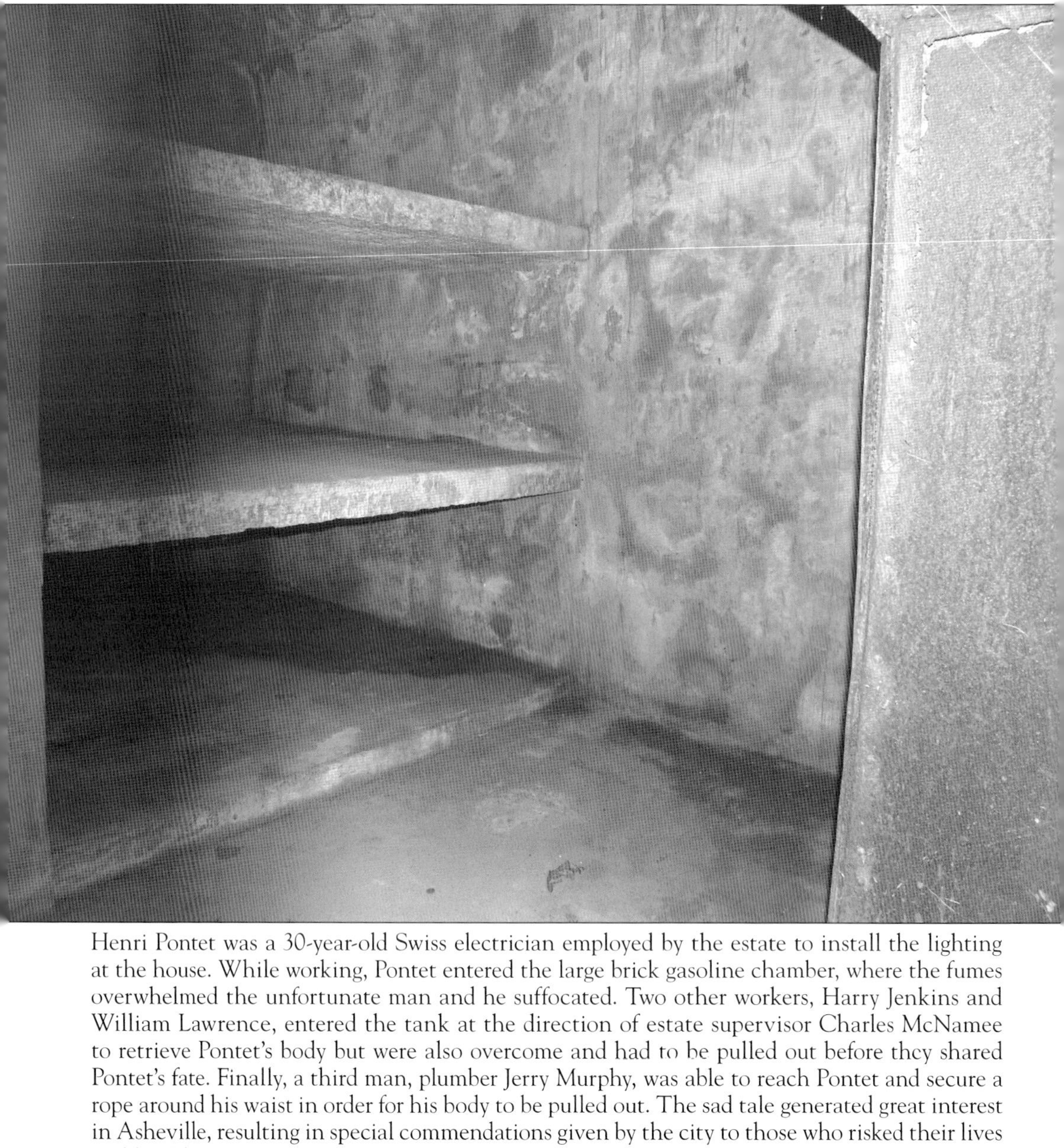

Henri Pontet was a 30-year-old Swiss electrician employed by the estate to install the lighting at the house. While working, Pontet entered the large brick gasoline chamber, where the fumes overwhelmed the unfortunate man and he suffocated. Two other workers, Harry Jenkins and William Lawrence, entered the tank at the direction of estate supervisor Charles McNamee to retrieve Pontet's body but were also overcome and had to be pulled out before they shared Pontet's fate. Finally, a third man, plumber Jerry Murphy, was able to reach Pontet and secure a rope around his waist in order for his body to be pulled out. The sad tale generated great interest in Asheville, resulting in special commendations given by the city to those who risked their lives and health to retrieve Pontet's body. Pontet was taken to Riverside's receiving vault (pictured), where he was kept for two weeks until arrangements could be made by his family in Switzerland to transport his remains back home.

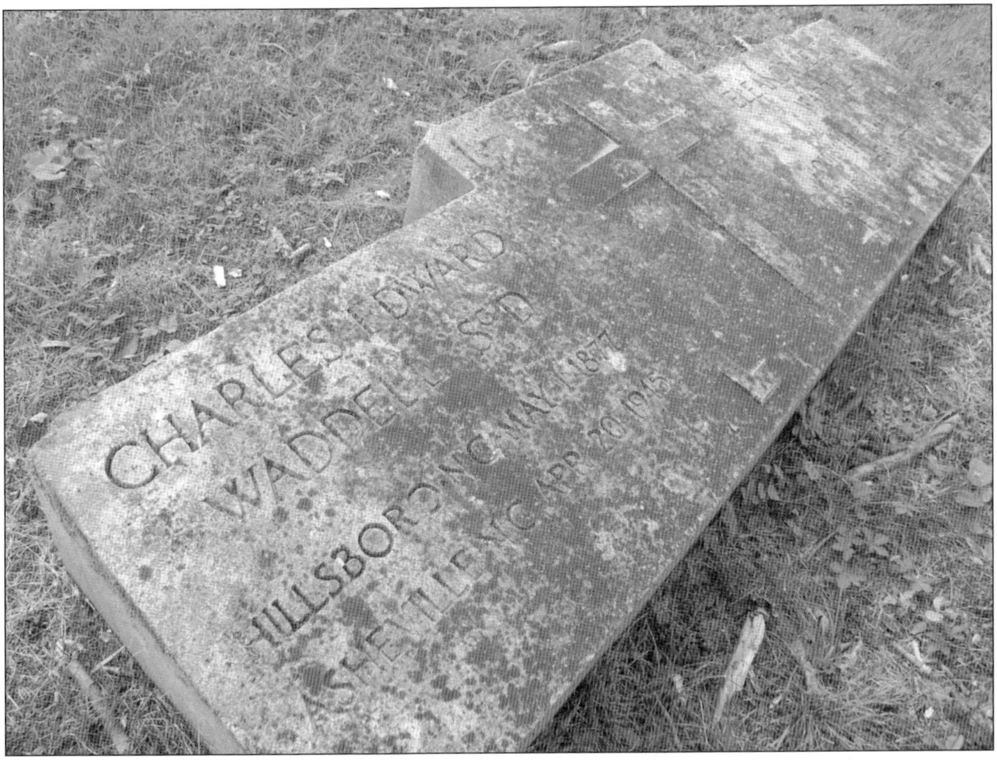

Charles Waddell was hired by Charles McNamee in 1901 to become the consulting engineer and electrician for the Biltmore Estate. He continued in this capacity for several years before establishing his own firm, Charles E. Waddell & Company. Waddell was very active in Biltmore Village's civil affairs and served as the Sunday school superintendent at All Souls Church.

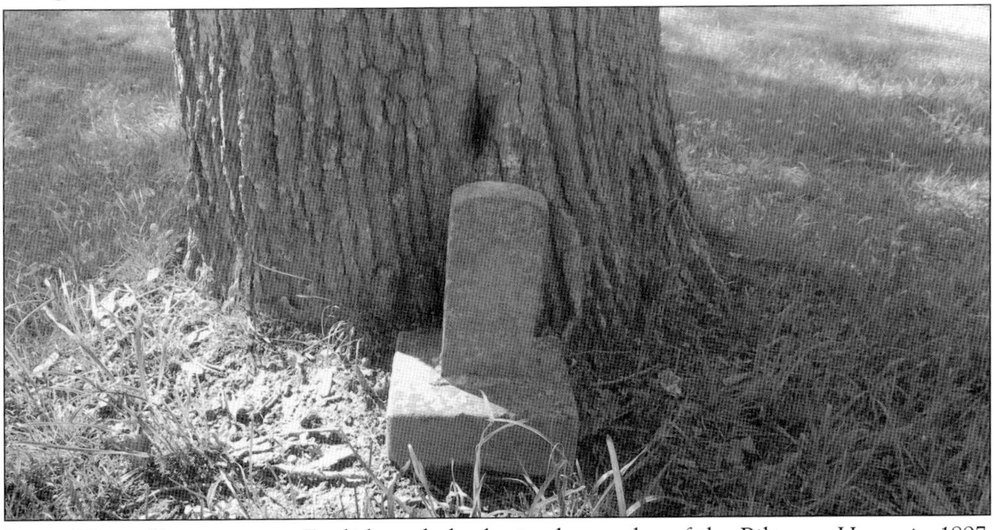

James Wagstaff was a young English underbutler in the employ of the Biltmore House in 1897. Wagstaff was among a number of employees who distrusted the concept of indoor plumbing and preferred instead to drink from the nearby spring, resulting in an outbreak of typhoid fever among them. Wagstaff passed away from the illness and was buried in Riverside at George Vanderbilt's expense.

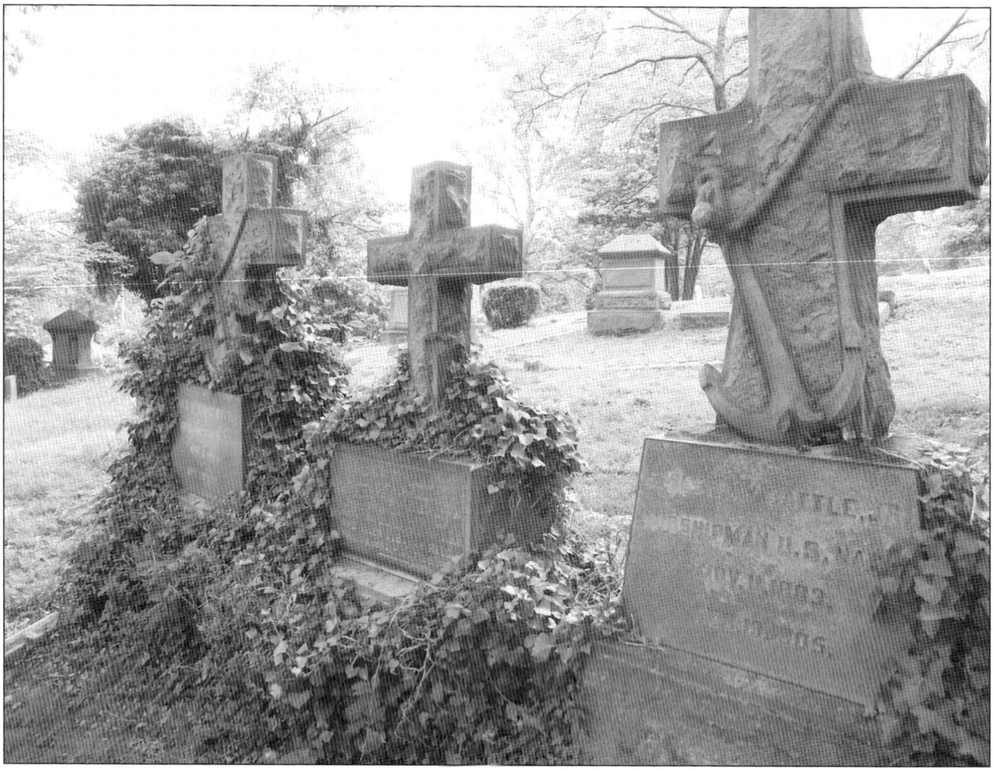

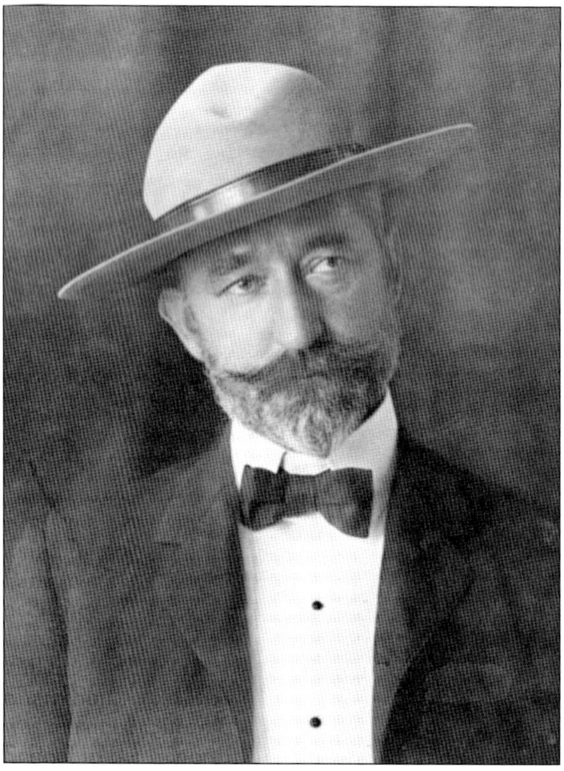

One of the most influential doctors in the history of North Carolina was the famously dapper Dr. Samuel Westray Battle. Dr. Battle was a former Navy surgeon who had retired due to an injury to his hand. The Navy's loss was Asheville's gain, as Battle became one of the leading promoters of Asheville as a health destination. This led prominent individuals such as Edwin Grove and Maria Kissam Vanderbilt, matriarch of the Vanderbilt family, to come to Asheville as patients of the renowned physician. On a trip to Asheville to accompany his ailing mother, George Vanderbilt fell in love with the area and the idea for the Biltmore Estate was born. Battle continued to serve the Vanderbilts after their move to Asheville and attended the birth of George's daughter Cornelia in 1900. (Left, NCC.)

Six

OUR FOEMAN'S MERIT

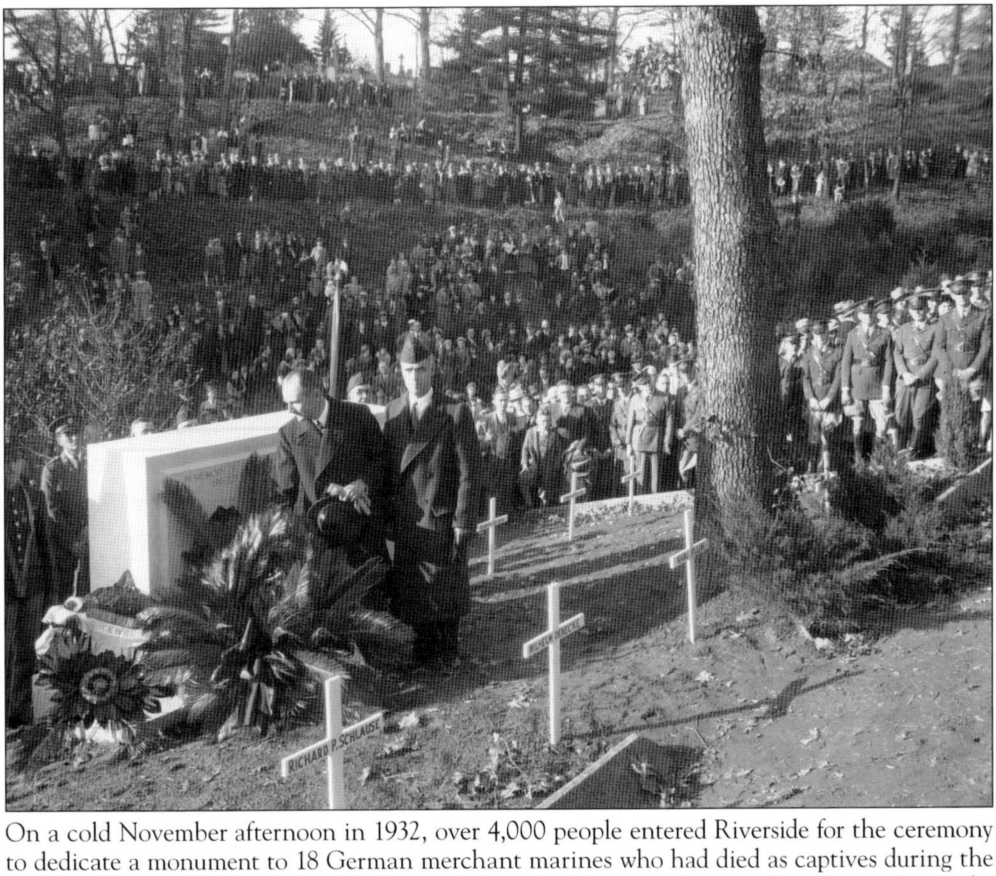

On a cold November afternoon in 1932, over 4,000 people entered Riverside for the ceremony to dedicate a monument to 18 German merchant marines who had died as captives during the First World War. This service honoring the fallen enemy, the largest to take place in Riverside, has often been described as Western North Carolina's finest moment. (E.M. Ball.)

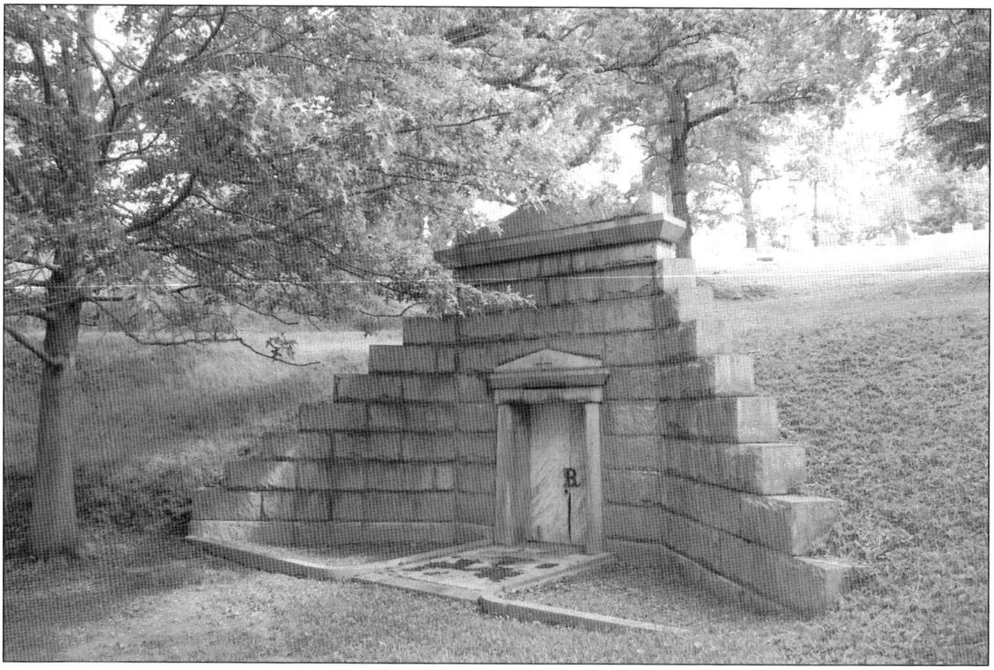

The unique Rumbough-Baker mausoleum is set into the hillside overlooking the final resting place of the German sailors. The mausoleum was designed by John Gulick Baker, an inventor who held over 60 patents in his lifetime, for himself and his daughter's family. His son-in-law, James E. Rumbough, was the only mayor in the history of Montford, from 1893 until 1904.

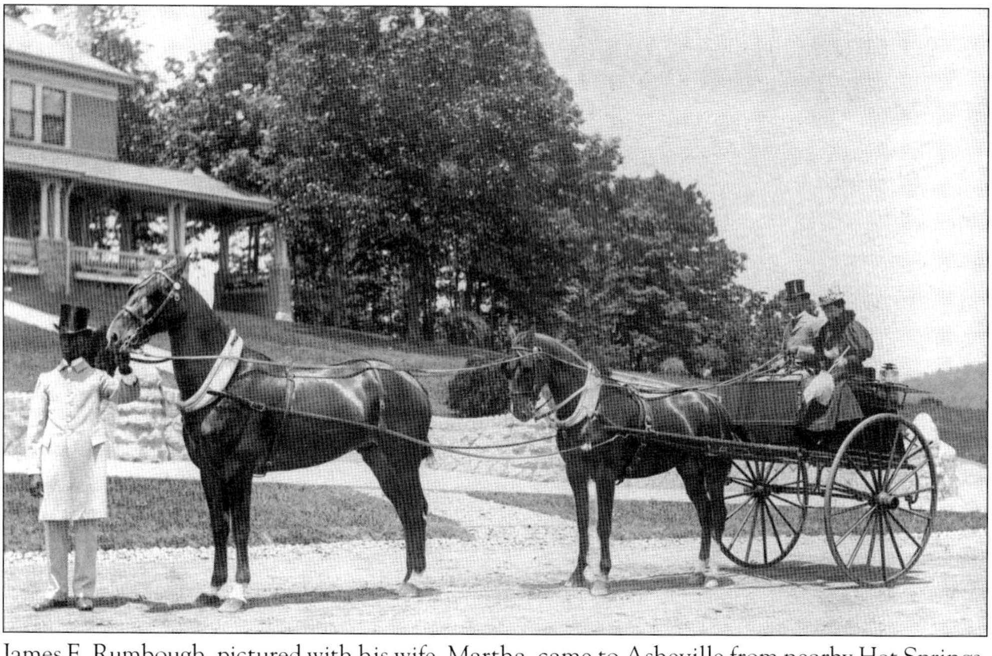

James E. Rumbough, pictured with his wife, Martha, came to Asheville from nearby Hot Springs, North Carolina, in 1880. In Hot Springs, the Rumbough family owned the Mountain Park Hotel. They negotiated a contract with the War Department in 1917 to house the German detainees within the hotel and its grounds for the remainder of the war. (NCC.)

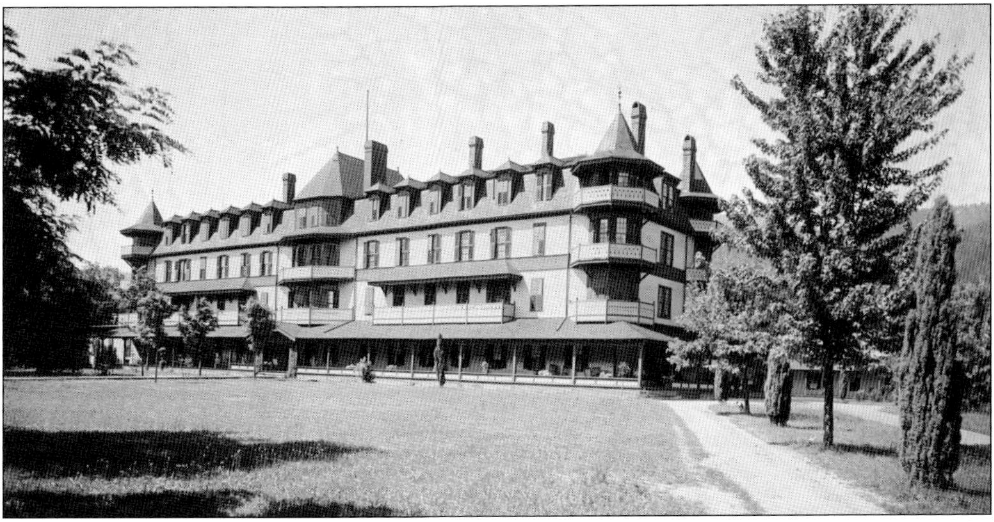

The Mountain Park Hotel was built in 1886 by stagecoach operator James H. Rumbough. The 200-room hotel was a portrait of elegance, with stables, tennis courts, a golf course, and the natural hot springs that drew visitors from around the country. Declining revenues leading up to World War I, however, led to the hotel's use as an internment camp. It burned down a few years later in 1920. (LOC.)

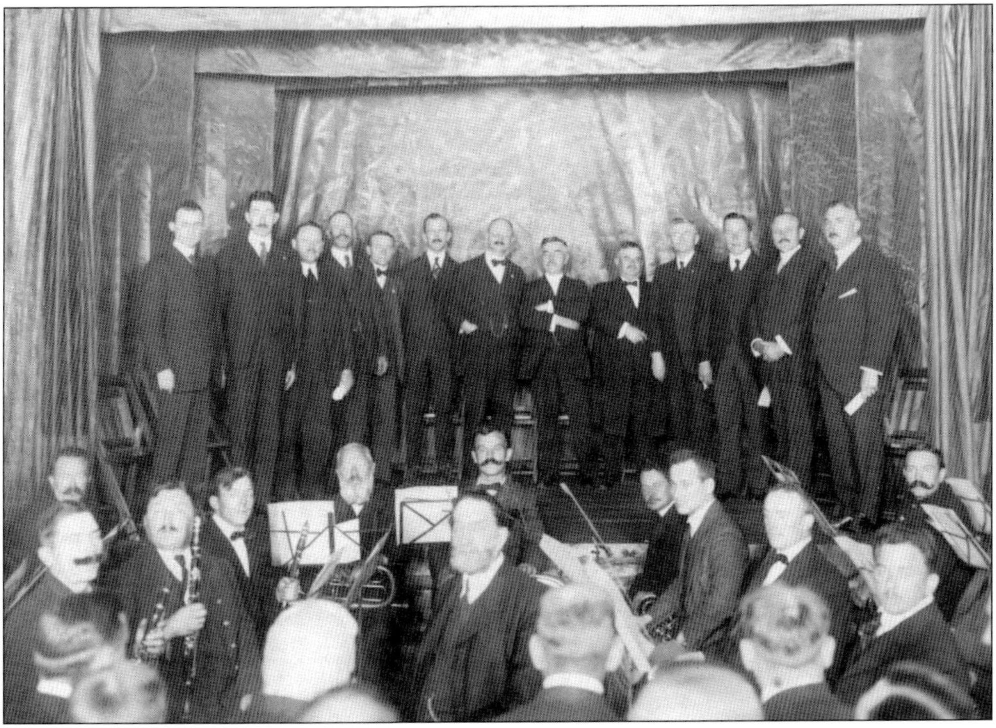

The German prisoners were classified by the US government as "enemy aliens" after being taken captive when the United States declared war on Germany on April 6, 1917. Of the 2,200 who came to Hot Springs, most were civilians who had taken refuge in American harbors after Great Britain and Germany went to war. Included in this number were members of the German orchestra pictured here. (ATC.)

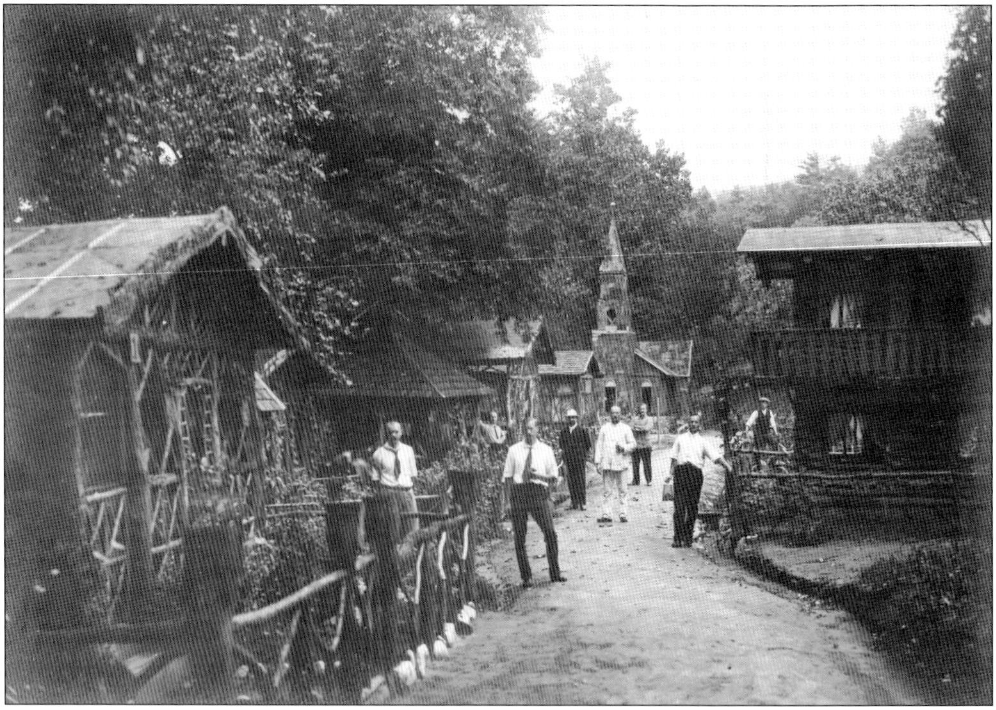

During World War I, German detainees were brought to the Mountain Park Hotel from Ellis Island, New York, to remove them from the public eye and major population centers. The officers were housed in the hotel itself, while the sailors and other civilians built an "Alpine village" from scrap lumber and recycled tin on the hotel grounds. By all accounts of the time, the internment camp was a decent place and was referred to locally as "the prison from which no one wanted to escape." The Germans were welcomed by the locals as a source of excitement, and the German brass band held weekly concerts. As evidenced in the below photograph, the Germans interned in Hot Springs fared much better than their compatriots back in Germany, often having time for recreation and revelry. (Both, ATC.)

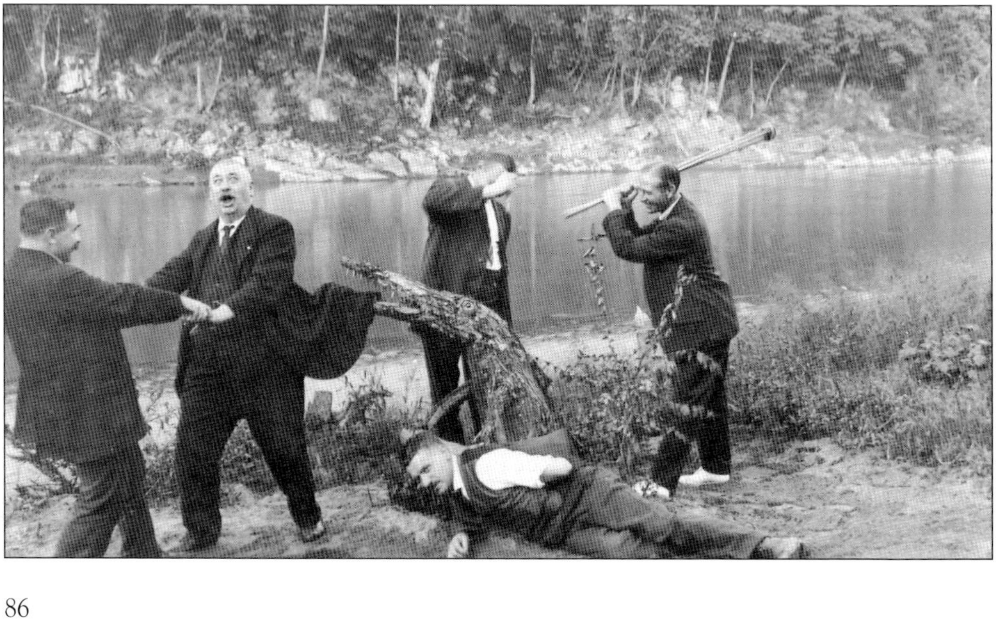

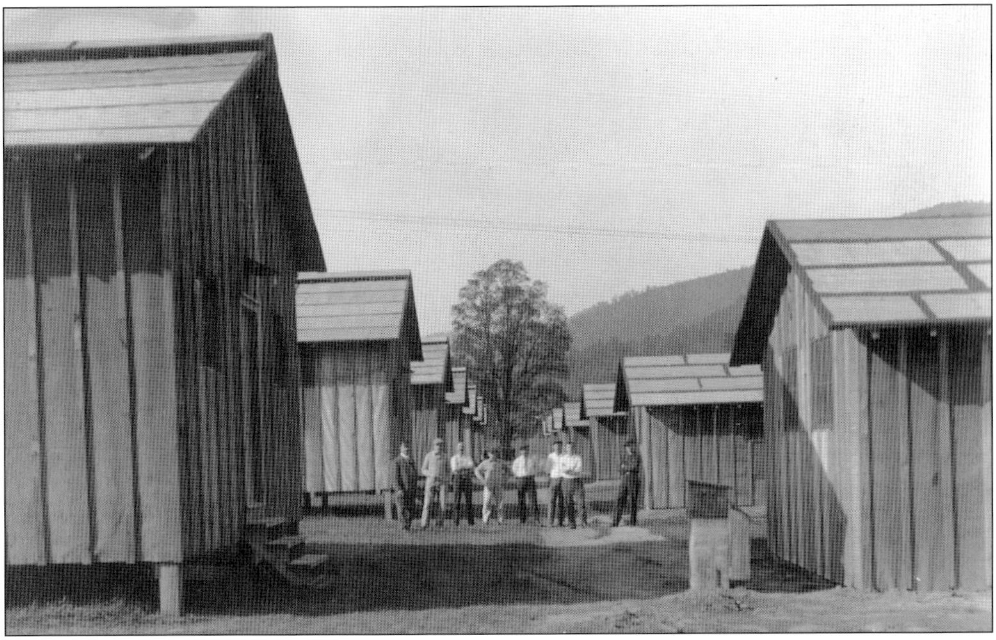

The men continued in the Hot Springs detention facility for a little more than a year with little incident when an outbreak of typhoid fever swept through the camp in August 1918. The close quarters and inadequate medical facilities contributed to the spread of the fever, and over 200 men were infected. (ATC.)

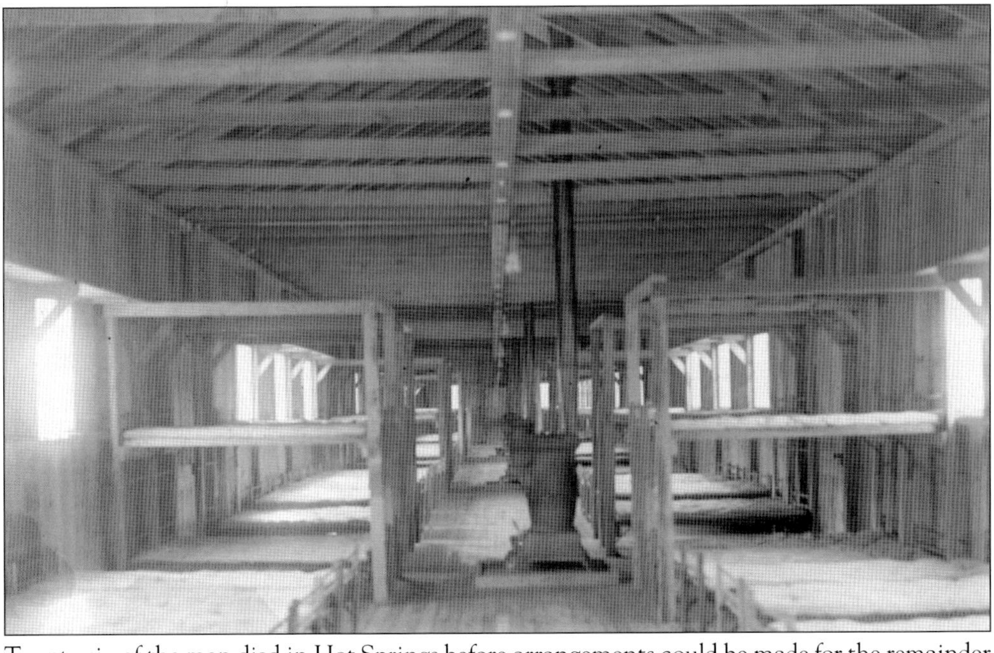

Twenty-six of the men died in Hot Springs before arrangements could be made for the remainder to be moved to Asheville. In all, 186 men made the trip on a specially fitted two-section Southern Railroad train. Some died en route, and the rest were brought to the hospital at Kenilworth. Over the next several months, 18 Germans died in Asheville and were brought to Riverside for burial. (ATC.)

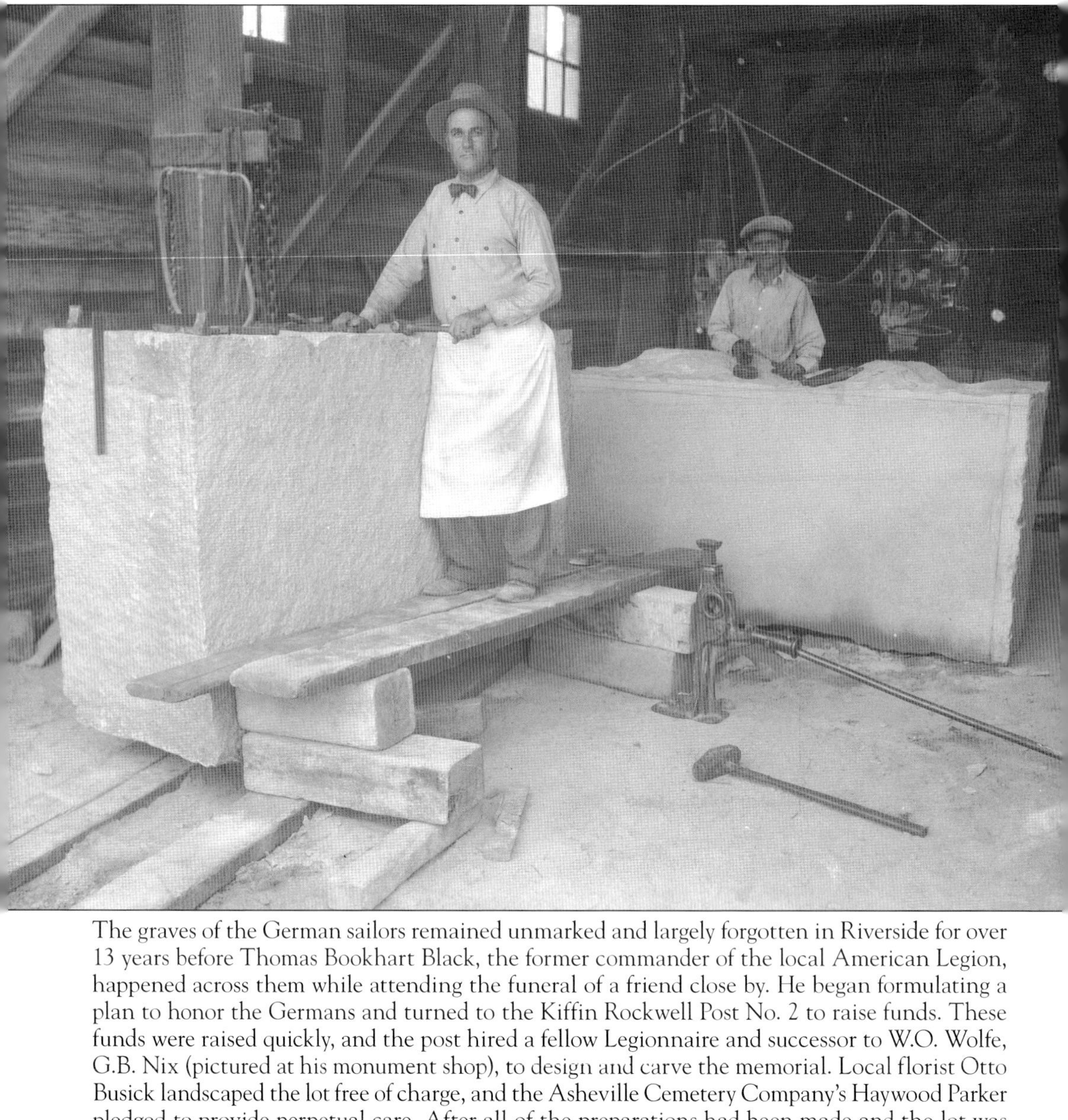

The graves of the German sailors remained unmarked and largely forgotten in Riverside for over 13 years before Thomas Bookhart Black, the former commander of the local American Legion, happened across them while attending the funeral of a friend close by. He began formulating a plan to honor the Germans and turned to the Kiffin Rockwell Post No. 2 to raise funds. These funds were raised quickly, and the post hired a fellow Legionnaire and successor to W.O. Wolfe, G.B. Nix (pictured at his monument shop), to design and carve the memorial. Local florist Otto Busick landscaped the lot free of charge, and the Asheville Cemetery Company's Haywood Parker pledged to provide perpetual care. After all of the preparations had been made and the lot was completed, Thomas Black turned his attention to planning the large international ceremony to dedicate the memorial. (E.M. Ball.)

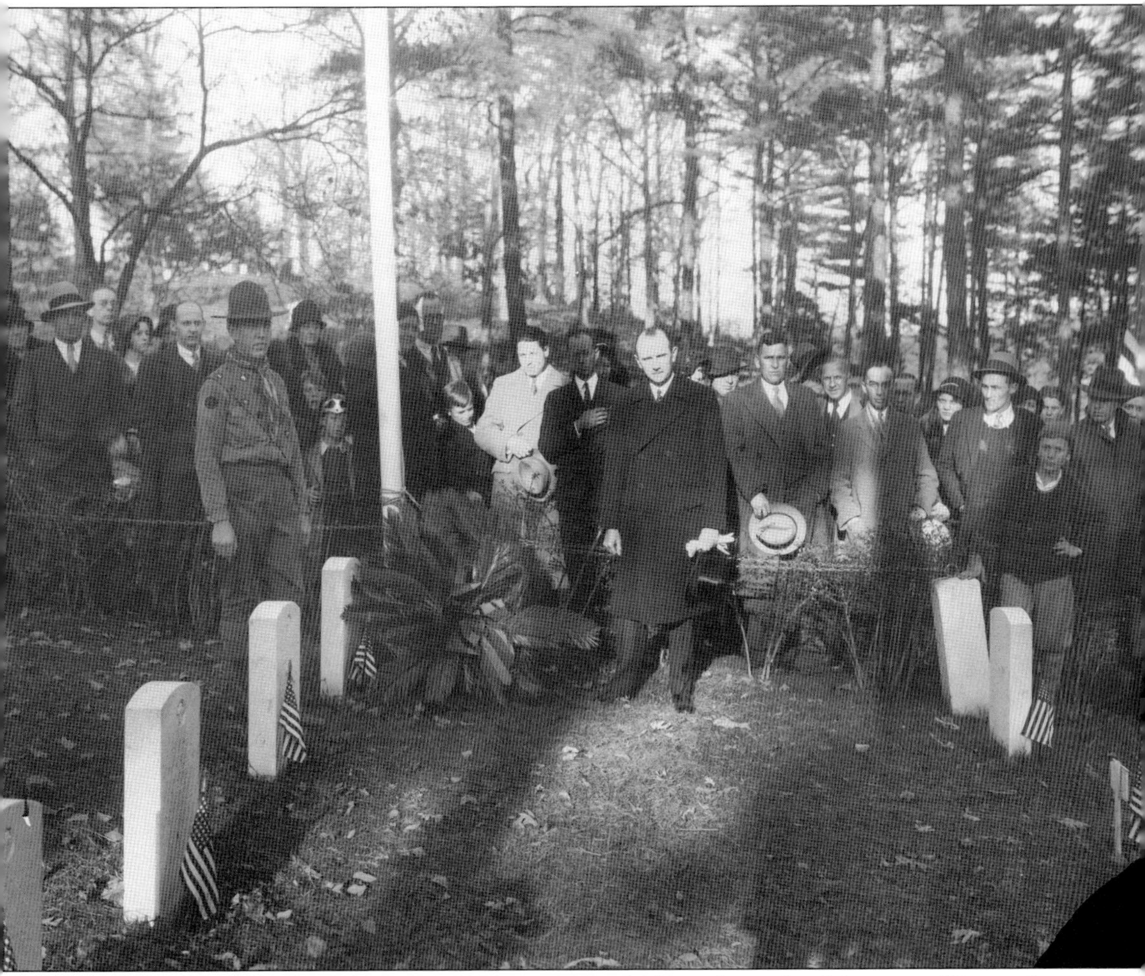

On November 20, 1932, a procession of over 2,000 people formed outside of the gates of Riverside. At the procession's head were members of the Kiffin Rockwell Post and of Der Stahlhelm, a German organization of former frontline soldiers. Each carried the flags of their respective homelands. Behind them were prominent Asheville citizens and, from left to right beside the flagpole, German consul Dr. R.L. Jaeger, German ambassador to the United States Dr. F.W. von Prittwitz, and German consul J.A. von Dohlen. The dedication service was broadcast nationally by NBC radio and in Germany via shortwave radio courtesy of the Reichs-Rundfunk-Gesellschaft. Thomas Black (pictured far left) was first to speak, promising the German people that their kindred would be "taken into the bosom of American . . . so their lives will not be forgotten." Dr. von Prittwitz followed with an address to the crowd promising an end to national antagonism and calling for the monument to stand as a symbol of the mutual promise for unity between the two countries in striving for peace and progress. (E.M. Ball.)

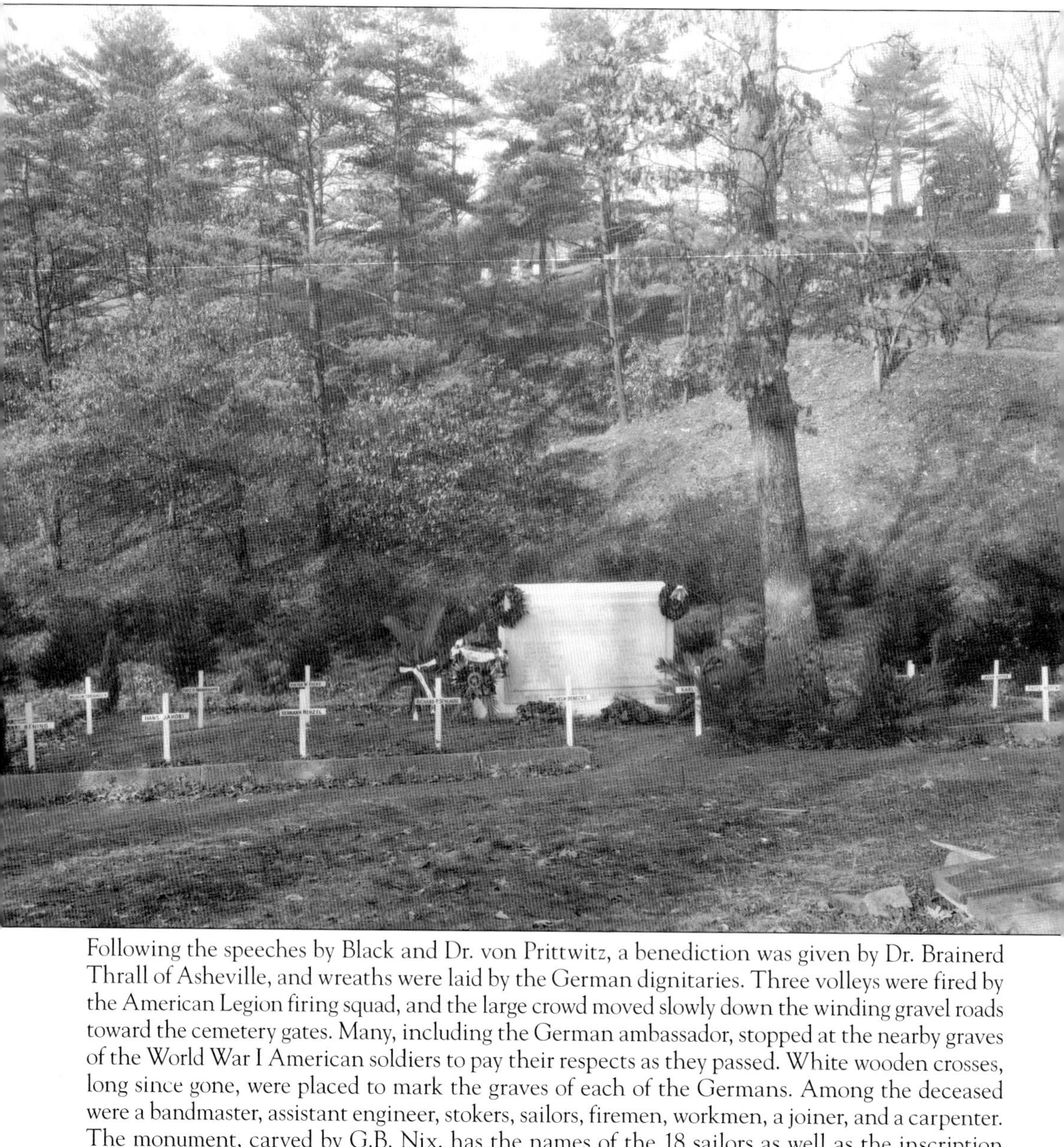

Following the speeches by Black and Dr. von Prittwitz, a benediction was given by Dr. Brainerd Thrall of Asheville, and wreaths were laid by the German dignitaries. Three volleys were fired by the American Legion firing squad, and the large crowd moved slowly down the winding gravel roads toward the cemetery gates. Many, including the German ambassador, stopped at the nearby graves of the World War I American soldiers to pay their respects as they passed. White wooden crosses, long since gone, were placed to mark the graves of each of the Germans. Among the deceased were a bandmaster, assistant engineer, stokers, sailors, firemen, workmen, a joiner, and a carpenter. The monument, carved by G.B. Nix, has the names of the 18 sailors as well as the inscription from Goethe: "Nicht grosser vorteil wusst'ich zu nennen als des feindes verdienst erkennen" (No greater gain for the human spirit than a sense of our foeman's merit). (E.M. Ball.)

Seven

Thomas Wolfe's Asheville

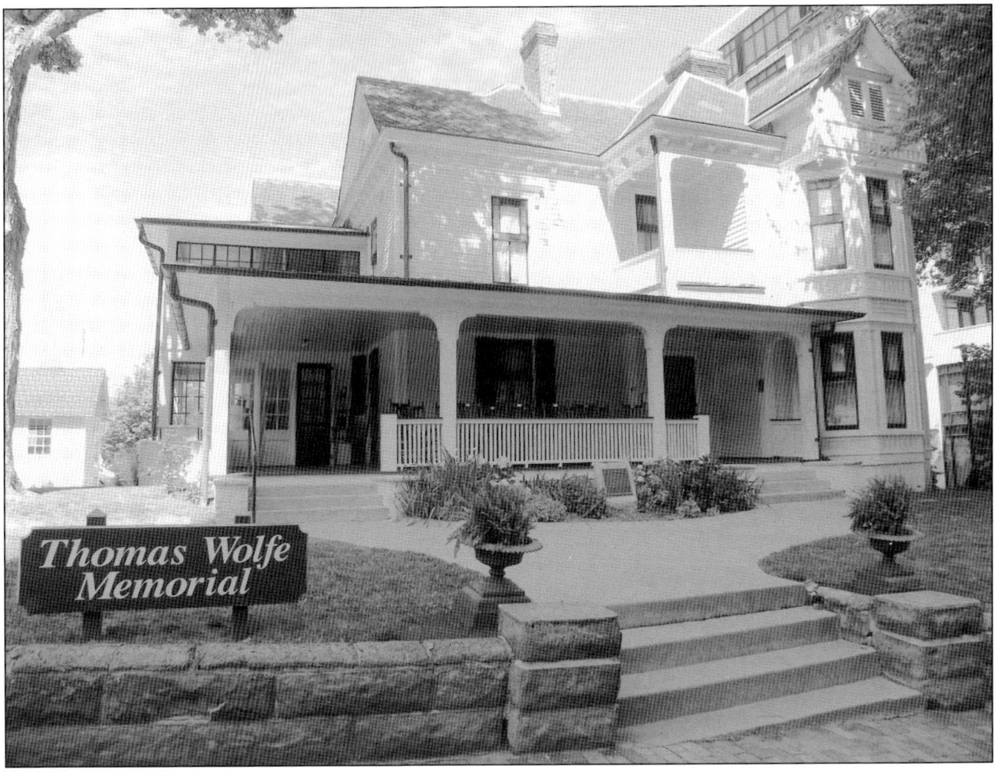

Thomas Wolfe both thrilled and scandalized the people of Asheville with the publication of *Look Homeward, Angel*, a semiautobiographical novel based on Wolfe's experiences growing up at his mother's boardinghouse, the Old Kentucky Home (pictured), and his perspective on those who shaped his childhood. Over 150 of the characters in the novel have been identified as being buried in Riverside.

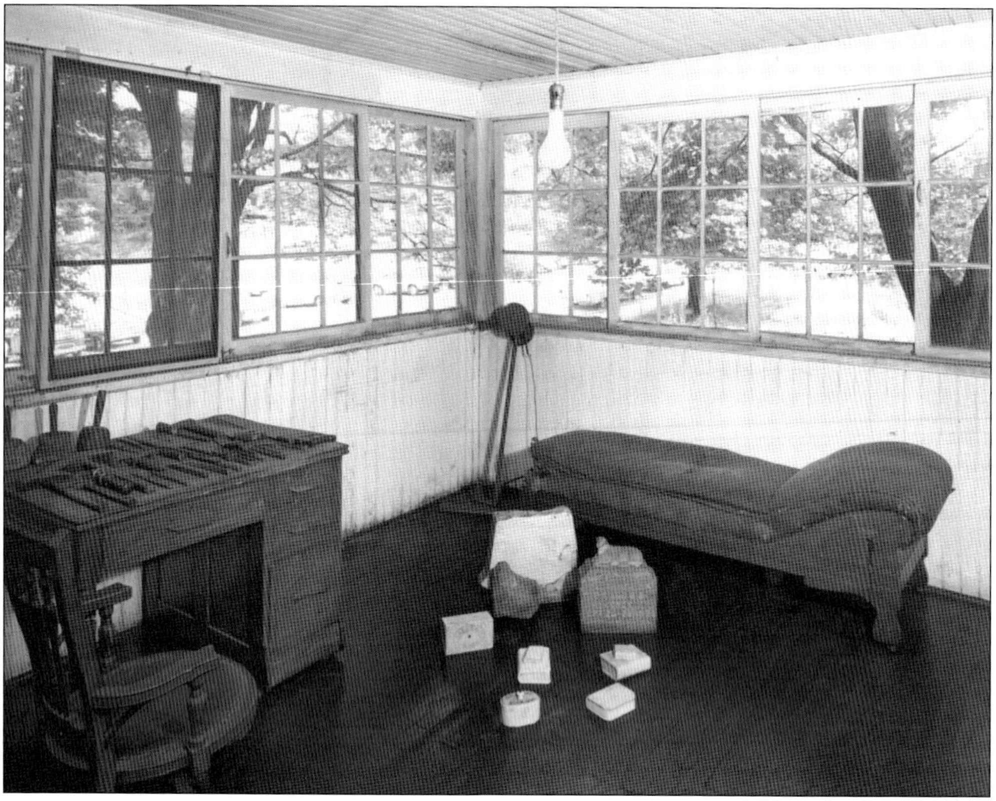

Thomas Wolfe will always be most closely associated with Riverside Cemetery because it was the place where he was laid to rest, but he spent many hours there during his life with his father, W.O., assisting in small ways with the family business. W.O. Wolfe's monument shop has been immortalized through his son's writings, and the man himself was cemented as one of the enduring characters of American literature, though his depiction as the hard-drinking, insecure W.O. Gant by Thomas is not a flattering one. W.O. was an excellent craftsman, and his work was much desired throughout the region, but he often felt in the shadow of his in-laws and of the more successful S.I. Bean. Pictured here are some of the tools used as a monument mason and an advertisement card for his business. (Above, TWC; below, RCA.)

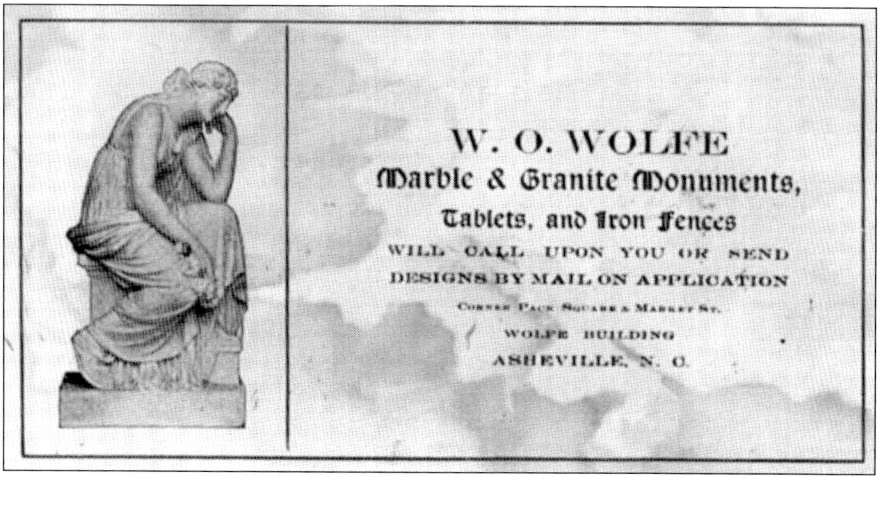

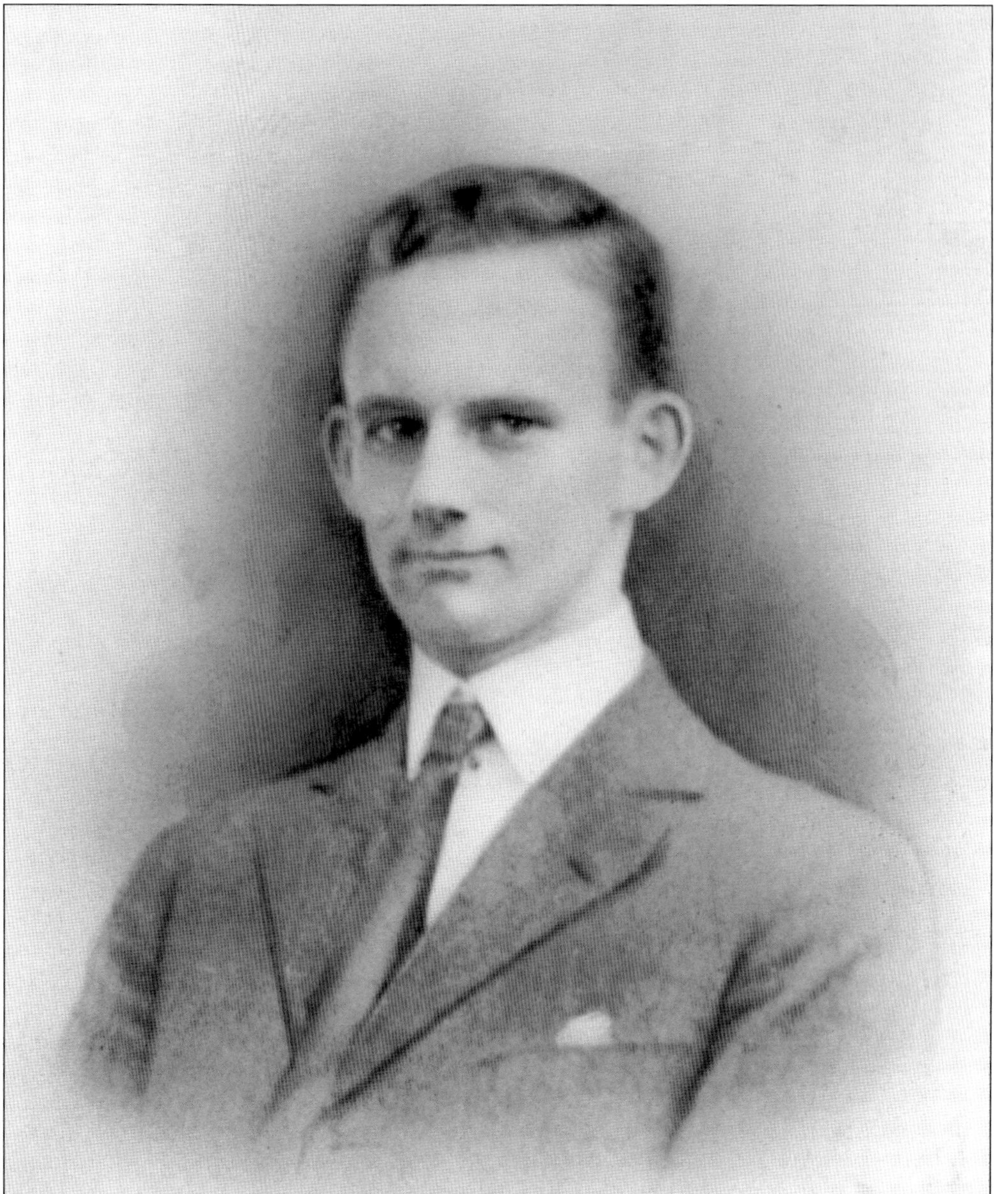

There was no greater influence in Thomas Wolfe's life than his older brother and mentor Ben, who pushed Tom to make the most of the opportunities afforded to him and to rise above the pettiness and greed that surrounded them. In 1918, the Spanish influenza pandemic reached Asheville and claimed Ben as one of its victims. In *Look Homeward, Angel*, Wolfe writes about Ben's death and burial at Riverside in what is still considered by many one of the most realistic and poignant depictions of death in modern literature. W.O. carved a small marker for his grave to match that of his deceased twin, Grover. Thomas wrote to his sister Mabel in a letter, "I think the Asheville I knew died for me when Ben died. I have never forgotten him and I never shall. I think that his death affected me more than any other event in my life. . . . Ben—he was one of those fine people who want the best and highest out of life, and who get nothing—who die unknown and unsuccessful." (TWC.)

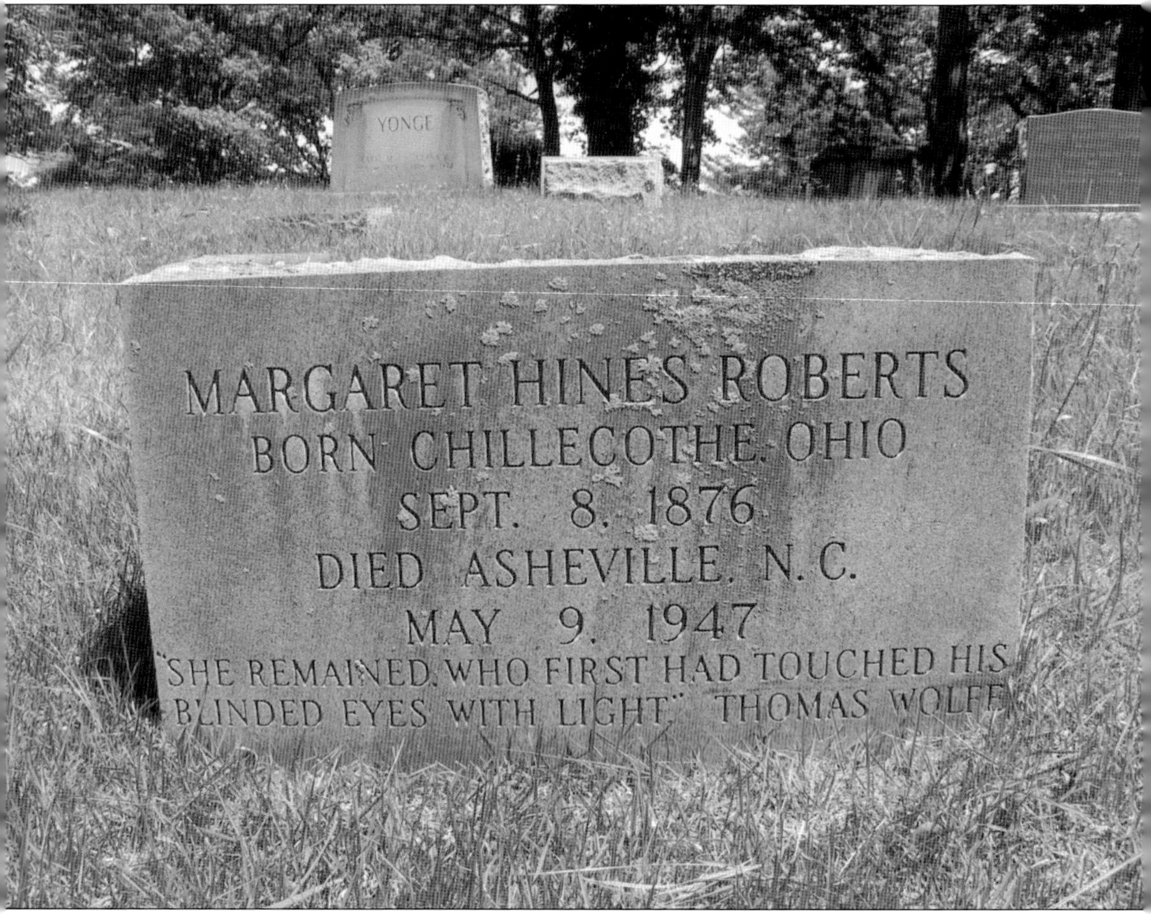

Margaret Hines Roberts was the beloved teacher of Thomas Wolfe at the North State Fitting School from 1912 until 1916. He worshipped her and wrote that she was "the mother of his spirit." Roberts was the first to recognize Wolfe's brilliance and pushed him to begin writing. Wolfe continued to seek her affection and approval even after they had a falling out because of his unflattering depiction of her husband, headmaster John Munsey Roberts, in *Look Homeward, Angel*. Roberts refused to speak to Wolfe for almost seven years, for although she thought his novel to be "powerful, beautifully written," she was afraid that his painful treatment of her husband would hurt and humiliate her family. They reconciled in 1936, two years before Wolfe's death. When she passed away in 1947, her husband had her buried within sight of their former pupil and inscribed the quote Wolfe had written for her—"She remained, who first had touched his blinded eyes with light"—upon her monument.

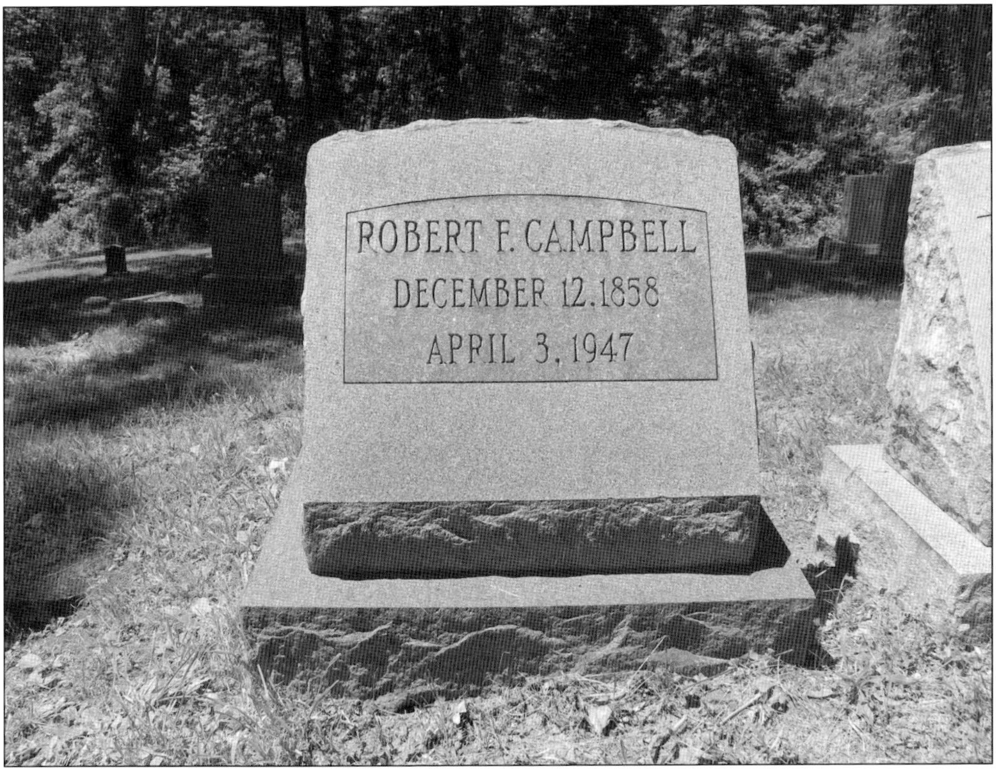

For over 45 years, Rev. Robert Fishburne Campbell was the minister of the First Presbyterian Church of Asheville, the church to which the Wolfe family belonged. During this time, Reverend Campbell presided over the funerals of many of Asheville's foremost citizens, including O. Henry, Gov. Zebulon Vance, and in 1938 the funeral of Thomas Wolfe.

NOLAND-BROWN COMPANY

Funeral Directors And Embalmers . Ambulance Service

283 BILTMORE AVE. **PHONES 65-4727**

Claude B. Holder, known as Horse Hines in Wolfe's *Look Homeward, Angel*, was the mortician at Noland-Brown Funeral Service. Holder is featured prominently in the novel, having many dealings with W.O. Wolfe in the course of his work. Holder was famously the mortician of the desperado Will Harris and the mummified "Duke" of Asheville, as well as serving for each of the Wolfe family. (NCC.)

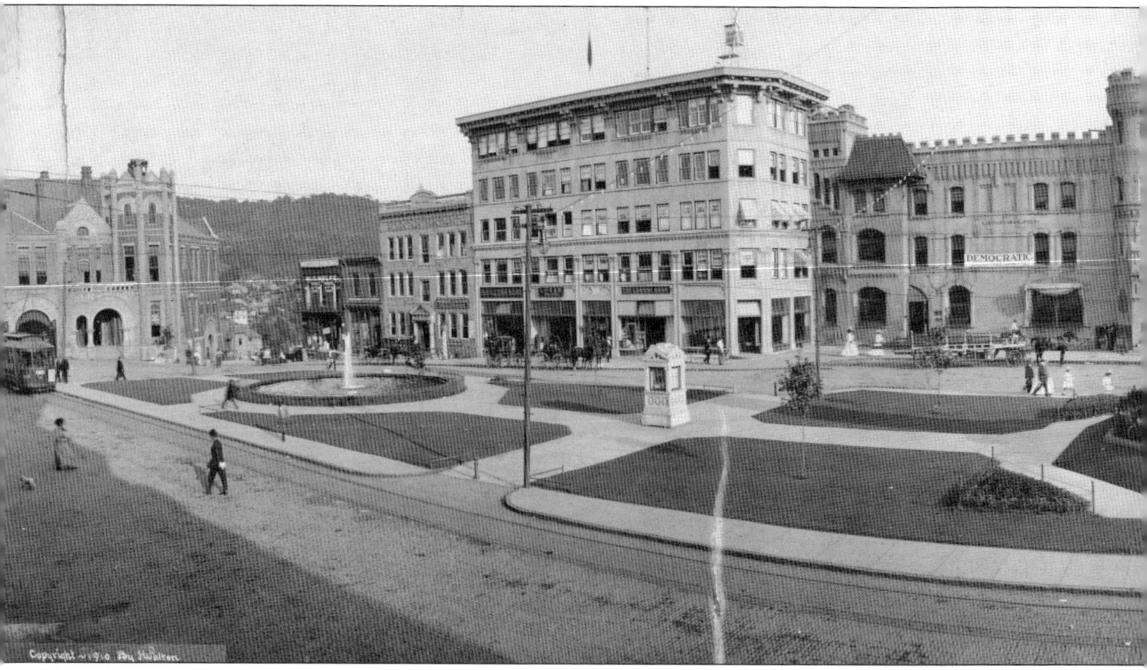

The public square, later named Pack Square in honor of George Willis Pack, was the center of life for Asheville during Thomas Wolfe's years. His father's monument shop was on the edge of the square where the Jackson Building, Asheville's first skyscraper, now stands. The square is easily recognizable because of the 65-foot-tall Vance Monument, designed by Richard Sharp

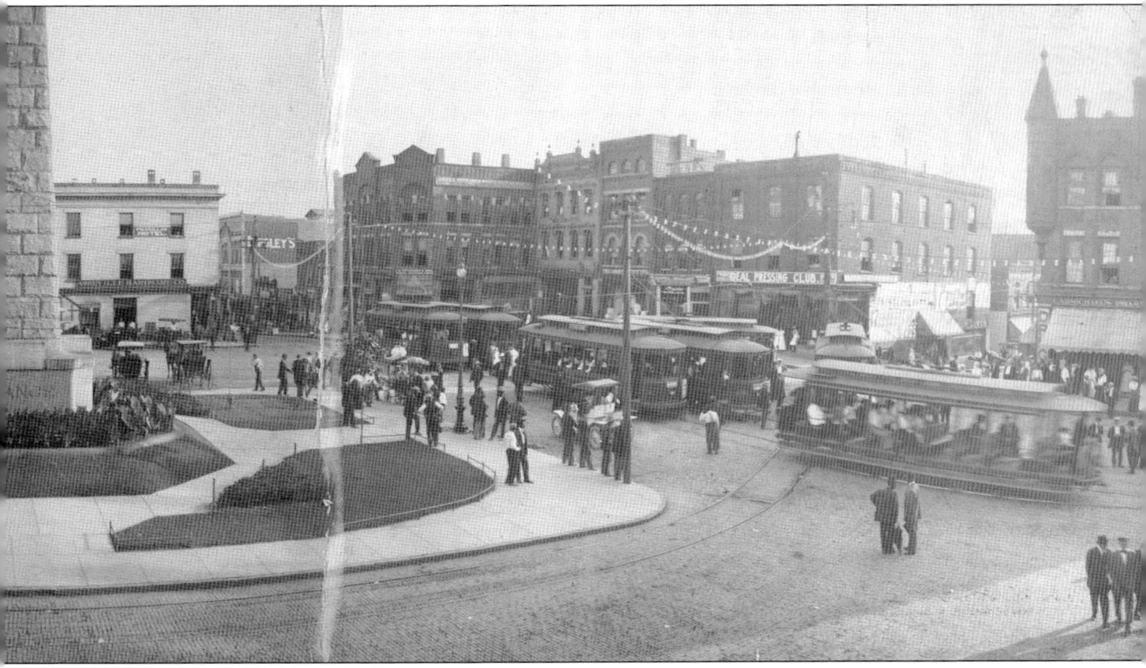

Smith and built under the supervision of J.A. Tennant, which has towered over the square since 1897. The square has hosted parades, protests, and even presidents in its time, and though it has often undergone changes to appearance, it is still the heart of Asheville's vibrant downtown to this day. (NCC.)

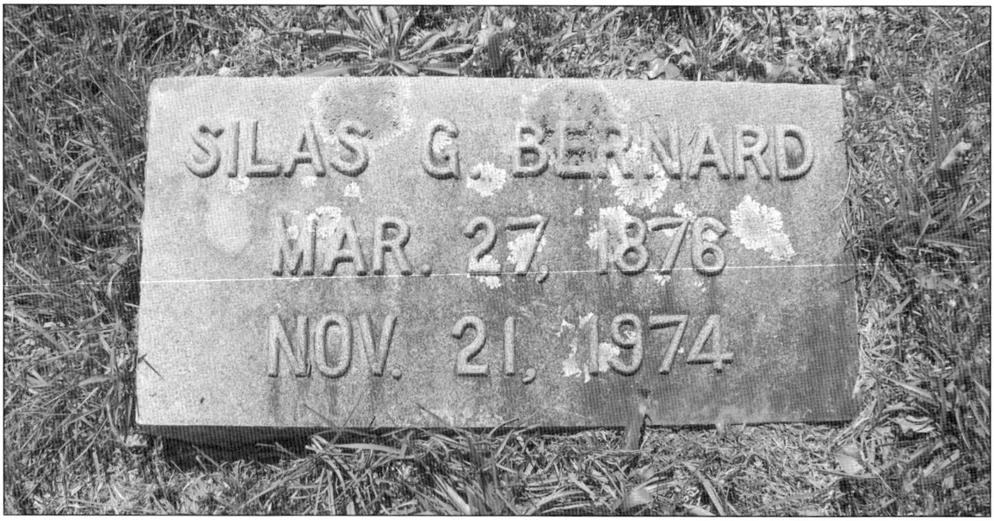

Thomas Wolfe is famously known for his long and laborious novels, but he did dabble in other forms of writing. His best-known short story, "Child by Tiger," is based on true events that happened in Asheville in his lifetime. In 1906, Charlotte outlaw Will Harris shot and killed five men in Asheville on the public square and Eagle Street. A 1,000-man posse was formed by police chief Silas G. Bernard (below, middle) and Harris was hunted down and shot over 100 times in a laurel thicket outside of the city. Harris was displayed in the Noland-Brown funeral home window before being interred in an unmarked grave in Riverside's notorious Section X, alongside horse thieves and murderers who had been previously executed by the state. (Below, NCC.)

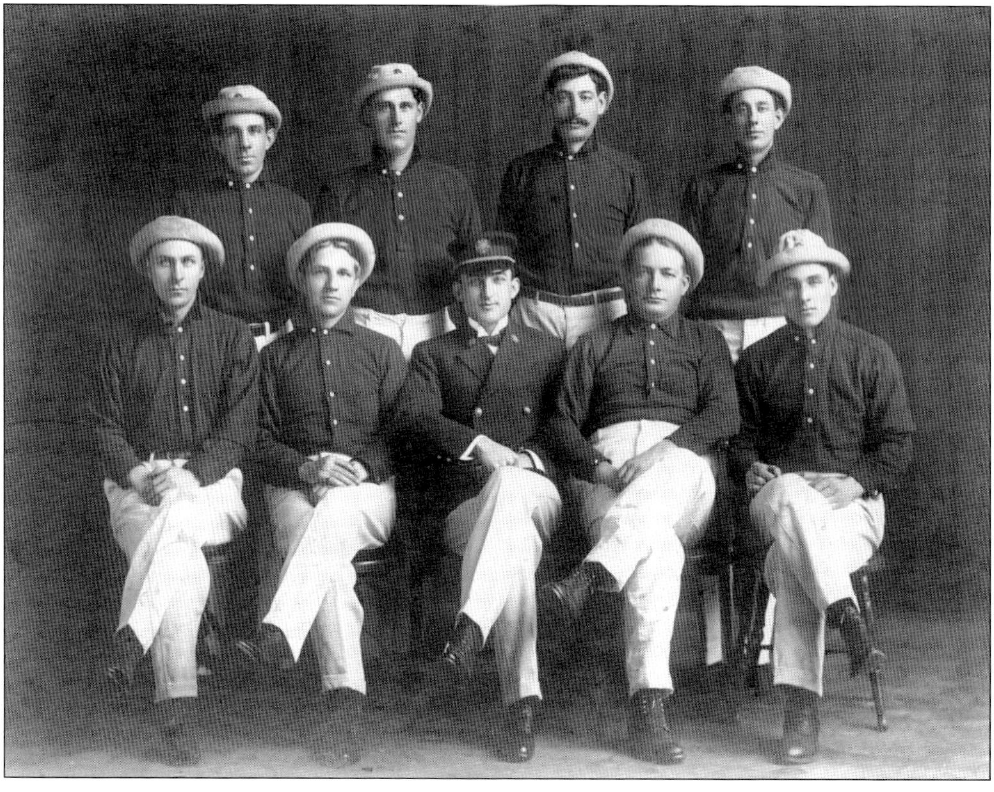

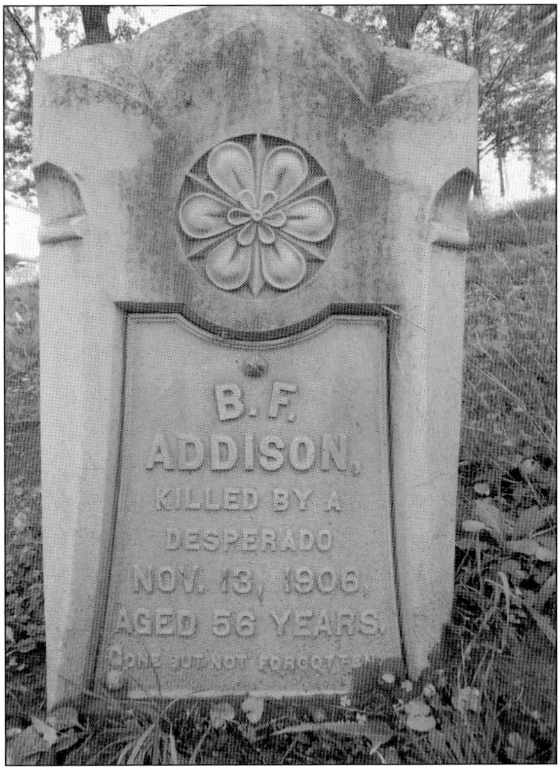

Two victims of what has since been dubbed "the Pack Square Shoot-out" were buried in Riverside in their family lots. James Bailey was a captain with the Asheville police force who responded to the report that Harris was in a drunken rage in the middle of Pack Square. When Harris saw the officer, he began to fire upon him. Bailey returned fire and then ducked behind a light pole to reload his weapon. Harris fired a shot through the pole, striking and killing Bailey. Benjamin Addison, an African American merchant on Eagle Street, stepped out of his shop to find the source of the commotion and was killed by a stray bullet from the outlaw. His unique zinc tombstone is inscribed "Killed by a Desperado."

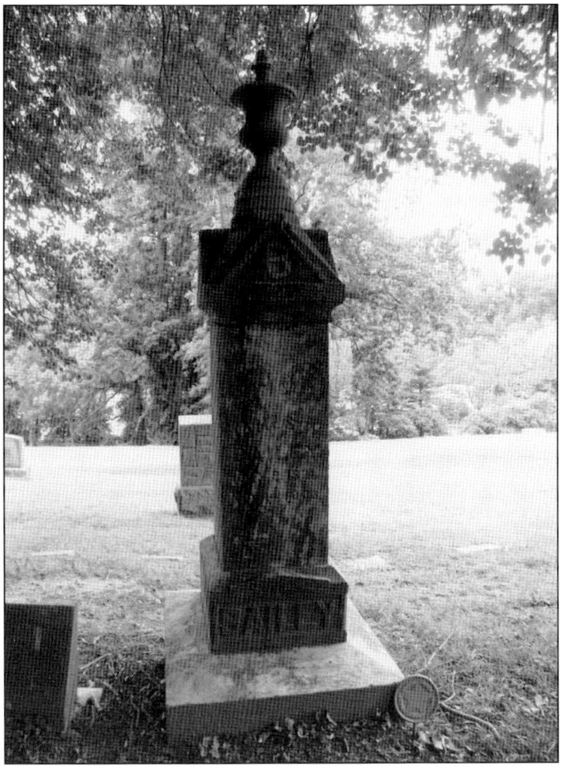

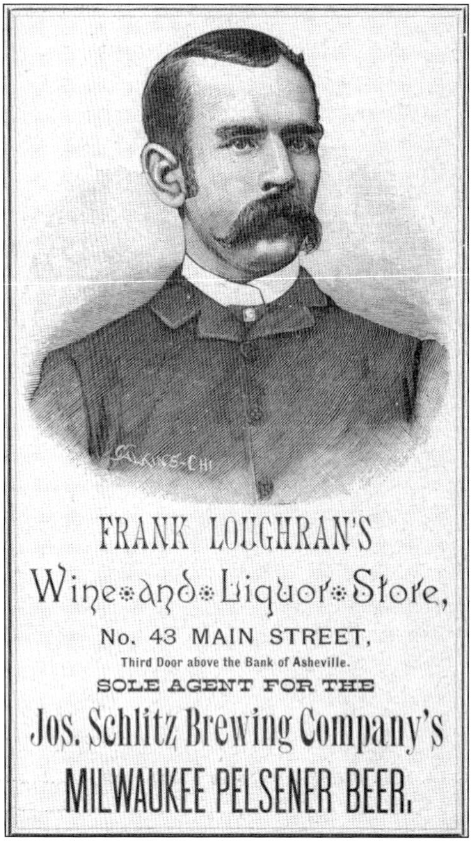

Frank Loughran and his wife, Adelaide, were hoteliers and saloon owners in downtown Asheville who owned a bar just off of Main Street on what is now known as Lexington Avenue. They were a well-known couple who entered into Wolfe's writings as Frank Moriarty and Princess Madeleine. Their bar, which stayed open as a speakeasy throughout Prohibition, was a notorious haunt of W.O. Wolfe. Wolfe was on the surface a staunch supporter of the Volstead Act but was rather different when it came to the actual practice. He was often carried home from Loughran's inebriated, which caused no end of humiliation to his wife, Julia. The bar has continued to operate under various names and owners and is the oldest continuously running bar in the region. (Left, PML.)

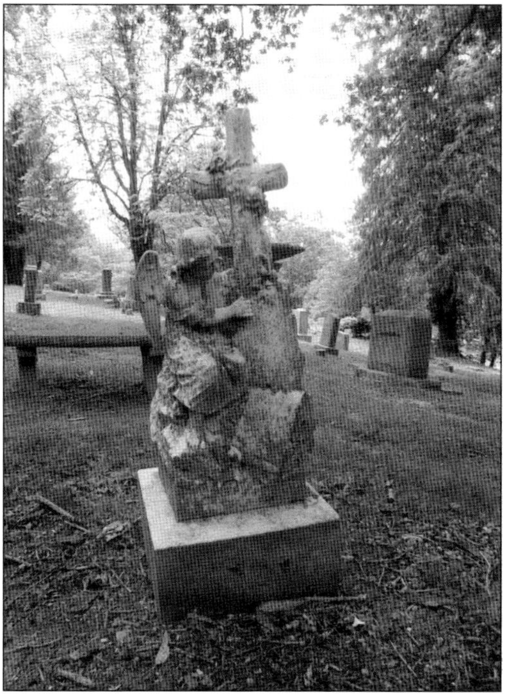

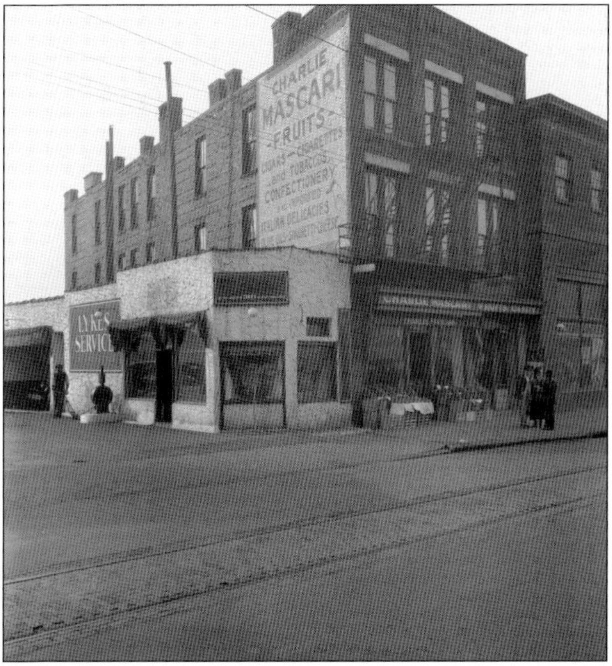

Charlie Mascari was the Italian grocer and produce seller on the square where Julia Wolfe did much of her shopping to feed guests at her boardinghouse. Mascari was a sharp businessman but was known by immigrants for his decency and willingness to go out of his way to help them set up their own businesses in pursuit of a better life. (E.M. Ball.)

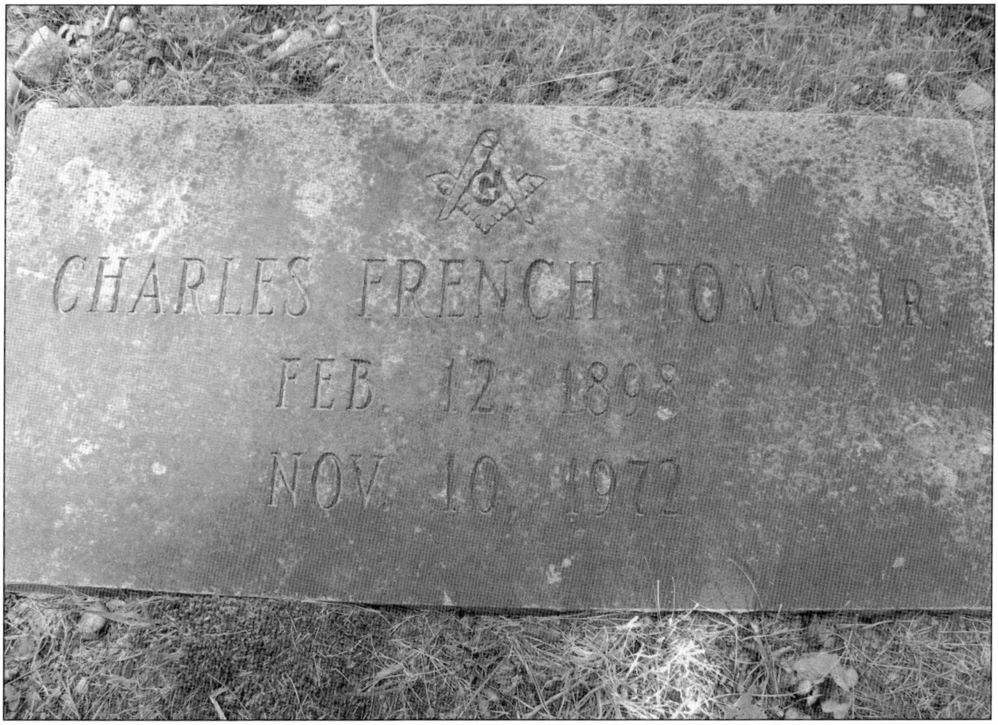

Charles French Toms, whom Wolfe renamed Tom French in his novels, was a wealthy Asheville boy who attended the University of North Carolina with Wolfe. His popularity and seemingly easy life irked Wolfe, who cast him as one of the main antagonists of *Look Homeward, Angel.* Toms lived in a fashionable Montford Avenue house near the cemetery, now the Lion and the Rose Bed & Breakfast.

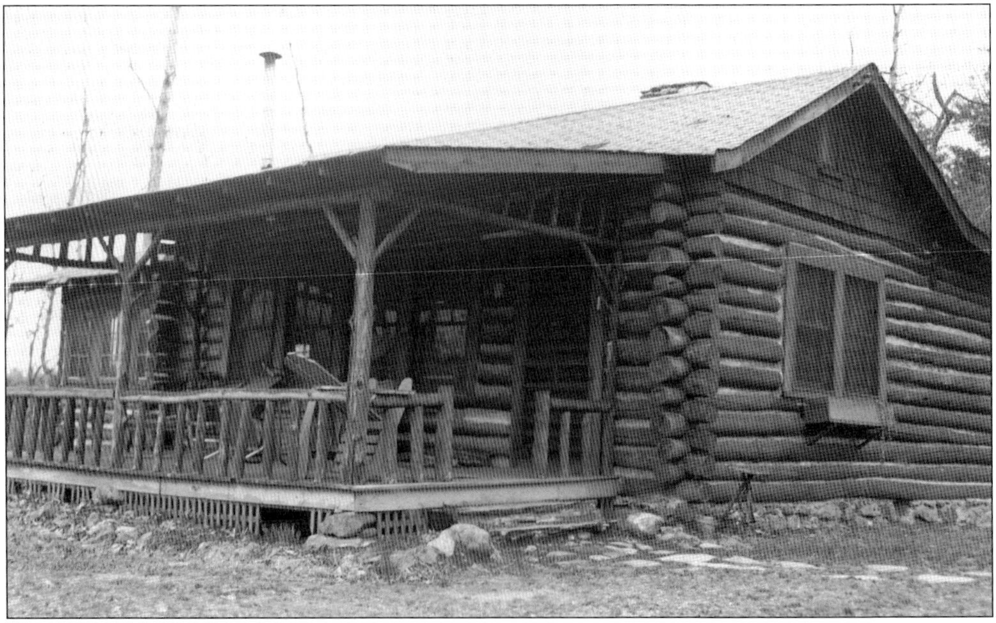

Max Whitson, Wolfe's college roommate, was a cartoonist who created the weekly panel *Trippy the Pup* and whose family built a small remote cabin in the Oteen area of Asheville. Upon hearing that Wolfe was looking for a place in Asheville where he could work away from the public, who were desirous to see Wolfe now that he had gained a degree of fame, Whitson offered the family cabin as a retreat for the novelist. In the summer of 1937, Wolfe lived and worked in the cabin in what was to be his last visit to his hometown. Today, the cabin is owned by the City of Asheville and is being renovated to become a writers' conference center and retreat. (Both, TWC.)

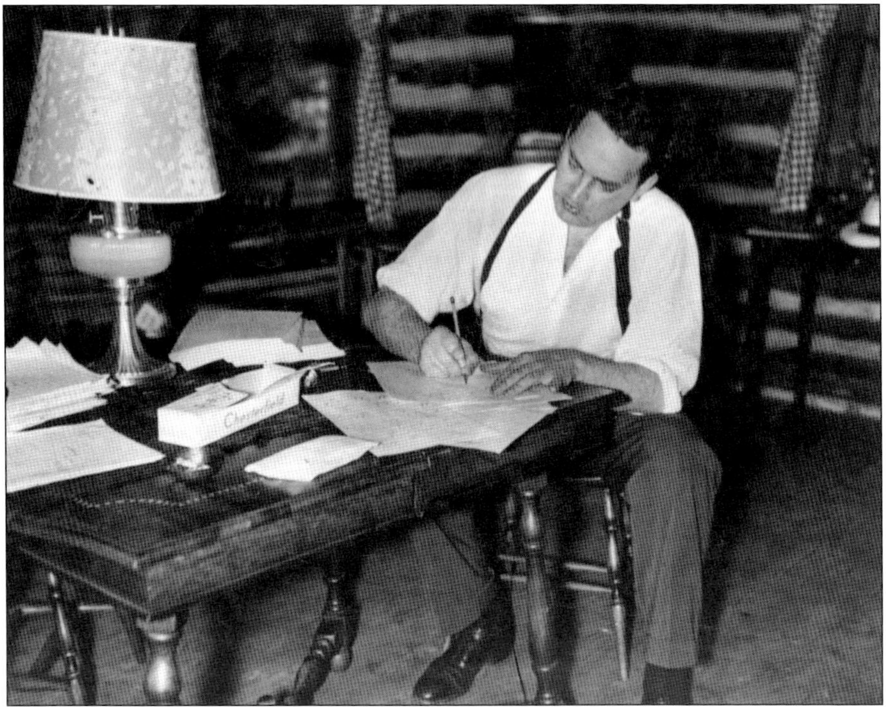

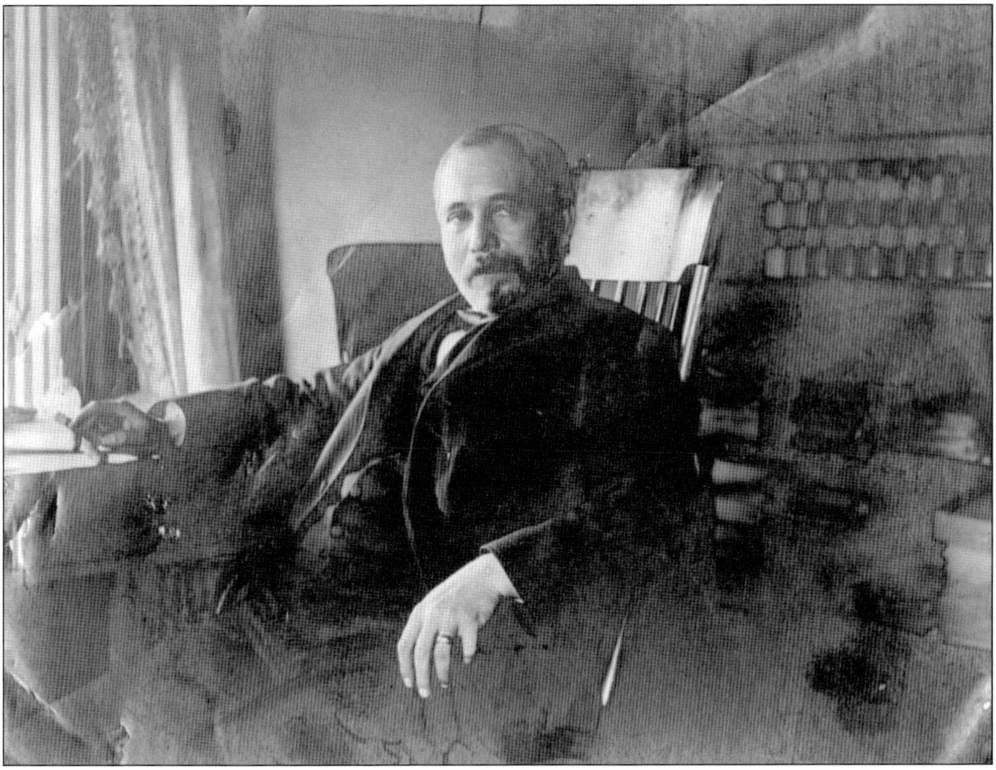

Dr. Karl Von Ruck, Von Zeck in *Look Homeward, Angel*, was a famous Asheville physician whose renowned Winyah Sanitarium attracted droves of tuberculosis patients to Asheville who hoped the cutting-edge treatments and wholesome mountain climate could bring them a cure. It was rumored that Wolfe contracted the tuberculosis that ended his life from one of the boarders at his mother's Old Kentucky Home who had come to Asheville for that very reason. (NCC.)

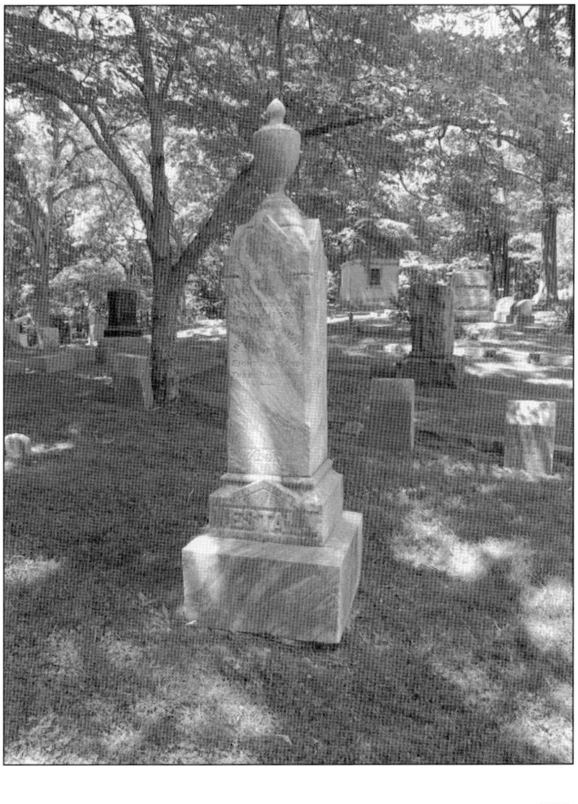

Thomas Wolfe's family on his mother's side was the Westalls, a highly successful though slightly peculiar group whom Wolfe skewered unmercifully in his writings. Wolfe's cousin Annie was the librarian of Pack Memorial Library. According to rumor, she took offense to her description as "hefty" in Wolfe's writings and refused to let the library carry any of his works until well after his death.

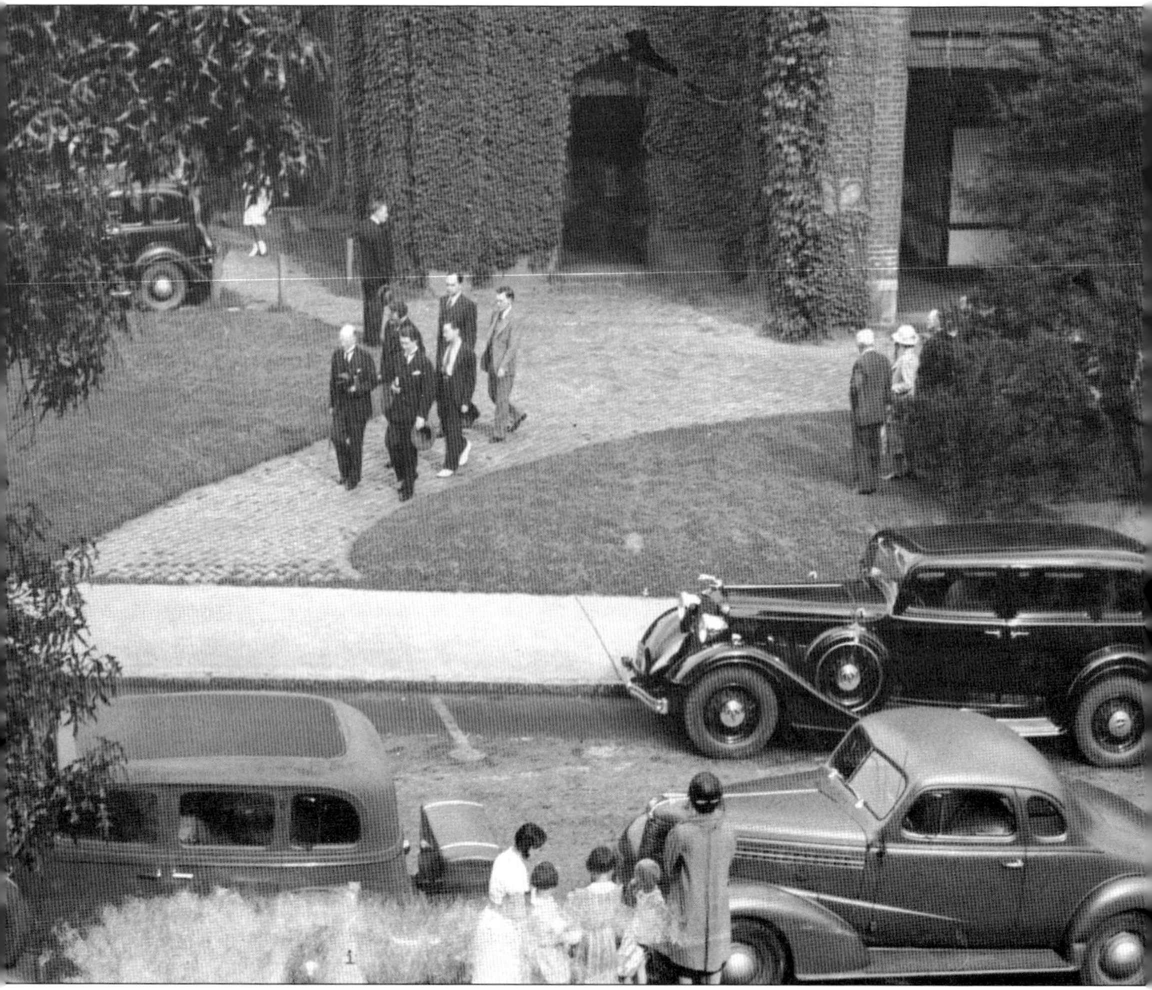

Thomas Wolfe passed away on September 15, 1938, of miliary tuberculosis at Johns Hopkins Hospital in Baltimore, just 18 days short of his 38th birthday. His body was brought back to Asheville by train to be interred in the family lot in Riverside. After a wake at his mother's boardinghouse, the Old Kentucky Home, the funeral service was held at the First Presbyterian Church in downtown Asheville. As the funeral procession wound its way from the church to the cemetery, men lined the streets with their hats doffed to honor Asheville's most famous son. Included in the list of honorary pallbearers is Wolfe's editor, Maxwell Perkins. (TWC.)

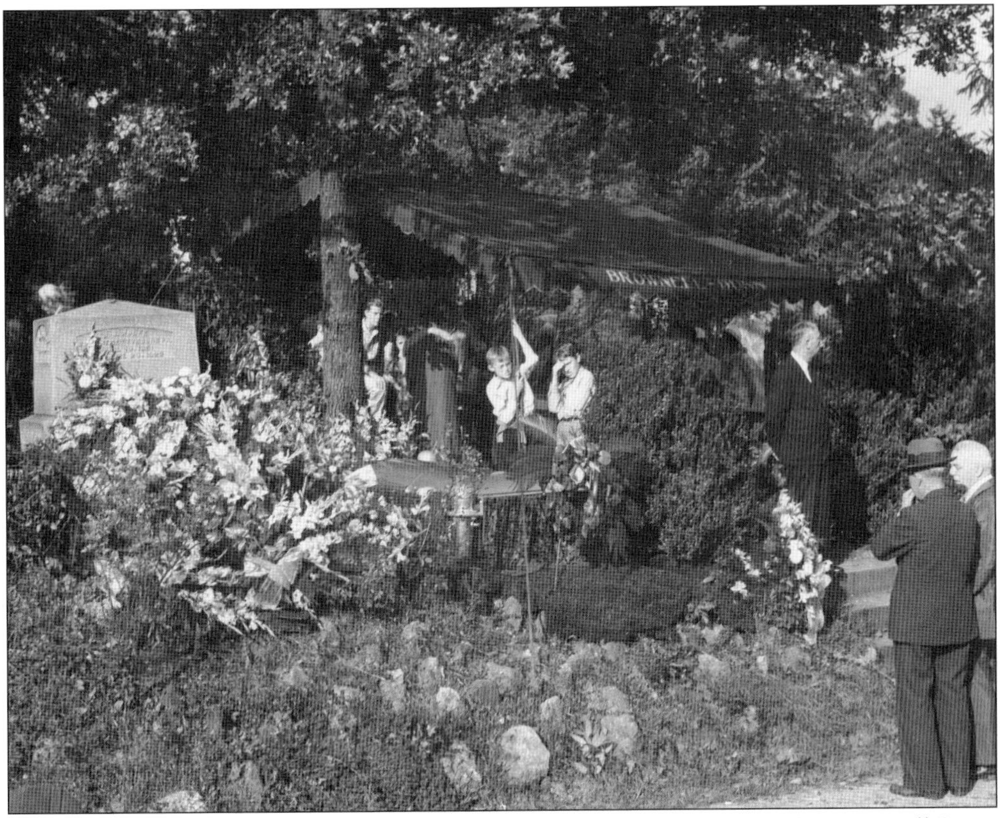

Wolfe was buried in the family lot beside the monument of his mother and father. Brownell-Dunn Funeral Home set up the service. Superintendent E.J. Atwood had a large oak tree cut down in the family lot to create the space for Tom. Retired minister Dr. Campbell performed the graveside service for the family, and a large number of mourners gathered. (TWC.)

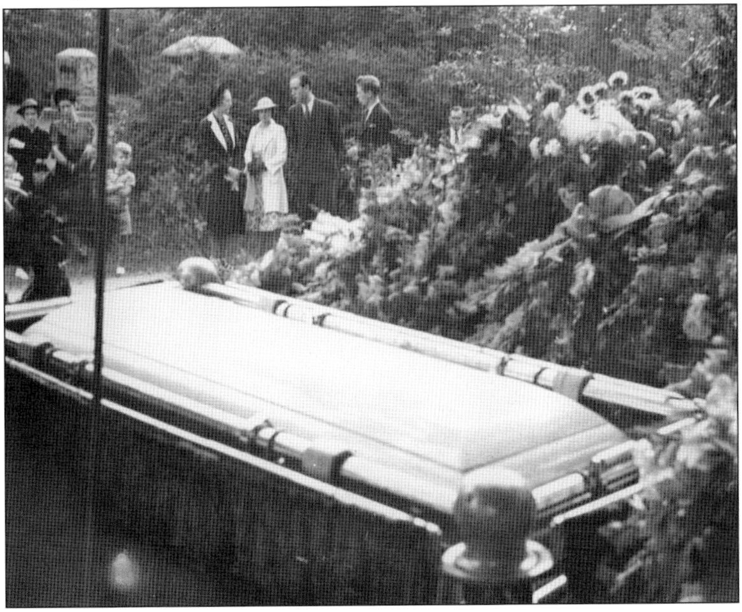

The graveside service at Wolfe's funeral in Riverside was a difficult affair for the Wolfe family. Only his mother, Julia, was able to remain stoic as the scriptures were read and hymns sung. Mabel, the sibling whom Wolfe was closest to after the passing of Ben, could not bring herself to attend the service, turning around her car and speeding away as soon as she saw the open grave. (TWC.)

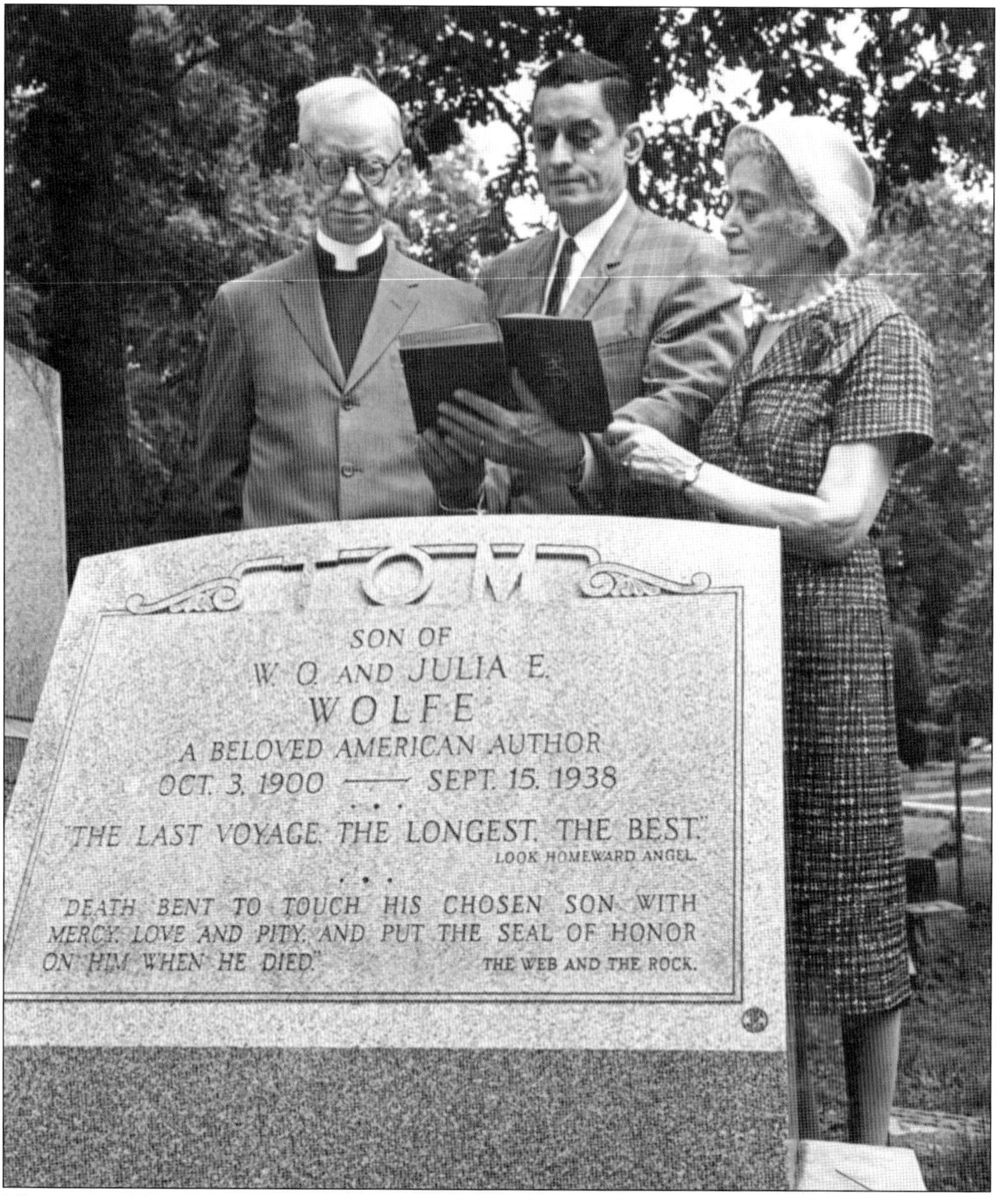

Thomas Wolfe's impact on Asheville through the years cannot be overstated. His celebrity and works helped to give an identity to the small mountain city that was always striving to become so much more. Even after obtaining international acclaim, Wolfe never quite felt accepted by those in his mountain home, even titling a second novel about Asheville *You Can't Go Home Again*, but he posthumously proved himself wrong. Wolfe was finally able to return home upon his death both literally and figuratively, and the Ashevillians who alternately loved and hated the author welcomed him with open arms. His grave remains one of the most visited in all of North Carolina with tens of thousands of yearly visitors. Pictured here are, from left to right, the Reverend Norvin Duncan, Dr. Roy Roberts, and Fannie Gross saying a prayer at a memorial ceremony at Wolfe's gravesite in 1964. (TWC.)

Eight

The Remarkable Women of Asheville

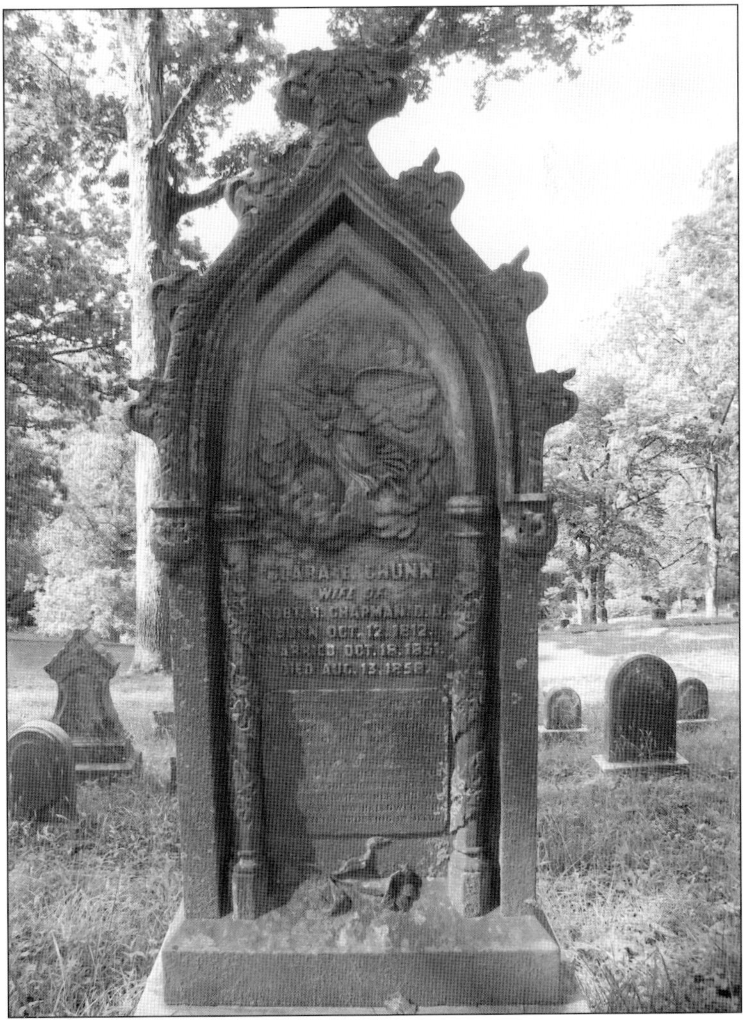

Asheville has long had a reputation for strong, forward-thinking women, from the hearty pioneers of the early days to the progressive politicians of today. Clara Chunn was a prominent citizen of Asheville whose family settled in the area later named Chunn's Cover in her honor. Her elaborate monument was originally located in the Episcopal churchyard on Church Street before being relocated to Riverside in 1917.

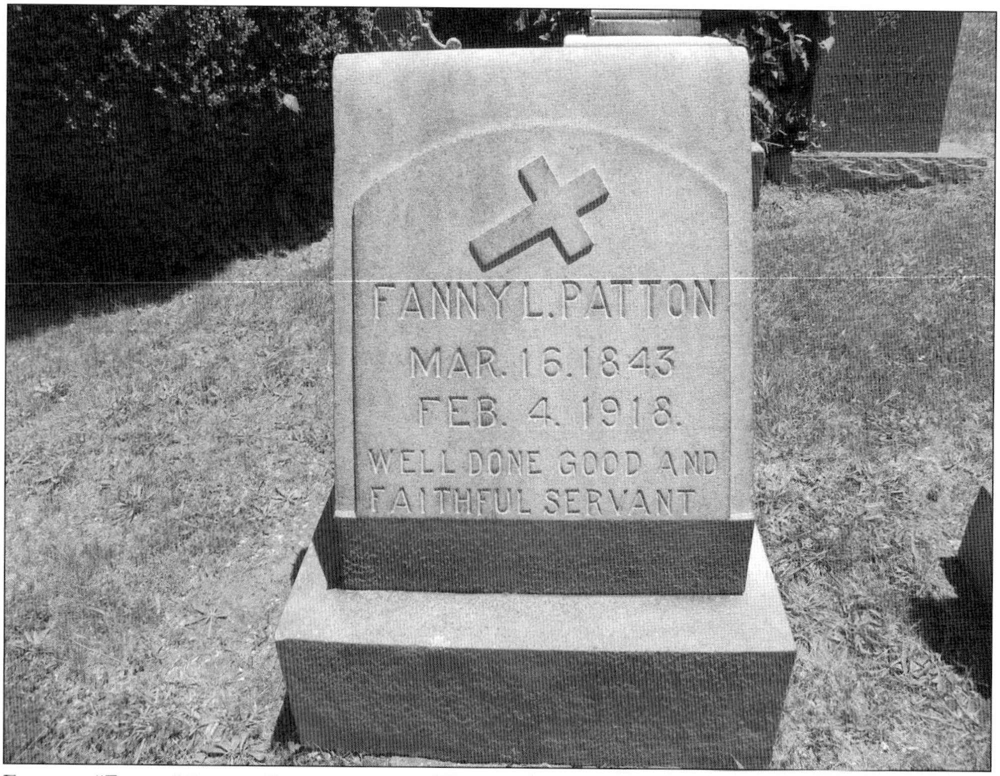

Frances "Fanny" Louisa Patton, sister of Riverside Cemetery founder T.W. Patton, was one of the most charitable women in the history of Asheville. She has been credited with the creation of the Asheville Library Association in 1879, which resulted in Asheville's public library system, and the Buncombe County Children's Home. She was also one of the four founders of Mission Hospital.

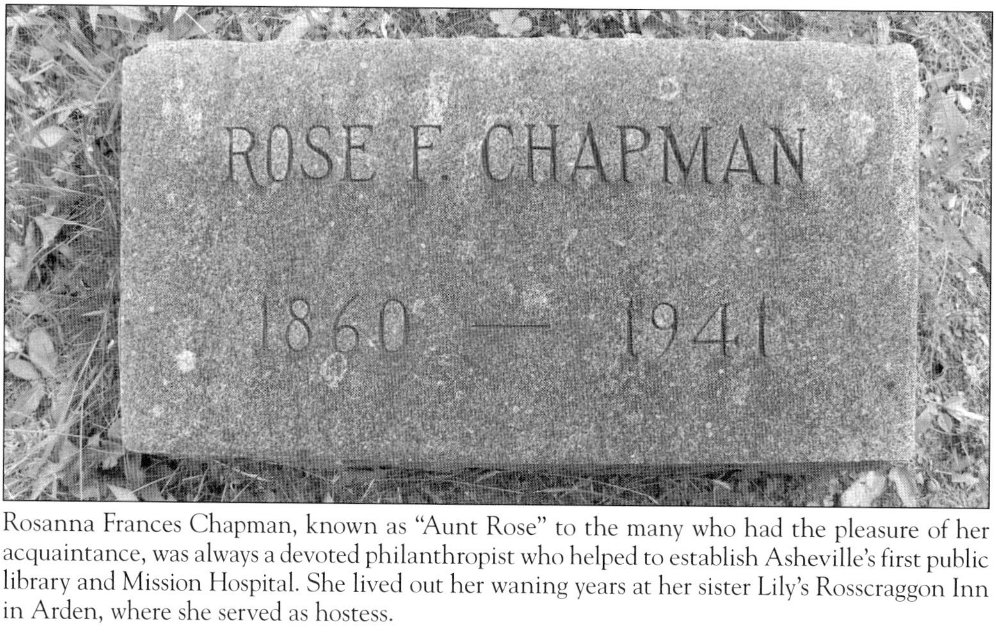

Rosanna Frances Chapman, known as "Aunt Rose" to the many who had the pleasure of her acquaintance, was always a devoted philanthropist who helped to establish Asheville's first public library and Mission Hospital. She lived out her waning years at her sister Lily's Rosscraggon Inn in Arden, where she served as hostess.

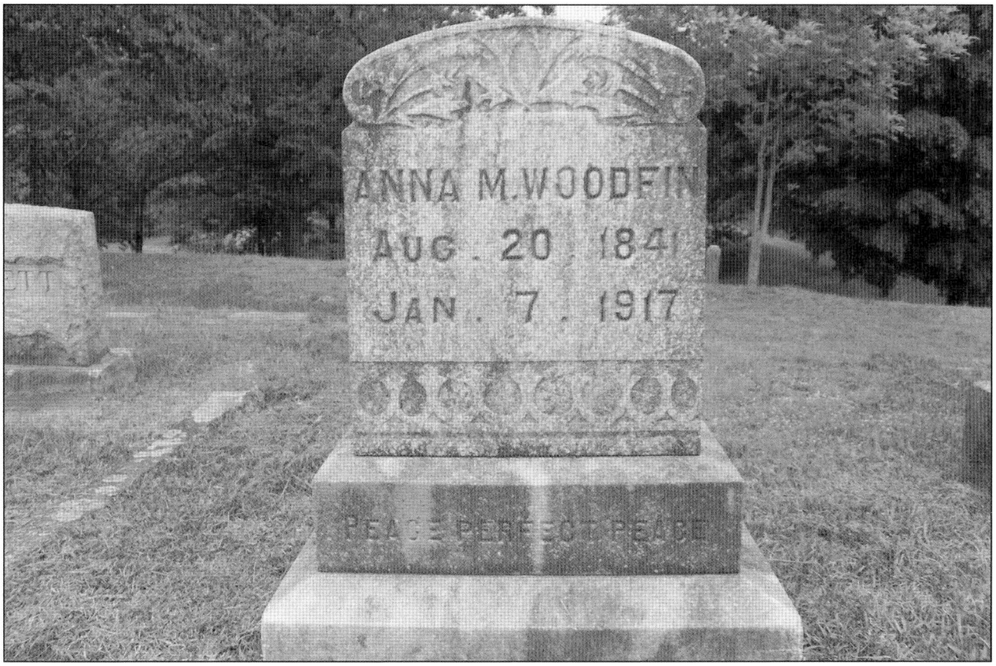

Anna Woodfin was the eldest daughter of Nicholas Woodfin, and as such was the owner of much of the property that was given to be Riverside Cemetery. Woodfin was known for her charity work and in the spring of 1884 founded the Asheville Flower Mission, of which she was the first president. This group delivered flowers, tracts, food, and clothing to the sick and destitute of Asheville. Woodfin, along with Fanny Patton, Rose Chapman, and Lily Carmichael, used this organization for the establishment of Flower Mission Hospital (later called Mission Hospital) on October 6, 1885. The hospital started as a small five-room cottage on Biltmore Avenue with Dr. William Hilliard serving as a volunteer physician, but it has grown to one of the largest hospital systems in the state, serving the 18 westernmost counties. (Below, NCC.)

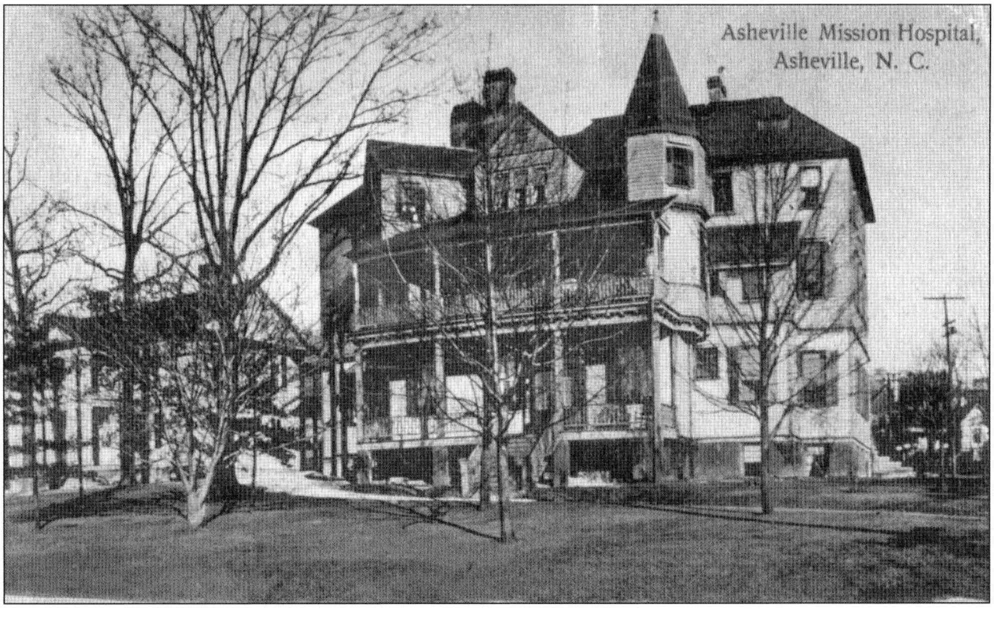

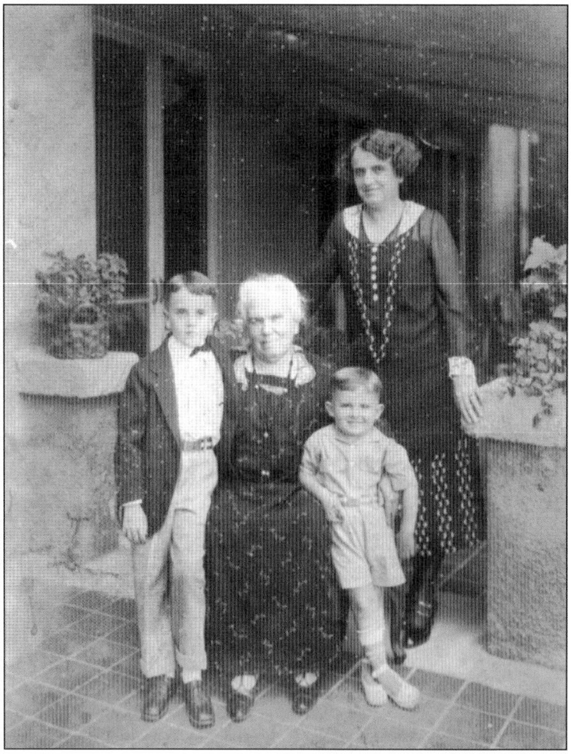

Leah Arcouet Chiles (right, with mother and children) was an accomplished artist and concert pianist before moving to Asheville and marrying James Chiles in 1914. Together, they managed the development and promotion of the town of Kenilworth for 11 years before James died unexpectedly. After his death, she continued his business and pursued a career in politics. She became one of North Carolina's first female mayors in 1928 when she was elected mayor of Kenilworth. (NCC.)

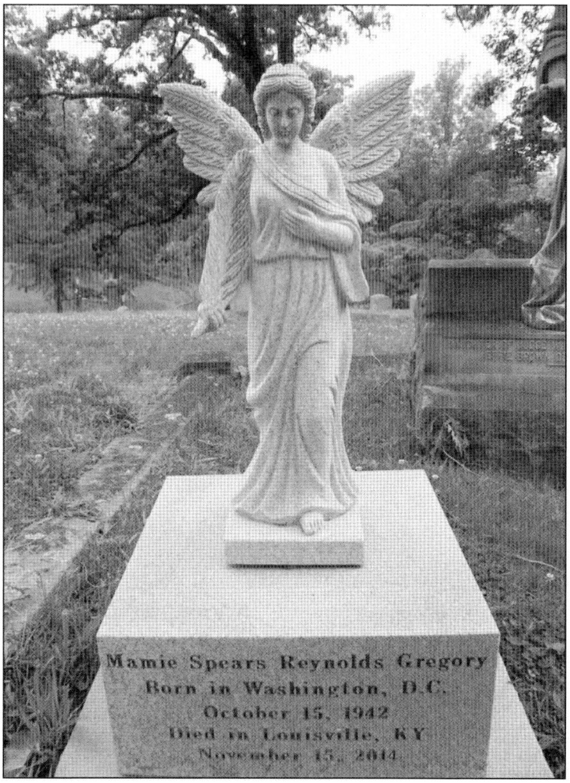

Mamie Spears Reynolds Gregory was a legendary Asheville heiress, daughter of Sen. Bob Reynolds and his fifth wife, Evalyn Washington McLean, and goddaughter of FBI director J. Edgar Hoover. The inheritor of $10 million at four years old, Gregory lived a life few could dream of. She threw lavish parties, bred both horses and dogs, became the first woman to qualify for the Daytona 500, and even owned a professional basketball team.

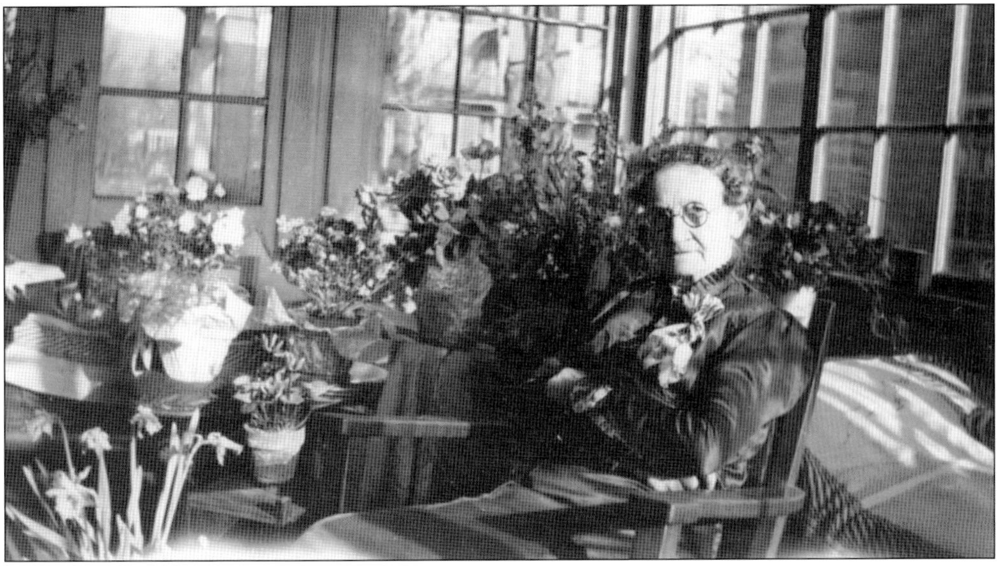

Julia Westall Wolfe was an Asheville businesswoman and owner of the Old Kentucky Home who was immortalized as Eliza Gant in the works of her youngest son, Thomas. Her portrayal in Thomas's writings as the pragmatic, hardworking mother of the large family plays well as the foil for her hard-drinking and overly dramatic husband, W.O. Julia, who was famous for her eye for real estate and business savvy, was quoted as saying there were only two perfect pieces of real estate in Asheville, the first being a piece of property on Valley Street that she had her eye on and the other being Riverside Cemetery. (Above, NCC.)

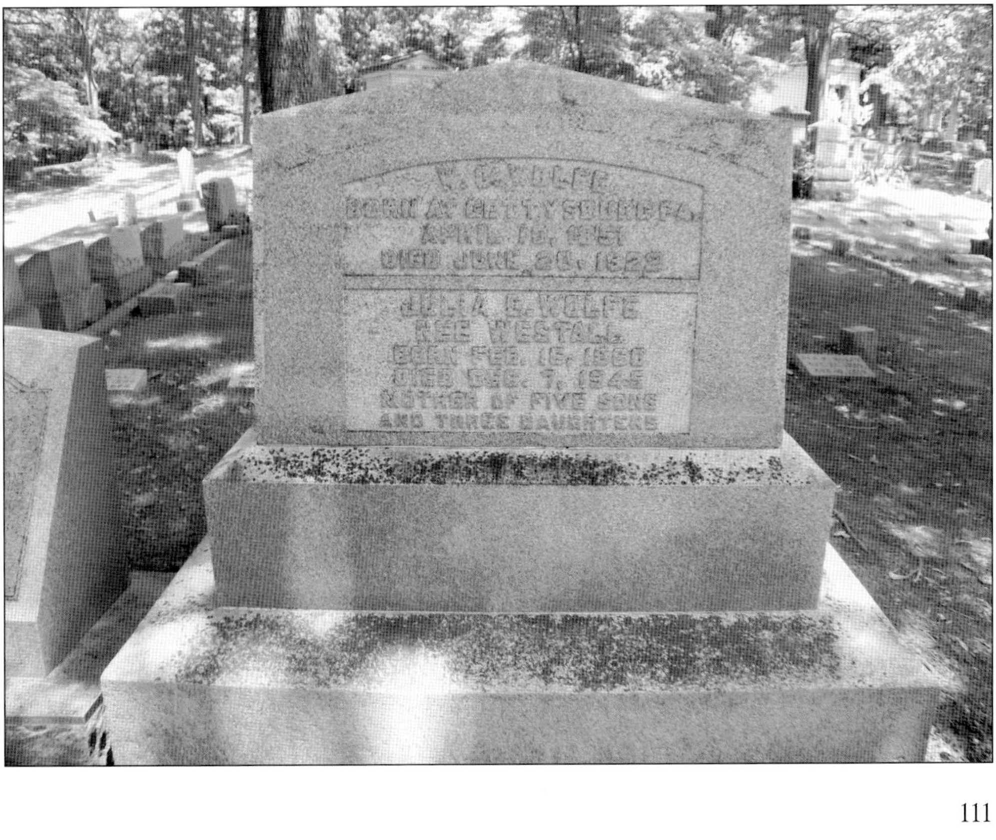

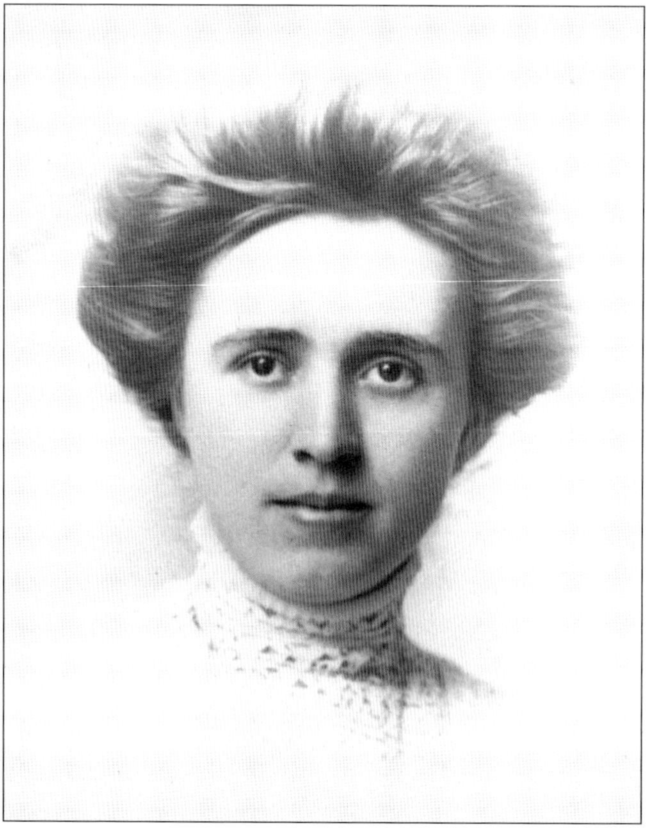

Lillian Exum Clement Stafford was a remarkable woman from a very early age. Born in 1894, Stafford was the first female attorney in North Carolina to have a practice without male partners. Her success continued when she was elected in a landslide to the North Carolina General Assembly at just 26 years of age, making her the first female legislator in the South before the passage of the 19th Amendment, which gave the right to vote. Affectionately called "Brother Exum" by her fellow legislators, she was a very effective representative who introduced 17 bills, almost all of which were passed. Stafford retired from politics after just one term to be a director at the state hospital at Morganton and to raise her daughter, Nancy. She died of pneumonia in 1925 at the age of 38. (Left, NCC.)

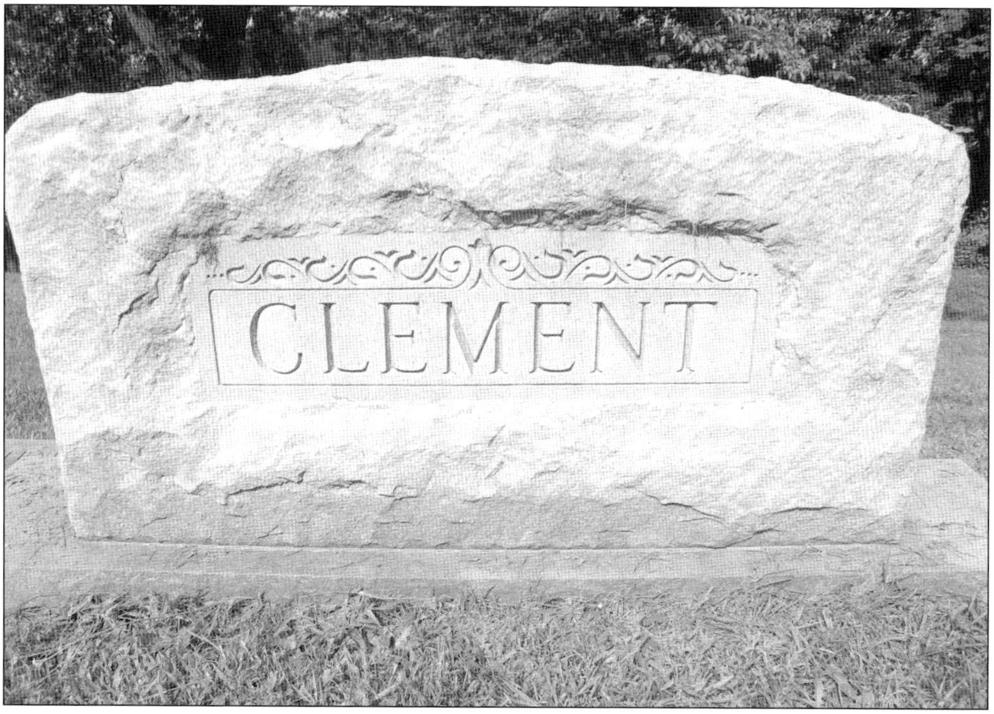

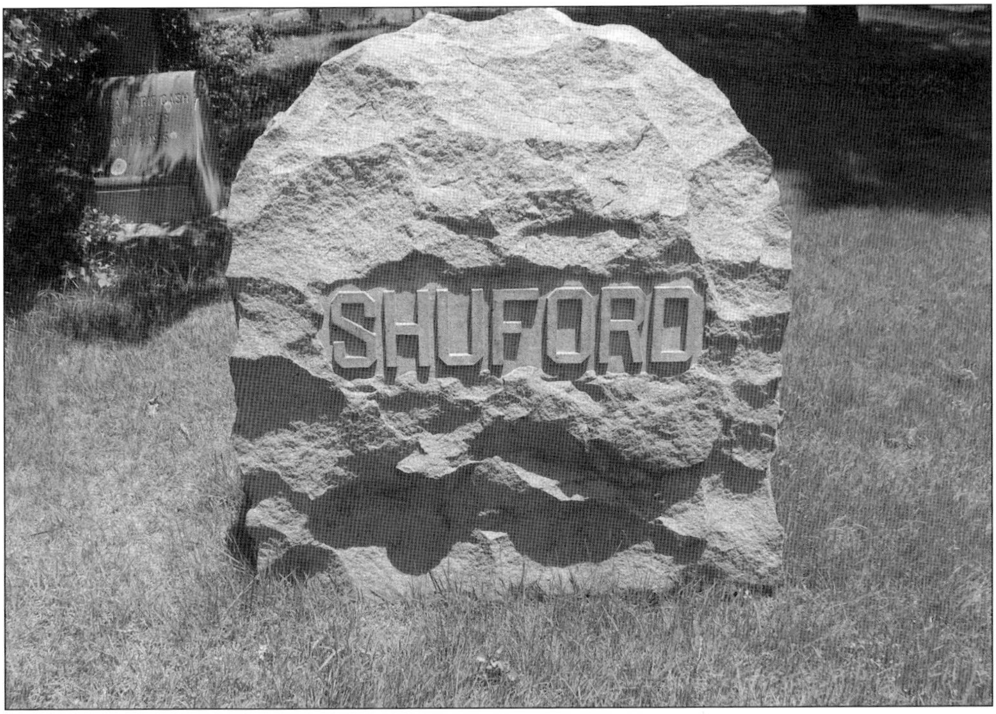

Dr. Mary Frances "Polly" Shuford was an Asheville physician who fought to establish a hospital for the African American citizens of Asheville during segregation, when blacks were not typically admitted to the local hospitals except for "colored wards," where the care was very poor. She was able to gather community support and establish the Asheville Colored Hospital in 1943, helping secure vital health care to an underserved community.

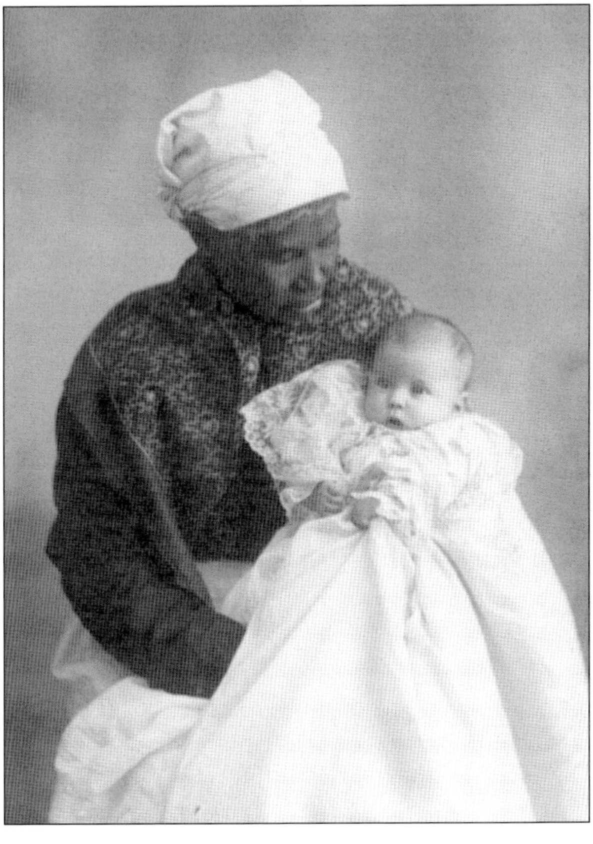

Tempie Avery was a well-known nurse and midwife who was born in Morganton in 1817. Tempie lived for over 100 years, spending much of her life in the service of the Woodfin family as both a slave and then a free woman. Following the Emancipation Proclamation in 1863, the Woodfin family granted her land just outside of Riverside Cemetery's future boundary. In 2017, the Montford Center was renamed the Tempie Avery Center in her honor. (NCC.)

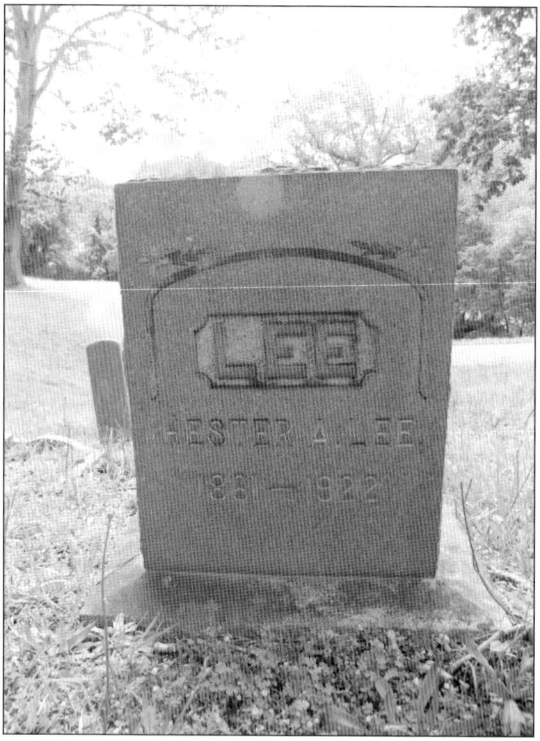

After her death in 1922, Hester Lee became half of the namesake of Stephens-Lee High School, the former Catholic Hill School, over which her husband Walter was principal. Stephens-Lee became the center of the African American community and was renowned for its classical music program, marching band, and athletics. The school closed during integration in 1965 and is now the Stephens-Lee Recreation Center.

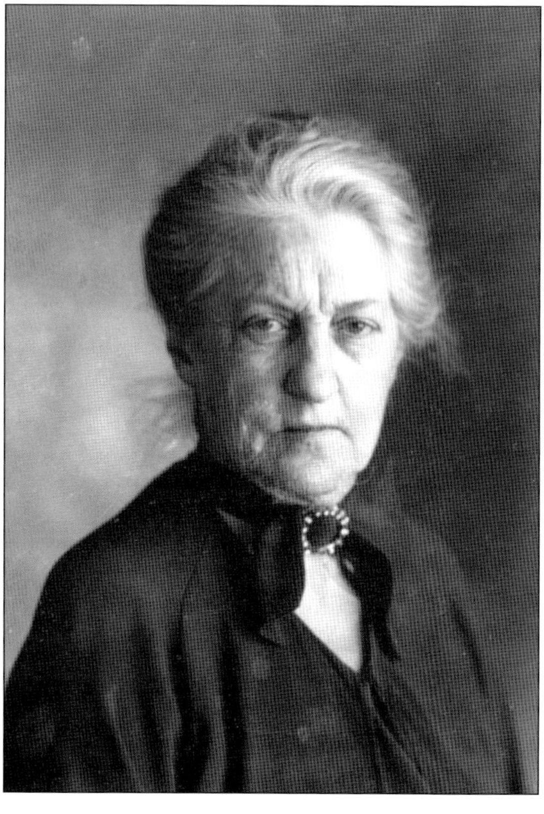

Queen Maude Carson was Asheville's first female principal at one of the three founding grade schools in the city, the Park Avenue School. Carson was a dedicated educator in the public school system for over 40 years. The school building, designed by architects Richard Sharp Smith and Douglas Ellington, was renamed Queen Carson Elementary School in her honor in 1935. (E.M. Ball.)

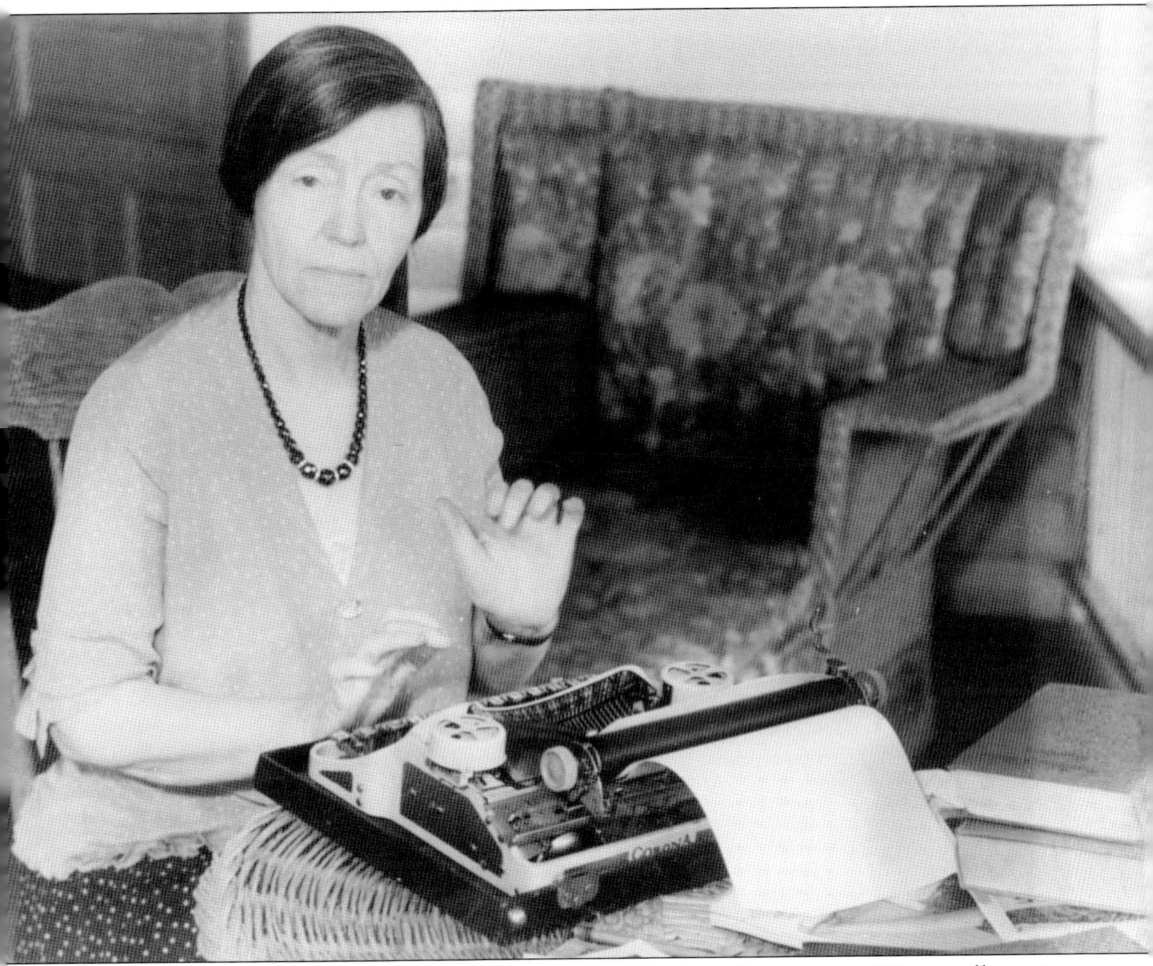

Sara Coleman Porter, second wife of author William Sydney Porter, was a Weaverville native and childhood friend of the beloved author. In 1905, the two began a courtship through letters in which Porter encouraged her to begin writing. She did and attained a fair degree of success under the pen name Sara Lindsey. W.S. Porter said that his days spent in Asheville with Sara were the happiest of his life and the only time he had ever felt at peace. After her husband's death in 1910, Sara Porter had him buried in Riverside in her family lot with a simple marker. Soon after, the Asheville Cemetery Company erected a signpost directing curious visitors to the location of his gravesite. Sara Porter, wishing to avoid the fame and notoriety associated with her husband, demanded that the signpost be removed. According to the writings of Haywood Parker, the staff would always acquiesce when Sara Porter came in and then replace the sign the second she stepped outside of the cemetery gates. (NCC.)

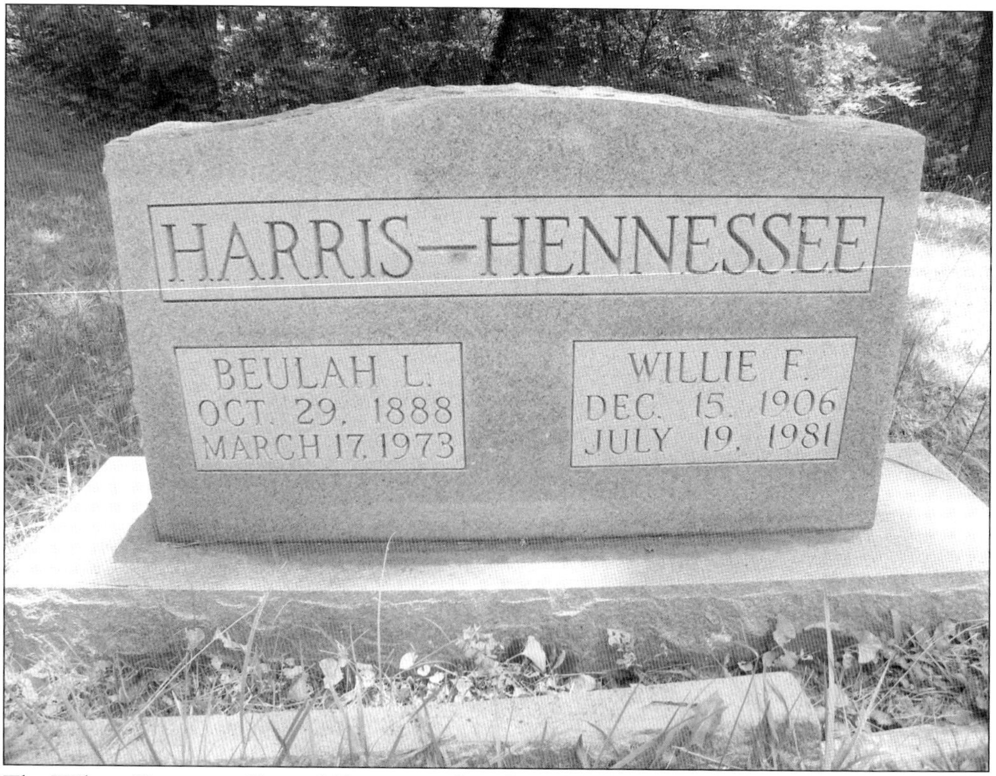

The Wilson-Hennessee Funeral Home in Asheville was begun by James Wilson, nephew of Isaac Dickson. When Wilson passed away, the business was taken over by Willie Ford Hennessee, an Asheville woman and entrepreneur. Besides managing the funeral home, Hennessee was also the owner of Willie's Beauty Nook, president of the North Carolina State Beauty Culturist & Cosmetologist Association, and the first African American voter registrar in Western North Carolina.

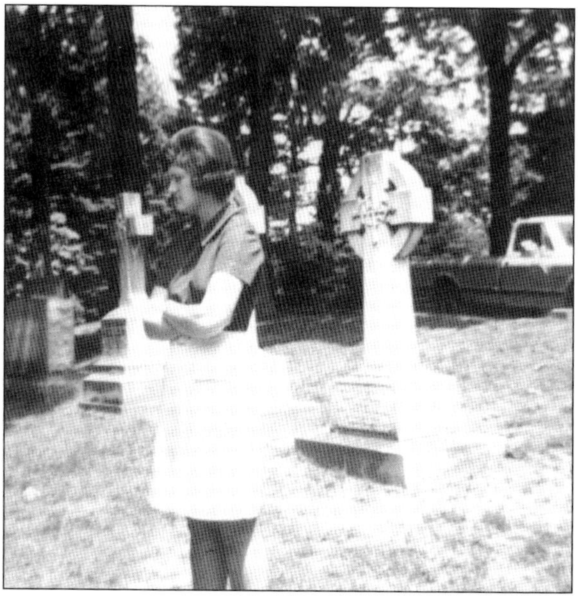

This 1972 photograph taken by Chick Hunter shows cemetery secretary Martha Greene as she oversees a funeral setup in Riverside's Section R. Greene, along with longtime cemetery foreman Robert Crayton, managed the day-to-day operations at Riverside for nine years after the unexpected death of Hunter in 1974. (RCA.)

Nine

Riverside Through the Ages

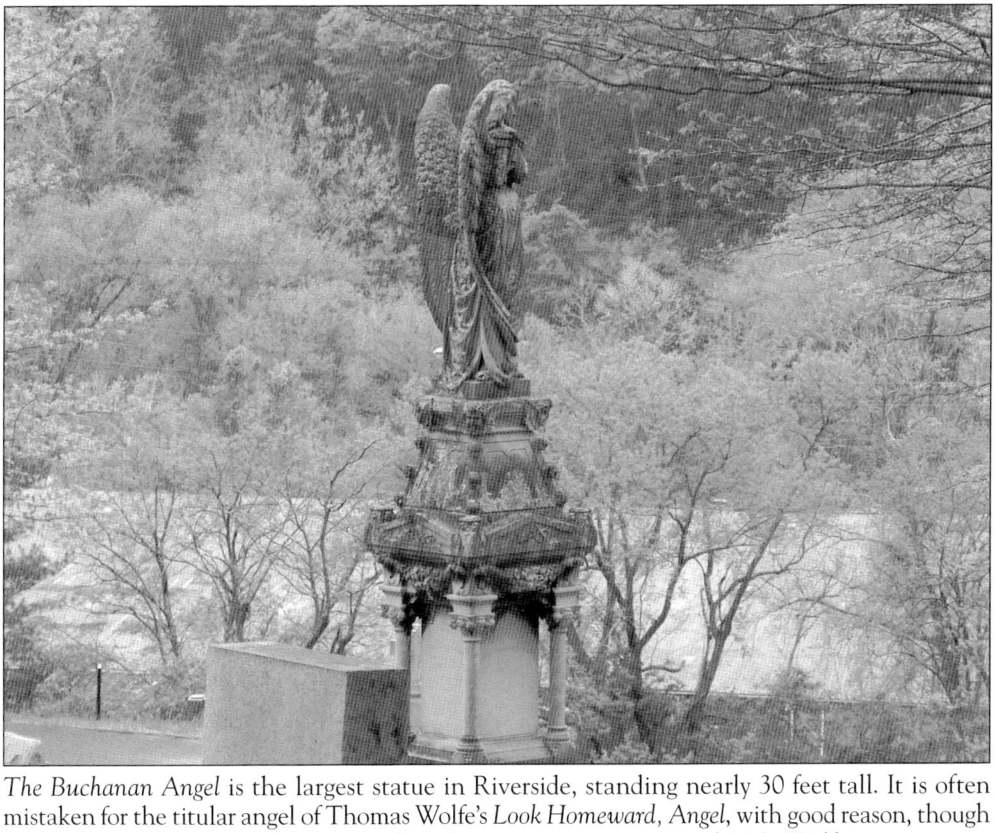

The Buchanan Angel is the largest statue in Riverside, standing nearly 30 feet tall. It is often mistaken for the titular angel of Thomas Wolfe's *Look Homeward, Angel*, with good reason, though historians have disagreed about whether the monument was one of W.O. Wolfe's creations or that of Biltmore stonecutter Fred Miles. From its lofty perch, the angel looks down on the French Broad River that gave Riverside its name.

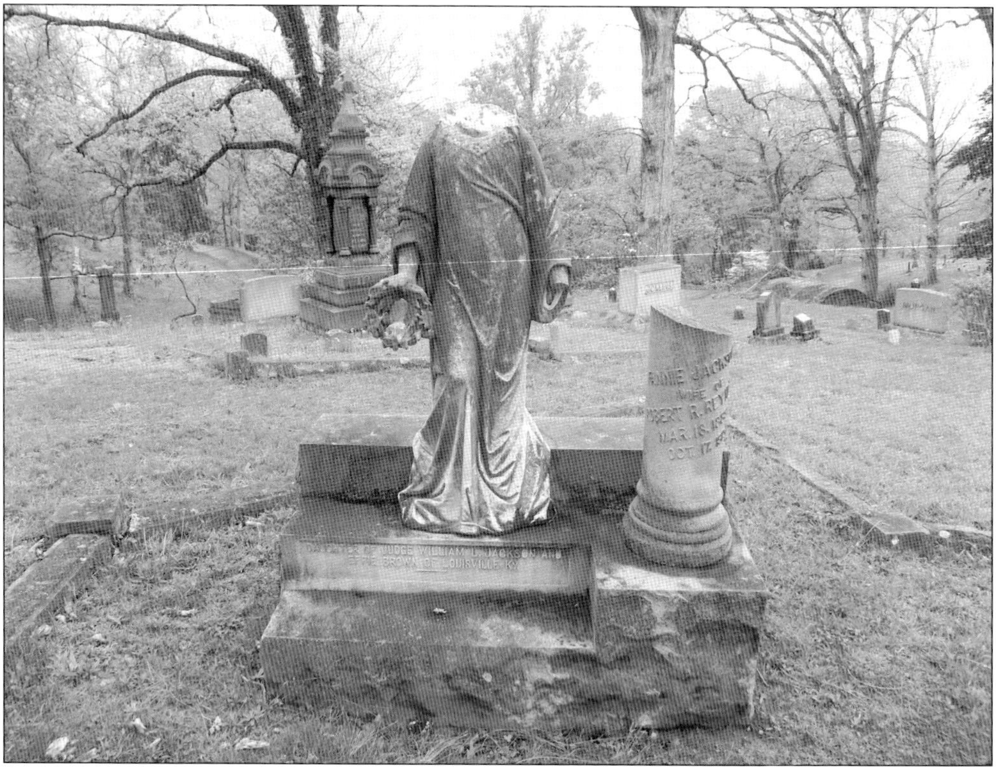

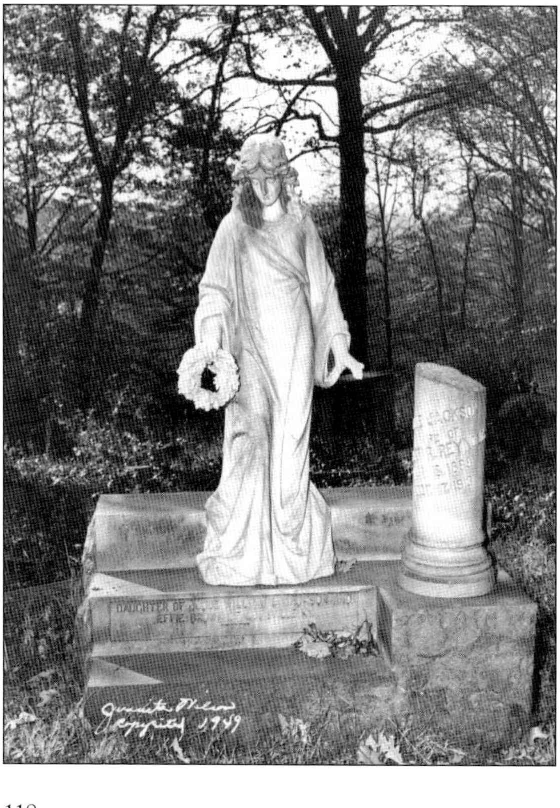

The Fannie Reynolds monument has attracted the attention of artists more than any other in Western North Carolina. Fannie was the first wife of Sen. Robert Rice Reynolds, who purchased the ornate monument to mark her grave after she passed away at 24. Though vandals stole the statue's head in 1950, the monument has remained a muse for photographers and painters for the better part of a century. The iconic statue has long been known as the "Headless Angel of Riverside," and depictions of it show up in art galleries all around the state. Pictured at left is the statue in 1949, just before its head was lost. (Left, NCC.)

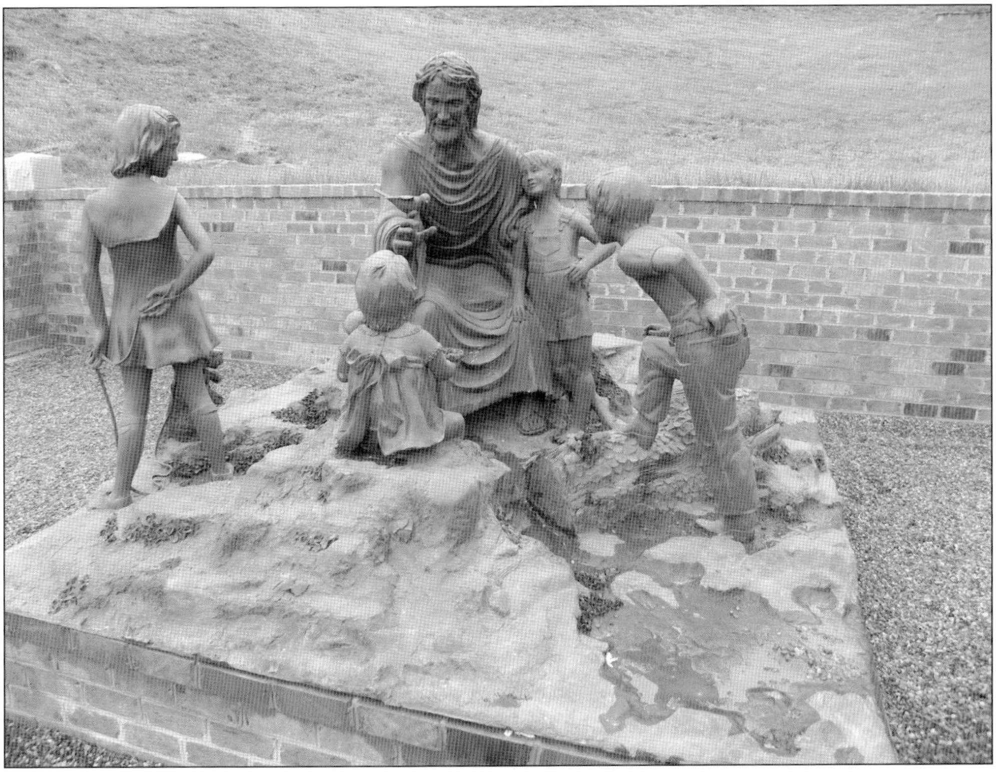

The Sparrow is a recent installation in Riverside, erected for the Reeves family. Sitting inside an impressive walled lot, the statue depicts Jesus surrounded by children, two of whom were modeled after the Reeveses' own. California artists Pat Hopper and Bill Minschew completed the statue after more than a year's work in 1975. It was moved from the Reeves business in California to its new home in Riverside in 2016.

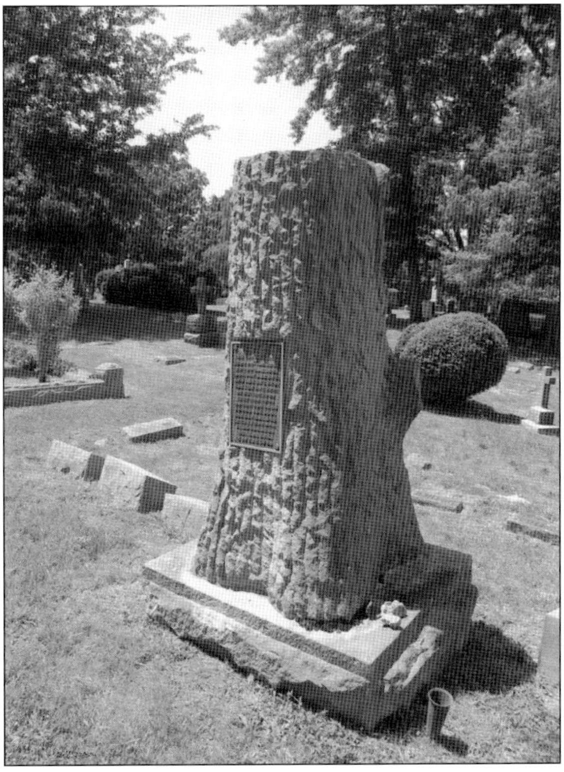

Scattered throughout Riverside are 18 monuments resembling tree trunks, such as the one pictured here. These monuments were placed on the graves of members of the Woodmen of the World organization, a fraternal society meant to benefit society and evoke images of woodmen clearing the land in order to provide for their families. The organization provided these markers to members from 1890 until 1930.

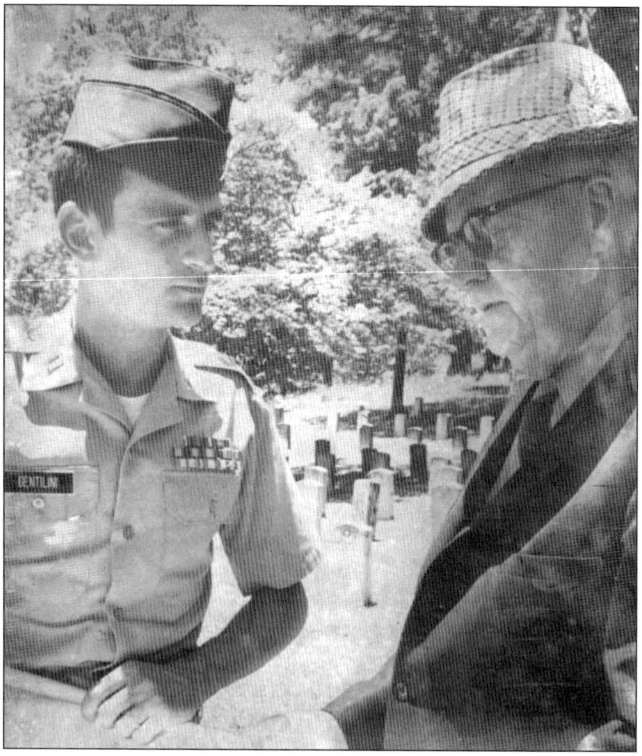

In this 1957 photograph, Chick Hunter discusses plans for Decoration Day ceremonies with Captain Gentilini at the front of the Veteran's Section of the cemetery. Elaborate Decoration Day ceremonies were often planned in Riverside by the very active Kiffin Rockwell Post No. 2 of the American Legion and attracted scores of visitors paying their respects to the military's fallen. (RCA.)

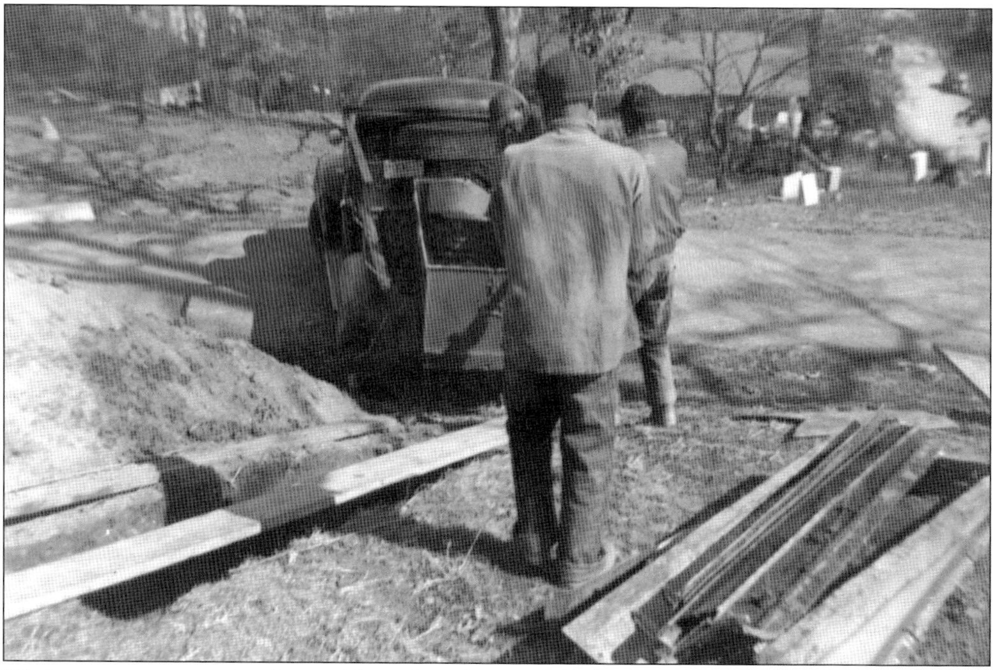

Workers prepare to unload a steel burial vault out of the back of their 1940 Studebaker pickup. Work in Riverside was difficult, with low pay and long hours. Often, workers were recruited from Asheville High School for the summer season. In the winter months, workers were more likely to come from the old Craggy Prison on work release. (RCA.)

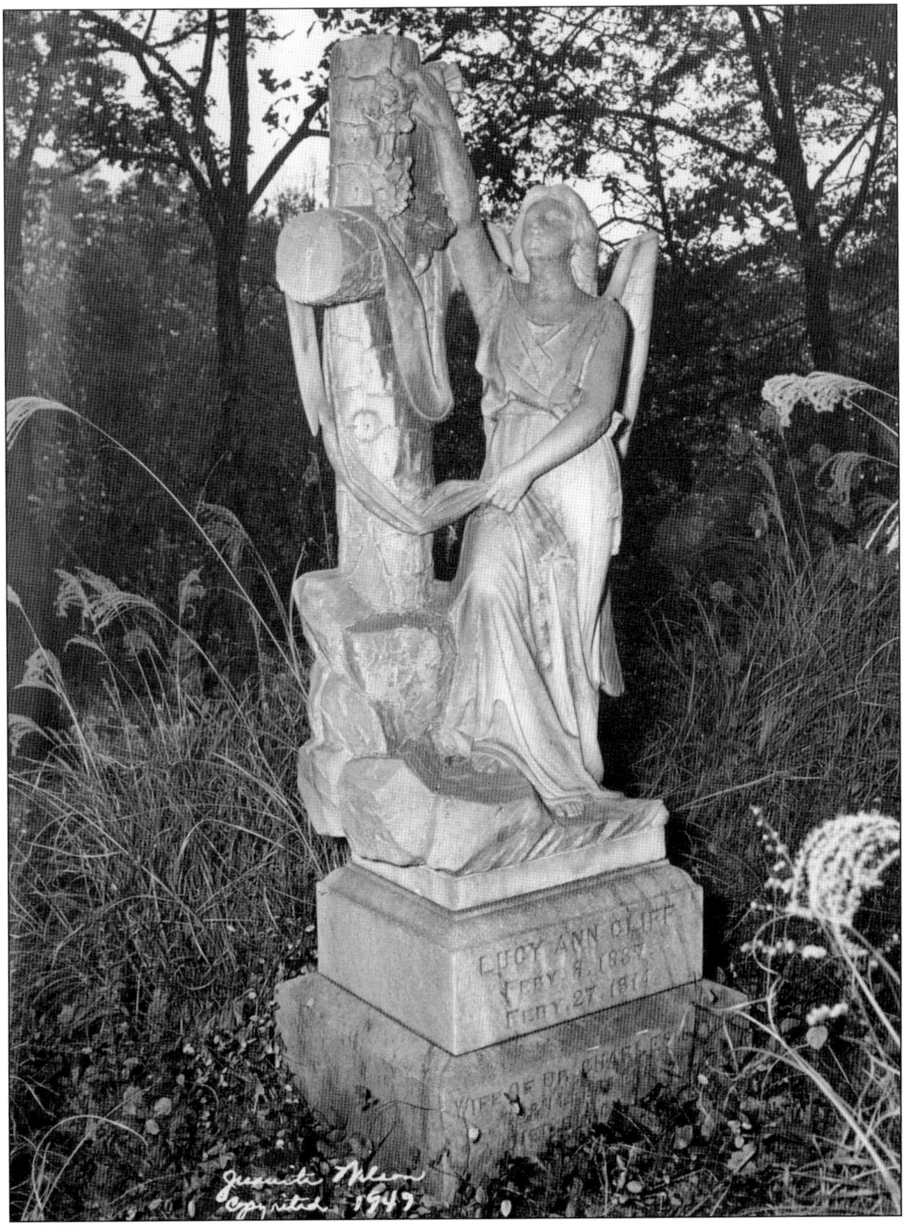

This angel marking the grave of Lucy Ann Cliff has been the subject of controversy amongst Wolfe scholars ever since it was mistakenly identified as the one from Thomas Wolfe's writings in a 1936 article in the *Asheville Citizen*. After reading the article, Wolfe refuted the claim that it was the "angel on the porch" and claimed that he had never laid eyes on it before, though that seems unlikely, since his father had displayed the Cliff angel at his shop before installing it in 1914 at Riverside. It was then decided amongst the scholars of the day that the angel from the novel was the one located in Oakdale Cemetery in Hendersonville, North Carolina, though Thomas Wolfe would never confirm this. Today, the consensus has been reached that it is most likely that Wolfe pulled attributes of all of the different angels from his memories in order to create the image of the one he describes in *Look Homeward, Angel*, much as he did with many of the living characters within. (NCC.)

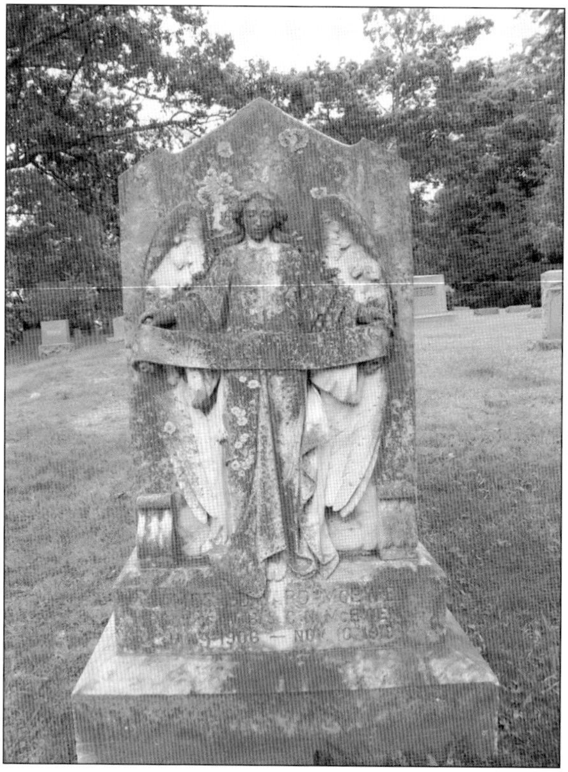

The McEwen monument, pictured here, marks the grave of 13-year-old Edward McEwen, son of the Connecticut lumberman Wooster Baird McEwen and his wife, Caroline Nichols, of Barnardsville. Edward died as a result of ptomaine poisoning in Norfolk, Virginia, while on a family outing. After the tragedy, the McEwen family moved the lumber business to High Point, North Carolina, where it still operates to this day.

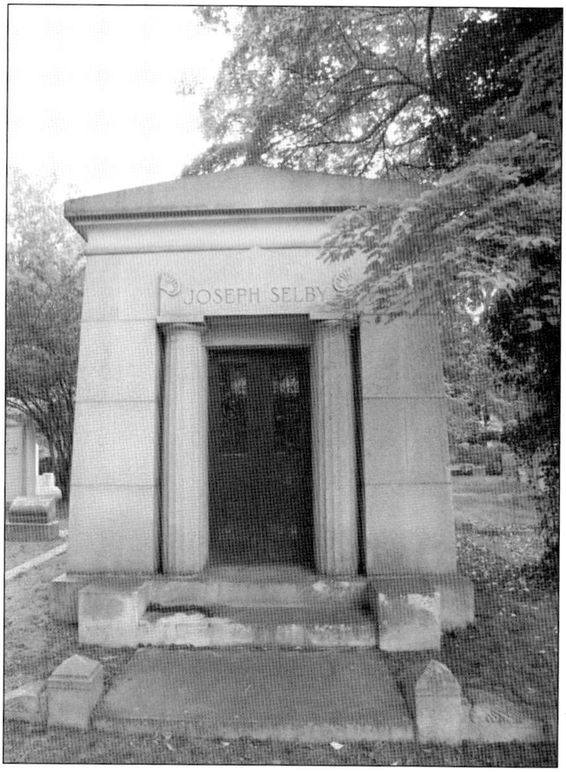

Riverside's 16 family mausoleums have always been some of the most eye-catching features of the garden cemetery. Pictured here is the Selby mausoleum in Section Q, the first that most visitors to Riverside encounter. The large stone "houses of the dead" have been a part of the cemetery's landscape since the gates were first opened in 1885 and continue being built to this day.

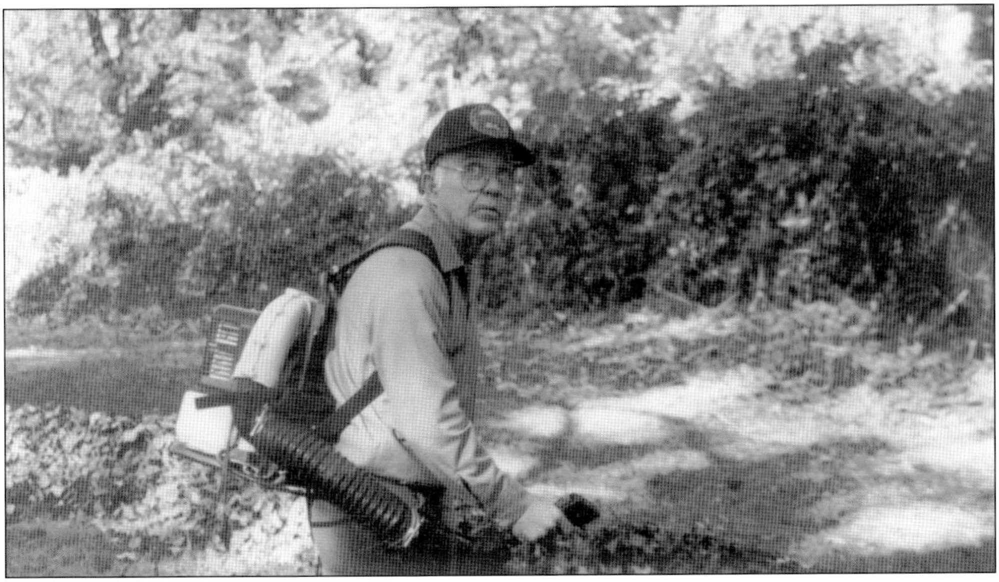

In 1952, when the City of Asheville took over management of the cemetery, crews of 20 laborers were employed to take care of the 87 acres of cemetery grounds. As technology advanced, the need for such a large workforce decreased. Now, the grounds crew at Riverside numbers just four. Pictured here is T.L. Ball, who worked at Riverside in the 1990s. (RCA.)

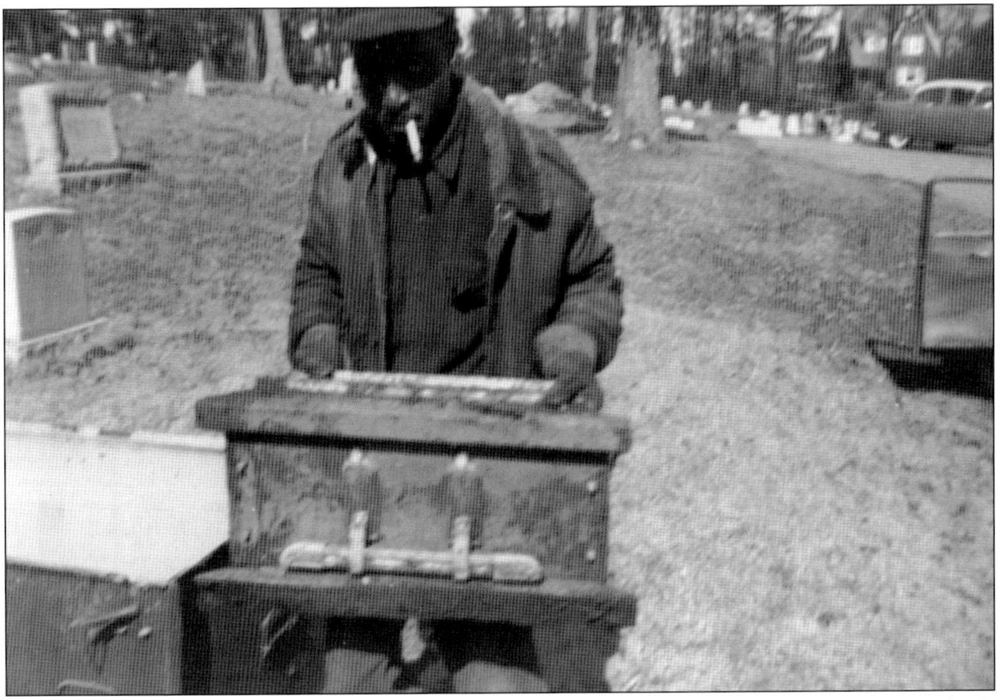

Riverside's early advertisements encouraged people to buy large lots in the cemetery, which boasted wide carriageways, perpetual care, and conveniences such as the water spigots dotting the hillsides. Often families would disinter their loved ones' remains and move them to the modern Riverside, as shown in this 1920s picture of a cemetery laborer waiting to reinter the casket of an infant into the new family lot. (RCA.)

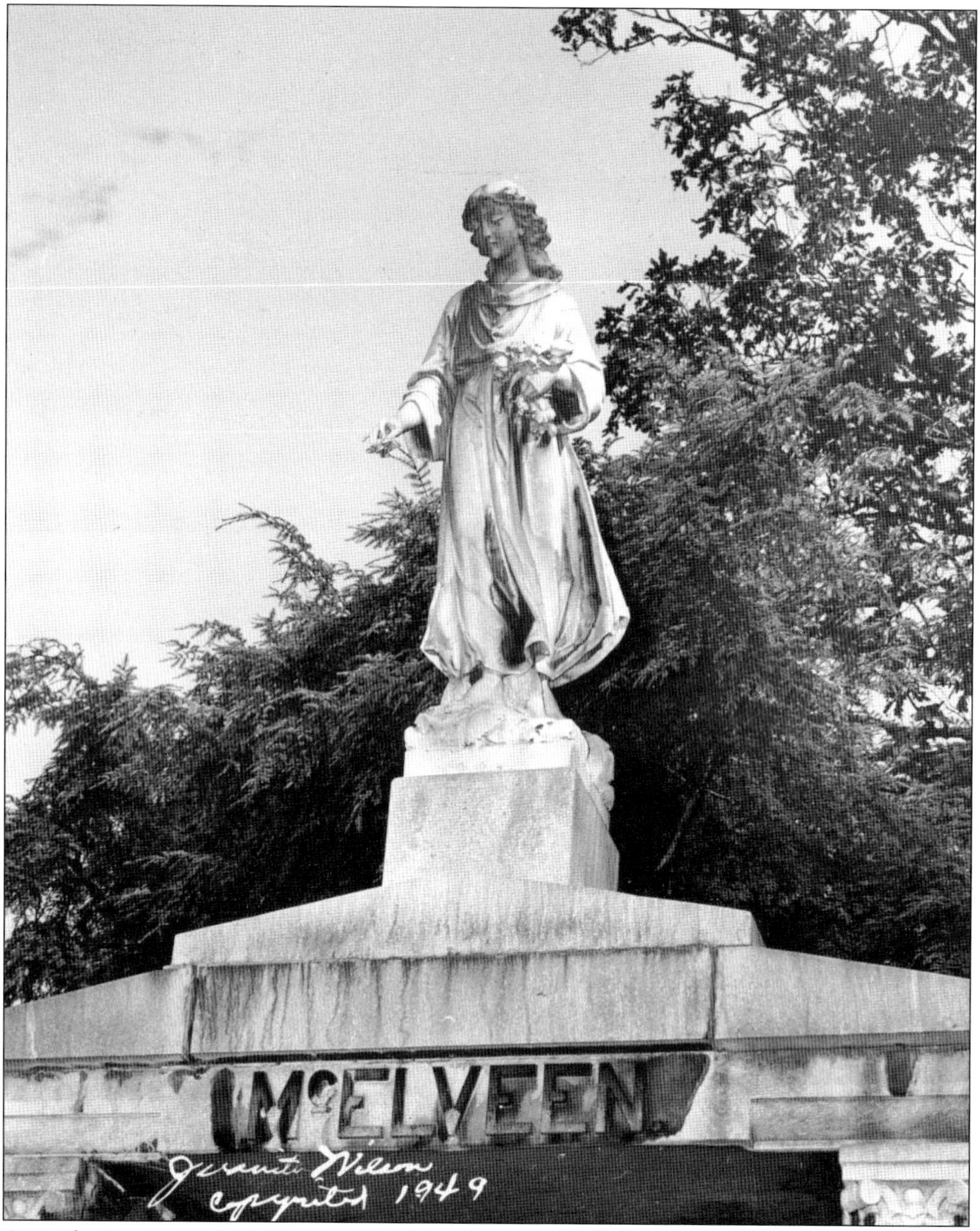

Atop the ivy-covered McElveen mausoleum sits one of W.O. Wolfe's Carrera marble angels. The angel is only visible at certain times of year, as the English ivy covers it during the summer months before being cut away again in the fall. Though Wolfe was a proficient stonecutter, he was never able to master carving faces so instead ordered his angels from Italy, where the art had been perfected. Of the angels installed by W.O. in Riverside, this one likely contributed the most to the conception of the angel in his son's novel *Look Homeward, Angel*. The mausoleum itself was built to entomb the first wife of wealthy Atlanta businessman George Wyche McElveen in 1900 and then his younger brother, Joseph, two years later. Since that time, the mausoleum has remained unused for interments, instead becoming one of favorite haunts of photographers and even serving as the backdrop for several weddings. (NCC.)

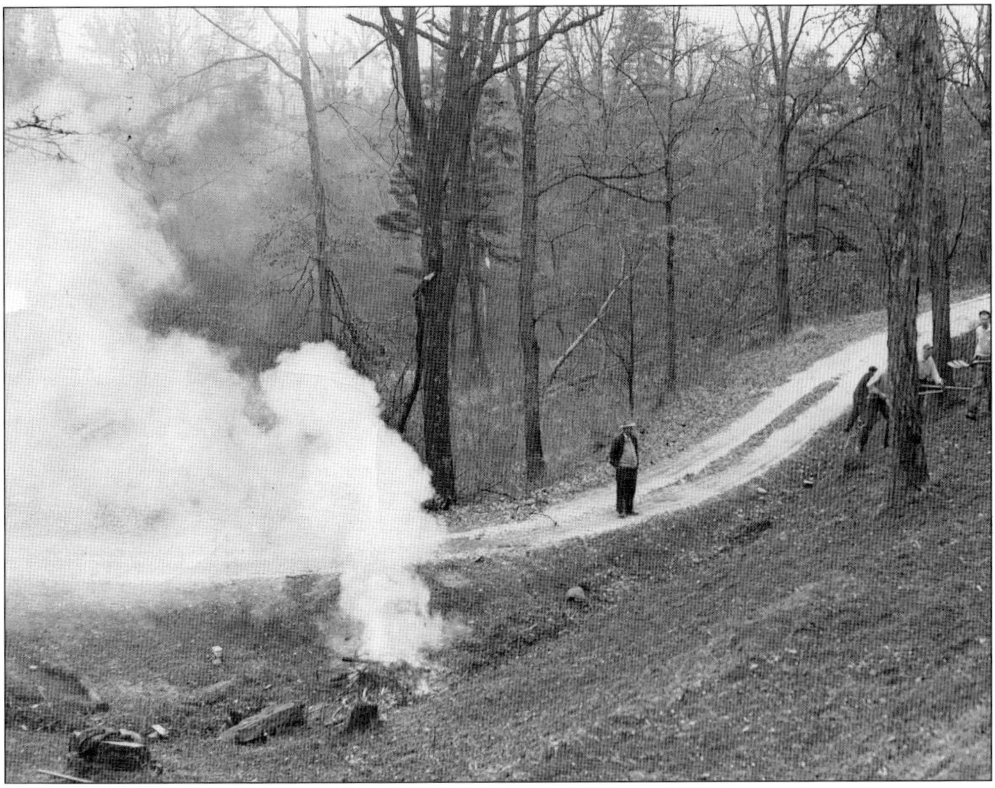

When the City of Asheville took over Riverside in 1952, Chick Hunter inherited a cemetery that had been left untended for 10 years and had fallen into disrepair. In a 1954 speech to the American Cemetery Association, Hunter stated that he refused to open any graves until the city crews were able to tame what had become a "vast wilderness." This photograph shows Hunter overseeing the removal of the undergrowth. (RCA.)

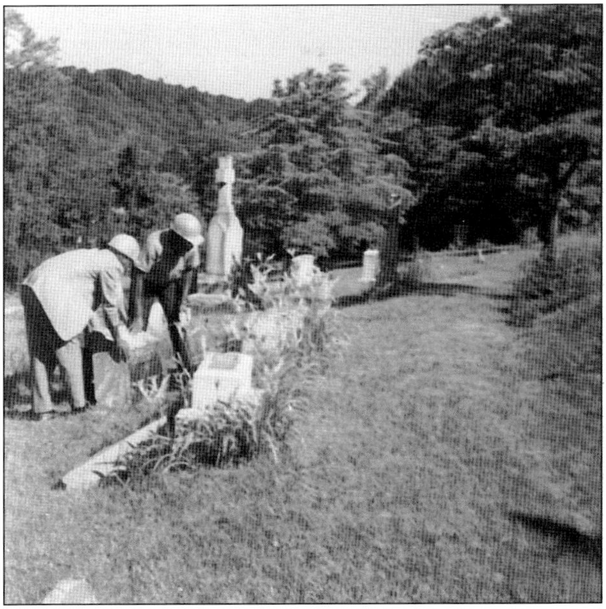

This 1970s photograph shows volunteers setting up monuments that had been toppled by vandals in Riverside's Section II. Volunteers have always played a large and welcome role in Riverside, assisting with the planting of trees and flowers, the restoration and cleaning of monuments, and cemetery tours to the many school groups that visit. (RCA.)

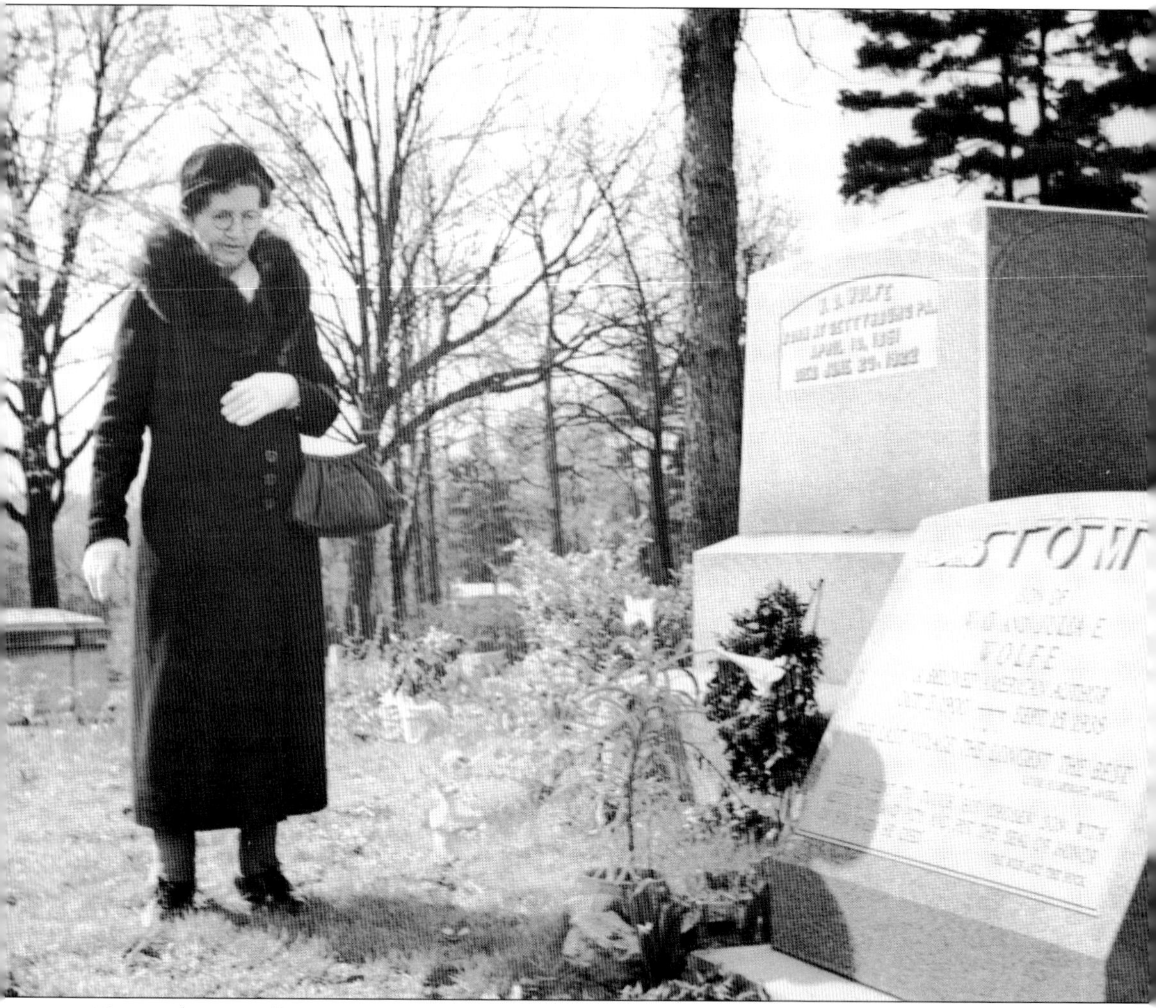

"Some things will never change. Some things will always be the same. Lean down your ear upon the earth and listen," writes Thomas Wolfe in *You Can't Go Home Again.* (Thomas Wolfe Memorial.)

Index